KU-223-917

New York by Area

Essentials

Published by Time Out Guides Ltd
Universal House
251 Tottenham Court Road
London W1T 7AB
Tel: + 44 (0)20 7813 3000
Fax: + 44 (0)20 7813 6001
Email: guides@timeout.com
www.timeout.com

Managing Director Peter Fiennes
Financial Director Gareth Garner
Editorial Director Ruth Jarvis
Deputy Series Editor Dominic Earle
Editorial Manager Holly Pick
Assistant Management Accountant Ija Krasnikova

Time Out Guides is a wholly owned subsidiary of Time Out Group Ltd.

© **Time Out Group Ltd**
Chairman Tony Elliott
Financial Director Richard Waterlow
Group General Manager/Director Nichola Coulthard
Time Out Magazine Ltd MD Richard Waterlow
Time Out Communications Ltd MD David Pepper
Time Out International Ltd MD Cathy Runciman
Production Director Mark Lamond
Group IT Director Simon Chappell
Head of Marketing Catherine Demajo

Time Out and the Time Out logo are trademarks of Time Out Group Ltd.

This edition first published in Great Britain in 2008 by Ebury Publishing
A Random House Group Company
Company information can be found on www.randomhouse.co.uk
Random House UK Limited Reg. No. 954009
10 9 8 7 6 5 4 3 2 1

Distributed in the US by Publishers Group West
Distributed in Canada by Publishers Group Canada

For further distribution details, see www.timeout.com

ISBN: 978-1-84670-103-0

A CIP catalogue record for this book is available from the British Library.

Printed and bound by Firmengruppe APPL, aprinta druck, Germany.

The Random House Group Limited supports The Forest Stewardship Council (FSC), the
leading international forest certification organisation. All our titles that are printed on
Greenpeace approved FSC certified paper carry the FSC logo. Our paper procurement
policy can be found at www.rbooks.co.uk/environment.

Time Out carbon-offsets all its flights with Trees for Cities (www.treesforcities.org).

New York Shortlist

The **Time Out New York Shortlist 2009** is one of a new series of annual guides that draws on Time Out's background as a magazine publisher to keep you current with what's going on in town. As well as New York's key sights and the best of its eating, drinking and leisure options, it picks out the most exciting venues to have opened in the last year and gives a full calendar of events from September 2008 to December 2009. It also includes features on the important news, trends and openings, all compiled by locally based editors and writers. Whether you're visiting for the first time in your life or the first time this year, you'll find the *Time Out New York Shortlist* contains all you need to know, in a portable, easy-to-use format.

The guide divides central New York into four areas, each containing listings for Sights & Museums, Eating & Drinking, Shopping, Nightlife and Arts & Leisure, and maps pinpointing their locations. At the front of the book are chapters rounding up these scenes city-wide, and giving a shortlist of our overall picks. We include itineraries for days out, plus essentials such as transport information and hotels.

Our listings give phone numbers as dialled within the United States. Within New York you need to use the initial 1 and the three-digit area code even if you're calling from within that same area code. From abroad, use your country's exit code followed by the number given (the initial 1 is the US's country code).

We have noted price categories by using one to four dollar signs ($-$$$$), representing budget, moderate, expensive and luxury. Major credit cards are accepted unless otherwise stated. We also indicate when a venue is NEW, and give **Event highlights**.

All our listings are double-checked, but places do sometimes close or change their hours or prices, so it's a good idea to call a venue before visiting. While every effort has been made to ensure accuracy, the publishers cannot accept responsibility for any errors that this guide may contain.

Venues are marked on the maps using symbols numbered according to their order within the chapter and colour-coded as follows:

❶ Sights & Museums
❶ Eating & Drinking
❶ Shopping
❶ Nightlife
❶ Arts & Leisure

Map key	
Major sight or landmark	
Hospital or college	
Railway station	
Park	
River	
Freeway	478
Main road	
Main road tunnel	
Pedestrian road	
Airport	✈
Church	✚
Subway station	Ⓜ
Area name	SOHO

Time Out New York Shortlist 2009

EDITORIAL
Editor Keith Mulvihill
Deputy Editor Edoardo Albert
Proofreader Mandy Martinez
Indexer Rob Norman

DESIGN
Art Director Scott Moore
Art Editor Pinelope Kourmouzoglou
Senior Designer Henry Elphick
Graphic Designers Gemma Doyle,
  Kei Ishimaru
Digital Imaging Simon Foster
Advertising Designer Jodi Sher
Picture Editor Jael Marschner
Deputy Picture Editor Katie Morris
Picture Researcher Gemma Walters
Picture Desk Assistant Marzena Zoladz

ADVERTISING
Commercial Director Mark Phillips
International Advertising Manager
  Kasimir Berger
International Sales Executive
  Charlie Sokol
Advertising Assistant Kate Staddon
Advertising Sales (New York)
  Julia Keefe-Chamberlain

MARKETING
Marketing Manager Yvonne Poon
Senior Publishing Brand Manager
  Luthfa Begum
**Sales & Marketing Director,
North America** Lisa Levinson
Marketing Designers Anthony Huggins,
  Nicola Wilson

PRODUCTION
Production Manager Brendan McKeown
Production Controller Damian Bennett
Production Co-ordinator Julie Pallot

CONTRIBUTORS
This guide was researched and written by Carmella Ciuraru, Toby Egan, Gabriella Gershenson, Keith Mulvihill, Jay Ruttenberg, Steve Smith, Bruce Tantum, Elisabeth Vincentelli and the writers of *Time Out New York*. Thanks to Elizabeth Barr, Brian Fiske, Alison Tocci, and all the contributors to past editions of the *Time Out New York Guide.*

PHOTOGRAPHY
Pages 7, 9, 14, 19, 64, 65, 79, 82, 133 Michael Kirby; pages 10, 21, 27, 35, 38, 39, 40, 43, 50, 51, 52, 53, 60, 61, 63, 67, 68, 69, 72, 75, 83, 92, 135, 140, 151, 156, 164, 165, 173, 177, 180 Ben Rosenzweig; page 28, 101, 106, 109 Alys Tomlinson; page 31 David Scheinmann; page 36 Ben Goldstein; page 45 Drew Toal; page 46 Mike Nelson; pages 47, 49 Shannon Taggart; page 48 Katie Ackerman; pages 54, 55, 62, 71, 80, 84, 89, 97, 107, 110, 112, 117, 118, 123, 125, 130, 142, 158, 159, 160, 161, 163 Jonathan Perugia; pages 87, 132 Jeff Gurwin; page 98 Michael Arnaud; page 115 Kyle Supley; page 126 Roxana Marroquin; page 144 David Rosenzweig; page 145 courtesy of the Metropolitan Museum of Art; page 162 Beth Levendis.

The following images were supplied by the featured artist/establishment: pages 44, 147, 166, 169, 178.

Cover photograph: Signs in Times Square. Credit: © Richard Cummins/Corbis

MAPS
JS Graphics (john@jsgraphics.co.uk).

About Time Out

Founded in 1968, Time Out has expanded from humble London beginnings into the leading resource for those wanting to know what's happening in the world's greatest cities. As well as our influential what's-on weeklies in London, New York and Chicago, we publish more than a dozen other listings magazines in cities as varied as Beijing and Mumbai. The magazines established Time Out's trademark style: sharp writing, informed reviewing and bang up-to-date inside knowledge of every scene.

Time Out made the natural leap into travel guides in the 1980s with the City Guide series, which now extends to over 50 destinations around the world. Written and researched by expert local writers and generously illustrated with original photography, the full-size guides cover a larger area than our Shortlist guides and include many more venue reviews, along with additional background features and a full set of maps.

Throughout this rapid growth, the company has remained proudly independent, still owned by Tony Elliott four decades after he started Time Out London as a single fold-out sheet of A5 paper. This independence extends to the editorial content of all our publications, this Shortlist included. No establishment has been featured because it has advertised, and no payment has influenced any of our reviews. And, for our critics, there's definitely no such thing as a free lunch: all restaurants and bars are visited and reviewed anonymously, and Time Out always picks up the bill.

For more about the company, see www.timeout.com.

Don't Miss
2009

New Museum of Contemporary Art

Sights & Museums

New York's cultural landscape has been busting at the seams with new construction and new openings over the past year. (We're loving the New Museum of Contemporary Art! p76) The variety of venues covers a lot of ground: the Museum of American Finance (p60), the Sports Museum of America (p61) and the Museum of Arts & Design (p148), to name a few. With so many ribbon-cuttings, we predict a run on oversize scissors. The one obvious down side to all this? The last thing you need is to add more must-see museums to an already long list. Below, we've given you a taste of some of the new stuff as well as the tried-and-true spots that New Yorkers have long loved. For more ideas about what to see and do check out the sightseeing chapters. And start planning a return trip!

Sights

At press time New Yorkers were gearing up for one of the most highly anticipated (and inspired) public works projects in the city's history: the High Line, a 1.5-mile defunct elevated train track on the west side, is being converted into a verdant urban walkway and should be ready for visitors near the end of 2008. 'It will have quite an industrial feel of steel and concrete,' said one of the overseers. 'You'll actually be walking on concrete planks between this wild looking landscape.' Many of the seeds being planted are those collected from the plants that were growing wild up there before restoration began, so that the 'accidental landscape' will be recreated.

Speaking of getting high, we've got some good news for you: two iconic rooftop vantage points are standing at the ready to satisfy your on-top-of-the-world cravings. Recently, the Empire State Building (p122) expanded its night-time hours to 2am, every day of the week. If taking in the city from the 102nd floor isn't enough then we suggest you head over to the Top of the Rock observation deck (it debuted in late 2005), perched on Midtown's Rockefeller Center (p124). One of the most impressive elements of the art deco tower is the unparalleled 360-degree views of Manhattan it affords and of course, going one up on the Empire State, it allows a view of, well, the Empire State Building.

Speaking of panoramas, believe it or not, you can take in the entire city of New York in just a few minutes at the Queens Museum of Art (p164). More than 40 years ago, an exact scale model of NYC was built to serve as the centrepiece of an amusement park ride at the 1964 World's Fair in Queens. Though the gondolas were eventually removed, the panorama remains. In 1992 approximately 60,000 of the 895,000 structures were refurbished, and in early 2007, the Lilliputian New York underwent a long-overdue upgrade. Now, visitors are treated to a fun, 13-minute multimedia tour of the sprawling metropolis.

Further Downtown, tourists are still visiting Ground Zero in droves. Construction at the former site of the World Trade Center towers is moving more rapidly and the Freedom Tower is rising a little more each month.

Museums

In January 2008, the Museum of American Finance moved to its new Wall Street digs. The various exhibits at the 30,000-square-foot institution have one thing in

Metropolitan Museum of Art

common: money! Visitors can marvel at antique piggy banks, old-fashioned cash registers and a curvaceous couch made of $30,000 worth of nickels. Noteworthy artefacts include a 1908 Ford Motor Company stock certificate signed by Henry Ford, ticker tape from Black Tuesday and a bond that belonged to President George Washington, believed to be the first official use of the dollar symbol by the federal government.

If finance is not your thing, no worries: New York's museums are among the best in the world. More than 60 institutions hold collections of everything from Gutenberg bibles (three of them) and ancient Etruscan jewellery to Plains Indians buckskins and salsa records, while others feature hands-on science exhibits. The buildings themselves are equally impressive and the list of must-see institutions just keeps getting longer. The recently opened New Museum of Contemporary Art (p76) threw open its doors not among the cultural giants along Uptown's Fifth Avenue, but Downtown on the Bowery. The building, which looks like gleaming boxes stacked one atop the other, will be the first art museum built from the ground up in lower Manhattan.

Yes, this new addition to Downtown will keep locals and visitors agog but rest assured that the old stalwarts won't be fading into the background anytime soon. For starters, the Metropolitan Museum of Art recently unveiled a redesign and reinstallation of the museum's stellar Greek and Roman collections. The luminous, double-storey atrium with its newly raised glass roof, surrounded by monumental figures of Hercules and Dionysus, is as eye-popping as the $220 million price tag to remake the wing. The renovation yielded in

SHORTLIST

Best new
- Museum of American Finance (p60)
- High Line (p9)
- New Museum of Contemporary Art (p76)

Best for cool kids
- Whitney Museum of American Art (p143)
- Washington Square Park (p91)
- Museum of Modern Art (MoMA) (p122)
- P.S.1 Contemporary Art Center (p164)

Best free
- Staten Island Ferry (p62)
- Walk across Brooklyn Bridge (p55)

Best historic
- Lower East Side Tenement Museum (p76)
- Fraunces Tavern Museum (p60)

Best outdoor fun
- Central Park (p135)
- Cloisters (p154)
- New York Botanical Garden (p158)

Best super cheap
- TKTS (p116)
- Carousel in Central Park (p140)

Best treasures
- American Museum of Natural History (p148)
- Metropolitan Museum of Art (p141)

Best USA!
- Statue of Liberty (p62)
- Ellis Island Immigration Museum (p62)

Best view
- Top of the Rock (p124)
- Empire State Building (p122)
- Circle Line Cruises (p127)

THIS IS YOUR NEW YORK.™

In the heart of historic Rockefeller Center®,
Top of the Rock Observation Deck is
New York's most beautiful view from
a thrilling 70 stories up.

Discover your New York
at Top of the Rock.

TOP OF THE ROCK™
OBSERVATION DECK
at Rockefeller Center®

50th Street between 5th and 6th Avenues
Open daily from 8am to midnight
For tickets call 212-698-2000 topoftherocknyc.com

excess of 30,000 square feet of new space, almost doubling the area devoted to classical art. Most of the 5,300 or so objects now on view had been left languishing in storage for decades.

Across the park at the American Museum of Natural History, some really (really) old friends are finally getting the recognition they deserve: Neanderthals, in all their skeletal glory, stand alongside modern day interpretations of these long dead human cousins. The newly opened Hall of Human Origins uses fossil records and DNA evidence to trace the connections between modern man and our earliest ancestors (and a few distant relations), with rare hominid fossils and artefacts, engaging video segments and realistic dioramas.

In recent years, another favourite New York institution, albeit one that may not be on the radar for those living outside Manhattan, has undergone a welcome transformation. In 2006, the Morgan Library (p111), which had shut its doors for three years to embark on its largest growth spurt since 1928, finally ushered in a new era. The expanded museum, designed by Pritzker Prize-winning architect Renzo Piano, has doubled the amount of exhibition space and added a number of new amenities to the old complex's three buildings. We'll be frank here: the Morgan is not the Met or the Museum of Modern Art (MoMA), but its welcoming atmosphere, small, easily digestible galleries, unusual artworks (ancient Mesopotamian seals, anyone?) and historical display of Pierpont Morgan's personal library make it a rare treat. Thanks to the expansion, the museum is now able to display more of its 350,000 objects than ever before.

Making the most of it

Keep in mind that visiting several venues in a single day can be exhausting. Similarly, it's self-defeating to attempt to hit all the major collections during one visit to an institution as large as the Met or the American Museum of Natural History. So plan, pace yourself and don't forget to snack often: a host of excellent museum cafés and restaurants afford convenient breaks. Delicious refuelling spots include Sarabeth's at the Whitney Museum of American Art (p143); the Jewish Museum's Café Weissman; and a more formal option, the recently opened Modern (p124) at MoMA.

Brace yourself for the local admission prices; they can be steep (tickets to the recently renovated MoMA cost $20 per adult). This is because most of the city's museums are privately funded and receive little or no government support. Even so, many of them, including MoMA, the Whitney and the Guggenheim, offer at least one evening a week when admission fees are either waived or switched to a voluntary donation. Most museums also offer discounts to students and senior citizens with valid IDs. And although the Met suggests a $20 donation for adults, you can pay what you wish any time you visit.

Most New York museums are closed on major US holidays. Nevertheless, some institutions are open on certain Monday holidays, such as Columbus Day and Presidents' Day.

Security remains tight. Guards at all public institutions will ask you to open your purse or backpack for inspection; umbrellas and any large bags must be left (free of charge) in a cloakroom. Most museums are accessible to disabled people.

Allen & Delancey p76

WHAT'S BEST
Eating & Drinking

In the ever expanding New York City dining scene, only one thing remains constant: nothing stays the same. This past year saw the emergence of several fully-fledged trends and enough activity to tide less fickle cities over for a decade.

Perhaps the most surprising of these was the restaurant boom on the previously gastro-deprived Upper West Side. Marquee names are now flaunting their skills north of 59th Street: Daniel Boulud brought charcuterie, French classics and premium wine with Bar Boulud (p149); Chef Ed Brown showcased his seafood expertise (and more) with the eclectic Eighty One (45 W 81st Street, between Columbus Avenue & Central Park West, 1-212 873 8181); and John

Schaefer surprised critics and diners alike with his acclaimed new American eaterie, Dovetail (p150).

There was a notable migration of Downtown restaurants northward too. Upper West branches of East Village stalwart, the Mermaid Inn (p86), Chelsea's vegetarian darling, Blossom (p106), and the West Village cupcakery Magnolia Bakery (p98) came to the 'hood last year. And in another happy development, the owners of the Clinton Street Baking Company (p77), welcomed Community Food & Juice (p150), a farmer-friendly comfort food eaterie and juice bar, to upper Broadway.

Speaking of farms brings us to another core element of the year in dining: farmers. Some restaurants have been putting an emphasis on supporting small farmers. (Not only do these restaurants buy local but their decor often evokes a rustic, farm-like ambience). In addition to Community Food & Juice, other practitioners include Peter Hoffman of Back Forty (190 Avenue B, at E 12th Street, 1-212 388 1990) in the East Village, a first-rate gastropub with cask-drawn ale, grass-fed burgers, and a commitment to serving Greenmarket goods (and yes, antique farming tools decorate the walls). An upscale version of th149s style of dining would be BLT Market (1430 Sixth Avenue, at Central Park South, 1-212 521 6125) at the Ritz Carlton, which sticks to the foods of the season.

Substance is great, but all of that earnestness hasn't put a damper on New Yorker's sense of style – dining is still very much a fashion-forward activity. Especially Downtown. Case in point is Allan & Delancey (p76), winner of *Time Out New York*'s 2008 best new restaurant award. The art of behaving frivolously and eating well while doing so is also alive in the West Village at scene-heavy restaurants such as Bar Blanc (p95), the project from the immensely talented chef Cesar Ramirez, and Commerce (p95), which serves former Montrachet chef Harold Moore's luxurious menu in an 'only in New York' deco setting. Though Bar Blanc is all white-and-chrome minimalism, while Commerce is warm woods and antique lighting, they both represent a slice of Manhattan's opulent dining scene.

For all of the new trends, the year in dining also has us welcoming back old friends. 2nd Ave Deli (p134), which had been closed for 2 years since losing its East Village lease, has finally relocated to 33rd Street. The menu

SHORTLIST

Best new
- Allen & Delancey (p76)
- Commerce (p95)
- New York City Hot Dog Company (p67)
- Dovetail (p150)

Best cocktails
- Pegu club (p67)
- Death & Co. (p86)
- Home Sweet Home (p78)
- Tailor (p68)

Best design
- Buddakan (p106)
- Merkato 55 (p96)
- The Modern (p124)

Best dessert
- Tailor (p68)
- P*ONG (p96)
- Kyotofu (p128)

Best for brunch
- Shorty's .32 (p67)
- Clinton Street Baking Company (p77)
- Baltazar (p66)
- Community Food & Juice (p150)

Best for hanging with hipsters
- Rififi (p88)
- Café Habana (p73)

Best for outdoor
- Plunge (p96)
- Central Park Boathouse (p140)
- New Leaf Café (p156)

Best New York deli
- 2nd Avenue Deli (p134)
- Katz's Delicatessen (p78)

Best view
- Bouchon Bakery (p149)
- Top of the Tower (p136)

Best wine bars
- Gottino (p96)
- Xai Xai Wine Bar (p129)
- Bin No. 220 (p63)

PIER 17
Seaport NYC

Seaport
Music
Festival

12 months
4 seasons
1 iconic venue
superior music

www.southstreetseaport.com

remains the same, and its devotees have not been disappointed – the legacy of chopped liver, pastrami on rye and matzo ball soup goes on. In the upscale department, French chef-restaurateur Alain Ducasse has come back to New York City with two new restaurants. (One might recall that his first two Gotham attempts, now defunct – Mix New York and Alain Ducasse at the Essex House – were given lukewarm receptions.) The first is Adour Alain Ducasse (p131) at the St Regis New York, whose hallmarks include a computerised wine list in the former Lespinasse space. In another legendary location (the former home of La Cote Basque) Ducasse has unveiled Benoit (60 W 55th Street, between Fifth & Sixth Avenues, 1-646 943 7373), a white-table cloth establishment that specialises in brasserie classics.

Eat your veggies

One of New York City's weak spots is the relative dearth of new vegetarian dining options. Though we appreciate what we already have, it is always a thrill to learn that another meat-free spot is joining the ranks. This year, the ever-popular Chelsea restaurant Blossom (p106) has brought its seitan scallopine and Brazilian mock-beef stew to the Upper West Side. Broadway East (p76), located where the Lower East Side meets Chinatown, is possibly Manhattan's first self-proclaimed 'flexitarian' eaterie. That means it isn't entirely vegetarian, but animal-friendly foods dominate the menu choices. That said, old reliable choices continue to draw regulars: the A-list includes Pure Food & Wine (54 Irving Place, between 17th & 18th Streets, 1-212 477 1010), and Counter (105 First Avenue, between 6th & 7th Streets, 1-212 982 5870).

Drink up!

If you think all of the activity in the restaurant world has left the drinking scene neglected, think again. There is a renaissance underway on all booze fronts: beer, wine and liquor. In the hops department, brew-dedicated bars continue to open. Among our new favourites is Spitzer's Corner (p78), which offers more than three dozen beers on tap in a superlative LES perch. Wine bars proliferate too, and they're becoming increasingly specialised. Gottino (p96), a fantastic enoteca in the West Village, offers an all-Italian list with small plates that alone are worth a visit. Terroir (413 E 12th Street, between First Avenue and Avenue A, no phone), the latest project from the owners of neighbouring Hearth in the East Village, serves only wines that best express the land and conditions whence they came. Perhaps most unique is Xai Xai Wine Bar (p129) in Midtown, exposing New Yorkers to the wines of Africa.

Even with all of these riches, there's still something bigger flourishing on the inebriation front: cocktails. Whether it's the chem-lab flair of Eben Freeman at restaurant and lounge Tailor (p68), who fashions 'solid' (ie non-liquid) cocktails and serves his bourbon with smoked Coke, or the old-school stylings of mixologist Jim Meehan at the East Village speakeasy PDT (113 St Marks Place, between First Avenue & Avenue A, 1-212 614 0386), you needn't look any further than Manhattan for a memorable, expertly shaken drink. If you can't choose between beer, wine and hooch, check out Huckleberry Bar (588 Grand Street, between Leonard & Lorimer Streets, 1-718 218 8555) in Williamsburg,

Brooklyn, which was voted 2008's best new bar in *Time Out*'s Eat Out Awards, for a well executed melding of the three.

Tips for dining out

A word of warning: snagging reservations can be tough, especially at weekends. Super-trendy spots can be booked weeks in advance but the majority require only a few days' notice or less. Most restaurants fill up between 7pm and 9pm. If you don't mind eating early (5pm) or late (after 9.30pm), your chances of getting into a popular place will improve. Alternatively, try to snag a hard-to-land reservation by calling at 5pm on the day you want to dine and hope for a cancellation. Dress codes are rarely enforced, but some ultra-fancy places require men to don a jacket and tie. If in doubt, call and ask. And remember: you can never really overdress in this town.

Have a smoke

A strict citywide smoking ban has changed the way smokers carouse: some go to bars and restaurants that allow smoking, but these are few and far between. The only legal places to smoke indoors are either venues that cater largely to cigar smokers (and actually sell cigars and cigarettes) or spaces that have created areas specifically for smokers. Try Circa Tabac (32 Watts Street, between Sixth Avenue & Thompson Street, 1-212 941 1781) or Club Macanudo (26 E 63rd Street, between Madison & Park Avenues, 1-212 752 8200). If it's warm and you want to drag while you drink, the outdoor spaces at Boxcar Lounge (168 Avenue B, between 10th and 11th Streets, 1-212 473 2830), or the hookah lounge Karma (51 First Avenue, between 3rd and 4th Streets, 1-212 677 3160) are good choices.

Merkato 55 p96

FASHION WORTH FIGHTING FOR

PURE DESIGNER IN EVERY CATEGORY **40-70% OFF** RETAIL EVERYDAY

Century 21
DEPARTMENT STORE

Charlotte Moss p146

WHAT'S BEST
Shopping

We've included an array of depots for affordable gems, vintage treasures and everything in between. But before you part with hard-earned cash, take this tactical spending tip: arrange your retail excursions by neighbourhood.

Street by street

Before *Project Runway*, there was New York's Lower East Side and, in more recent years, Nolita. These cluttered and cloistered streets – particularly the area bordered by Houston to the north, Delancey to the south, Broadway to the East and Clinton to the west – have become a haven for small designers looking to start their own shops. Pocket-sized spaces mix with now-familiar names (Calypso, Steven Alan, A Détacher), and you'll have to sharpen your elbows to compete with the fashionistas prowling the racks for emerging designers and the next big thing. A hive of indie designer activity for more than a decade, the Lower East Side has been a devoted midwife of talent, with many stores fostering fresh-faced designers. The first, which opened its doors in 1992, is TG-170 (p81), Terry Gillis's indie label incubator (she was one of the first to carry Built by Wendy) that still enjoys a cult following to this day. At weekends, a few blocks west, the Market NYC (p74) has become the best place Downtown to buy directly from designers. Housed in a school gymnasium, each vendor is given a five-by-seven-foot space

to show their wares, which range from jewellery to cocktail dresses to hats. Designers often alternate weekends, so there is always someone new to discover. As a result of its success, a carefully curated selection of the Market's best duds can now be found during the week at EDGE*nyNOHO (65 Bleecker Street, between Broadway & Lafayette Street, 1-212 358 0255), which showcases clothing, products and accessories from more than 65 designers. The best part? Many of the designers are on the premises to answer questions and broker deals, so you can say you knew them when.

Of course, some of you are much too label conscious to risk your hard-earned dollars on a bunch of no-names. Rest assured, there are miles upon miles of boutique-packed streets to satisfy the most designer-savvy shoppers. Label whores with cash to spend will find the latest fashions along Madison and Fifth Avenues – the blocks north of 50th Street are where you'll find some of the city's swankiest shops. Downtown hotspots include Soho (p64) and the West Village (p95) – where Bleecker Street has become a who's who among fashion greats, with the likes of Juicy Couture, Intermix, Cynthia Rowley, two Ralph Lauren stores and no fewer than three Marc Jacobs stores. The Meatpacking District (p95) is now counted among the city's fashion foundations. Here, look for Jeffrey, Girlshop, Scoop and three welcome new additions: Trina Turk (p99), Diane von Furstenberg (p97) and Yohji Yamamoto (p99).

Half price!

This being America's fashion capital there are numerous sample sales every week. To find out who's selling where during any given

SHORTLIST

Best new
- Yohji Yamamoto (p99)
- Charlotte Moss (p146)
- Matter (p70)
- Edit (p146)

Best antiques
- Garage (p108)
- Hell's Kitchen Flea Market (p129)

Best bargains
- Century 21 (p64)

Best chocolate
- Chocolate Haven (p97)
- La Maison du Chocolat (p147)

Best jewels
- Bulgari (p125)
- Doyle & Doyle (p79)

Best NYC looks
- Barney's (p146)
- Diane von Furstenberg (p97)
- Patricia Field (p89)

week, consult the Shopping section of *Time Out New York*. Top Button (www.topbutton.com) and the SSS Sample Sales hotline (1-212 947 8748, www.clothingline.com) are also great discount resources. Sales are usually held in the designers' shops or in rented loft spaces. Typically, loft sales are not equipped with changing rooms, so bring a courageous spirit and remember to wear appropriate undergarments.

If it's too rainy or cold to meander the streets, head to one of the city's shopping malls. The Shops at Columbus Circle (Time Warner Center, 10 Columbus Circle, at 59th Street), and the myriad stores in Trump Tower (Fifth Avenue, at 56th Street), Grand Central Terminal (p131) and South Street Seaport's cobblestoned Pier 17 (Fulton Street, at the East River) are convenient.

Rush p109

WHAT'S BEST
Nightlife

If you were to judge New York's nightlife by the Club World Awards – doled out annually to the nation's leading nightspots and parties – you would probably believe that our city's after-dark scene was going through a gilded age to rival the heyday of the long defunct (but much missed) niteries like Studio 54, the Paradise Garage and Twilo. After all, in the past year, Pacha (p130) won the award for best superclub, Cielo (p97) the one for best club and 'Dance. Here. Now.' at Cielo was voted the best party. And judging by attendance, most dance-music venues certainly seem to be going stronger than ever – on Fridays and Saturdays, for instance, the streets of the club-laden Meatpacking District are

crammed with pleasure seekers. So surely all is well in the city's clubbing universe?

Appearances can deceive. Take the superclub category: Pacha may have taken home the top prize – deservedly so, we might add – but it's the only such superclub in a town which used to always make room for three or four at a time. Its main competition, Crobar, closed last year, to be replaced by the thus-far underutilised Mansion (580 W 28th Street, between Tenth & Eleventh Avenues, 1-212 381 9096), a club that recently saw fit to send out a press release boasting that Spice Girls Geri Halliwell and Emma Bunton had attended one of its events. (Even ten years ago, that titbit would have been filed under

'Who cares?') Meanwhile, the massive Webster Hall (125 E 11th Street, between Third & Fourth Avenues, 1-212 353 1600) has been giving it a go, hosting hot-shot DJs like Sasha and Digweed, but it's still not much more than a grand, oversized fraternity house.

Then there's the city's attitude towards nightlife in general, and dance clubs in particular. The minutiae of the various laws that have an impact on clubs could fill up this guide book, but here's a telling statistic: in a town of eight million, there are currently 173 venues in NYC with a cabaret license, the document that allows dancing. (Yes, you need a license to dance in New York, which says something in itself.) As recently as the 1970s, the number was in the thousands. Obviously, things ain't what they used to be.

But NYC still clings to that 'city that never sleeps' tag and, while the scene could stand a bit of spit and polish, there are still more ways to dance the night away here than in all but a handful of world clubbing centres. Besides Pacha and Cielo, there's Sullivan Room (p94), an unpretentious spot that features some of America's best house-music talent, including the likes of Derrick Carter and Mark Farina. There's dive-bar supreme 205 (205 Chrystie Street, at Stanton Street, 1-212 477 6688), which hosts the mutant-disco likes of Rub-N-Tug and the DFA Records gang.

P.S.1's Warm Up (p164), a weekly summertime soirée held in a courtyard at a Queens museum, attracts thousands of kids who like nothing better than to boogie down to some pretty twisted DJs. Lovers of underground techno flock to the Bunker, a plucky little party held weekly in Williamsburg (back room of Galapagos Art Space, 70 North 6th Street, between Kent and

SHORTLIST

Best new
- Terminal 5 (p130)
- Studio B (p160)
- Highline Ballroom (p109)

Best for cabaret
- Metropolitan Room (p109)
- Joe's Pub (p90)

Best for gay
- Rush (p109)
- Element (Saturday nights) (p83)
- Studio Mezmor (p110)

Best for hipsters
- Cake Shop (p81)
- The Annex (p81)
- Nublu (p90)

Best for indie bands
- Arlene's Grocery (p81)
- Bowery Ballroom (p81)
- Delancey (p81)
- Mercury Lounge (p84)

Best for jazz
- Birdland (p119)
- Village Vanguard (p94)
- Smoke (p152)

Best for laughs
- Laugh Lounge nyc (p83)
- See Comedy Central (p115)

Best for megastar DJs
- APT (p99)
- Cielo (p97)
- Studio Mezmor (p110)
- Pacha (p130)

Best for rockers
- Continental (p89)
- Ace of Clubs (p89)
- Living Room (p83)

Best neo-burlesque
- Slipper Room (p85)

Best world music
- S.O.B's (p71)
- Zinc Bar (p94)
- Copacabana (p130)

Wythe Avenues, Williamsburg, Brooklyn). Studio B (p160), tucked away in an isolated corner of Brooklyn, is the centre of NYC's burgeoning electro-rock scene.

In the flesh

The end times for the recording industry loom. A punishing financial climate threatens to suffocate New York's cultural landscape. And, of course, the spot on the Bowery where CBGB once stood now houses a John Varvatos boutique. Yet somewhat counter intuitively, live music in the city is flourishing. For every venue squeezed out by rising rents a new one takes its place.

For larger seated shows, the iconic theatres uptown cannot be beaten. The palatial art deco totem Radio City Music Hall (p123), Harlem's decaying benchmark, the Apollo Theater (p157), and of course Carnegie Hall (plus its subterranean baby, Zankel Hall, p120) lend historic importance to even tedious performances. The rock scene's heart, however, beats Downtown and, increasingly, across the water in Brooklyn. The clubs dotting the East Village and Lower East Side are too many to count, but include the Living Room (p83) where you can hear folksy singer-songwriters, Nublu (p90) offering beat-heavy exotica and the avant-gardist fare of the Stone (Avenue C, at 2nd Street, no phone).

For medium-size acts, the Bowery Ballroom (p81) remains Manhattan's hub. In recent years, its owners have taken advantage of rock's resurgence by booking shows in a smattering of larger venues. Under the Bowery Presents rubric, the company regularly books Webster Hall (125 E 11th Street, between Third & Fourth Avenues, 1-212 353 1600), a huge club with gaudy trimmings, as

well as Terminal 5 (p130), an even larger space located along the city's western fringes. The Bowery's increasing forays into big-room bookings, which have included shows at mighty Madison Square Garden (p114) and the posh Hiro Ballroom at Maritime Hotel, have spurred the city's largest concert promoter, Live Nation, to increase its presence in clubs. Mid-size acts are now being booked at the Blender Bar at Gramercy Theatre (127 E 23rd Street, between Park & Lexington Avenues, 1-212 777 6800), as well as the newly renovated and renamed Fillmore East at Irving Plaza (17 Irving Place, at 15th Street, 1-212 777 6800). Other recent additions to the music scene include the Highline Ballroom (p109), in the Meatpacking District, and the Nokia Theatre Times Square (p118).

As in any town, Manhattan's most exciting music tends to emanate from its tiniest spaces. Joe's Pub (p90), the classy cabaret room tucked inside the Public Theater, continues to present great acts of all genres. Cheaper, grubbier and louder is Cake Shop, a three-year-old club on a particularly bustling strip of Ludlow Street. Cake Shop's ground floor houses a small record store and a colourful, vegan-friendly café. The modest stage and bar lie in the dingy basement. The sightlines are ghastly and there are certainly more comfortable places in which to hang out. But the booking is vibrant and on good nights the club has the sticky air of a high-school basement party: the ideal setting for a scruffy rock 'n' roll show.

Torch songs

Perhaps no other genre offers quite so diverse an array of performers as cabaret. Hip jazz types, grand old broads, bright young musical-theatre belters, semi-classical recitalists, female impersonators, neo-lounge singers and more, all share the same crowded rooms. In 2009 look for relative newcomer the Metropolitan Room (p109). If you're looking for a more classic experience, head to Café Carlyle or the Oak Room at the Algonquin Hotel. This is the New York of Woody Allen, where well-heeled daters can take in dinner and a show in a single package.

Hoot & holler

Looking for something to laugh about? You'll find it at one of the city's myriad comedy clubs listed in our special box Comedy Central (p115) as well as in *Time Out New York*. Visit Laugh Lounge nyc (p83) for a dose of the Downtown crowd; at Gotham Comedy Club (32 W 22nd Street, 1-212 367 9000) you'll hear late-night talk-show circuit comics. Step into the Upright Citizens Brigade Theater (307 W 26th Street, 1-212 366 9176) for top-notch improvisation and sketches.

Gay affair

Gay nightlife soldiers on despite the recent closures of some of the most popular queer clubs (like the Roxy and Mr. Black). One new-ish spot, Rush (p109) has opened up in Chelsea and is particularly popular with college age cuties. If you're in the mood to shake it in a big-time space with a deafening sound system, many of the large clubs like Element (p83), Pacha (p130) and Studio Mezmor (p110) have gay nights. Downtown's Chelsea and the East Village remain the go-to 'hoods for gays, with numerous cafés, bars and restaurants that will welcome you with open arms. In Midtown, Hell's Kitchen continues to rise as a night-time destination. Check out the Vlada Lounge (p129), a slick, laid-back setting for sipping cocktails.

The best source for all things gay is *HX* magazine, available at most eateries, bars and shops along Chelsea's Eighth Avenue, the city's queerest enclave.

Highline Ballroom

Lincoln Center p152

WHAT'S BEST
Arts & Leisure

In New York, it's easy to go on a binge: you can chase Tibetan dumplings with Belgian beer and finish an evening at a dessert-only restaurant; you can shop at a gigantic department store at 10am and an exclusive boutique at 10pm. And of course the city offers a smörgåsbord of cultural delights, all ready to be devoured – the only problem is how to winnow your choices to a manageable list. It's true that some tickets can be pricey but New Yorkers haven't lost their noses for a deal and bargains also abound if you look both online and at the TKTS (p116) booths. The range is extraordinary, from provocative plays staged in tiny Village basements to all-singing, all-dancing extravaganzas.

Theatre

For most Americans, Times Square is the centre of New York theatre. It's hard to disagree, though it certainly is not the whole of the picture. Musical theatre was born there, and it still thrives in the area between 42nd and 50th Streets. But there is a reason New York is America's first city when it comes to theatre: you can find something for every taste, from pure entertainment to avant-garde experiences, with every shade of stage magic in between.

Perennial favourites on the Great White Way include productions as diverse as *Spring Awakening*, *Chicago* and *Wicked*; two musical adaptations of popular films (*Shrek* and Elton John's *Billy Elliot*) are likely to join them when they start their runs in autumn 2008. Highly anticipated revivals include a new version of Rodgers and Hart's rarely seen *Pal Joey* in the fall of 2008 and the return of the Bob Fosse-themed revue *Dancin'* in spring 2009.

You can also find straight plays on Broadway, often lit up by awesome star wattage; in recent years, Julia Roberts, Patrick Stewart and Hugh Jackman have all appeared on the local boards. Since tickets for these shows often go fast, you may want to check websites such as theatermania.com and playbill.com in advance.

Yet Broadway is far from being the be-all-and-end-all of theatre in New York. As fun as high-budget productions are, sometimes you need a bit more intimacy; check out what's playing at the Duke on 42nd Street at (no.229, between Seventh & Eighth Avenues, 1-646 223 3010), Playwrights Horizons (416 W 42nd Street, between Ninth & Tenth Avenues, 1-212 279 4200), and Second Stage (307 W 43rd Street, at Eighth Avenue, 1-212 246 4422) for quality in a fairly classic mode. In the East Village, the Public Theater (p91), on Lafayette Street, offers a mix of new plays and classics with excellent production values; it also puts up a pair of free Shakespeare in the Park (p40) productions every summer in Central Park.

If you need something a little more challenging and iconoclastic – and much easier on the wallet – leave Times Square behind. Uptown, the Classical Theatre of Harlem (3940 Broadway, at 165th Street, 1-212 868 4444) presents high-octane stagings of classic works such as *Medea* and *The Cherry Orchard* at its small theatre on St Nicholas Avenue and 141st Street. But the historic centre for avant-garde and experimental

SHORTLIST

Best new festivals
- Honor! A Celebration of the African American Cultural Legacy (p155)
- High Line Festival (p9)

Best all-round space
- Symphony Space (p153)

Best concert halls
- Carnegie Hall (p153)
- Lincoln Center (p152)
- Merkin Concert Hall (p153)

Best for athletes
- Chelsea Piers (p110)

Best for cheap tickets
- TKTS (p116)

Best for dance
- Joyce Theater (p110)
- City Center (p120)

Best for eclectic shows
- Stomp (p91)
- Blue Man Group (p90)
- Bowery Poetry Club (p90)

Best long-running shows
- Avenue Q (p120)
- Wicked (p121)
- Billy Elliot (p120)

Best movie houses
- Film Forum (p99)
- Landmark's Sunshine Cinema (p85)
- Angelika Film Center (p94)

Best outdoor culture
- Shakespeare in the Park (p40)
- Midsummer Night Swing (p41)

Best small theatres
- Manhattan Theatre Club (p121)
- Performance Space 122 (p91)
- Flea Theater (p72)
- Kitchen (p110)

Best spectator sports
- US Open (p163)
- A Yankees game (p159)

YOU CAN'T STOP THE BEAT!
Original Formula!
Long-Lasting Hold!
Unbeatable Shine!
SEE IT LIVE!
hairspray
Cast subject to change.
Ticketmaster.com (212) 307-4100 • Groups: (800) BROADWAY
Neil Simon Theatre • HairsprayOnBroadway.com
ORIGINAL BROADWAY CAST RECORDING IN STORES NOW

Billy Elliot p28

theatre is the East Village. Look here for local companies such as Radiohole, Elevator Repair Company, the Nature Theater of Oklahoma and the National Theater of the United States of America, which often appear at venues like Performance Space 122 (p91), the aforementioned Public Theater and New York Theater Workshop (p91).

Film

Sure, you can come to New York and watch the same Hollywood blockbusters playing at your own neighbourhood's multiplex but, frankly, why bother? Instead, you can join savvy locals and explore the wonderful world of art-house films. They can be found at a variety of venues all over town, with local cinemaniacs favouring the Landmark Sunshine (p85) on the Lower East Side and the Lincoln Plaza Cinemas (across from Lincoln Center) on the Upper West Side. On its three (smallish) screens, Film Forum (p99) programmes a wide range of revivals and new indie features, while Anthology Film Archives – which recently replaced its legendarily uncomfortable seats – specialises in experimental programming. The Museum of Modern Art (p122) and the Lincoln Center Film Society's Walter Reade Theater also offer well-curated series and impeccable screening conditions.

Come summer, free outdoor screenings seem to pop up just about everywhere. The most popular ones take place in Bryant Park (located behind the public library on Fifth Avenue, at 42nd Street), where the crowds arrive early to grab a spot and enjoy a picnic before the movie begins. Check *Time Out New York* for other outdoors series such as RiverFlicks, Rooftop Films or Summer on the Hudson: Movies Under the Stars.

THE FUNNIEST SHOW IN THE WORLD!

MONTY PYTHON'S
SPAMALOT™

Photography by Simon Turtle & Joan Marcus

Visit Telecharge.com
or call 212-239-6200

Ⓢ Shubert Theatre · 225 West 44th Street
Grammy®-winning cast album on DECCA
www.MontyPythonsSpamalot.com

Classical music

'How do you get to Carnegie Hall?' a tourists asks a New Yorker. 'Practice, practice, practice,' is the answer. This may be the quintessential New York classical-music joke, but you *do* need to know how to get to the famous venue on 57th Street. This season, Carnegie Hall (p120) has lined up two major series that will actually spread out to citywide venues such as the Apollo Theater and the Cathedral of St John the Divine: the first is a sprawling tribute to Leonard Bernstein from September to December 2008 (p118); the second is a celebration of the African-American legacy, curated by soprano Jessye Norman, in March 2009 (see box p155).

Uptown, the Lincoln Center 'campus' (p152) encompasses several buildings and is home to the New York Philharmonic and two opera houses. After a long renovation, Alice Tully Hall reopens in February '09 with a month-long festival of wildly diverse programming: all tickets will be $25 or less. The Metropolitan Opera, now in its 125th season, continues to shake off its reputation for restrained shows by reaching out to directors such as Canadian experimentalist Robert Lepage (*La Damnation de Faust*, fall 2008) and staging new works such as John Adams's *Doctor Atomic* (fall 2008). And, of course, the Met can always be relied on for powerhouse singing: Anna Netrebko, Plácido Domingo, Renée Fleming, Deborah Voigt, Natalie Dessay, Juan Diego Flórez and Ben Heppner are only some of the stars scheduled for the 2008-09 season.

Across the plaza from the Met is the New York State Theater (p153), where City Opera has long been known for smaller budget,

imaginative stagings of classics and obscure Baroque pieces. The house is in a bit of a transition right now: it's starting extensive renovations in the fall of 2008, and a new general manager, the adventurous Gérard Mortier, is due to arrive in fall '09. In addition to these institutions, Lincoln Center also hosts several series such as American Songbook, Great Performers and Mostly Mozart.

Dance

New York is dance. On the one hand, resident companies such as Merce Cunningham, Paul Taylor, Trisha Brown and Alvin Ailey are among the world's best, and you can often catch visiting troupes such as the Kirov Ballet. On the other, you can discover cutting-edge choreographers such as Sarah Michelson, Christopher Wheeldon and Eiko & Koma in intimate venues that sometimes place you a few inches from the performers.

If classical and neo-classical fare are more your style, it's hard to beat American Ballet Theatre (at the Metropolitan Opera every spring) and New York City Ballet (at the New York State Theater in winter and spring); the Joyce Theater presents touring companies in various dance disciplines. Those interested in edgier fare should check out listings for Dance Theater Workshop (219 W 19th Street, between Seventh & Eighth Avenues, 1-212 924 0077), Danspace Project (131 E 10th Street, at Second Avenue, 1-212 674 8191), the Kitchen (p110) and Movement Research at Judson Church (55 Washington Square South, at Thompson Street, 1-212 539 2611). The latter is the home of the Judson Dance Theater, which revolutionised dance in the 1960s and continues to offer free showcases of new artists.

BROADWAY'S ALL-TIME KILLER HIT

CHICAGO

TELECHARGE.COM or 212-239-6200

CHICAGOTHEMUSICAL.COM ⑤ AMBASSADOR THEATRE · 219 WEST 49TH STREET
NEW YORK · LONDON

Calendar

Central Park SummerStage p40

Dates highlighted in **bold** are public holidays.

September 2008

1 Labor Day
Early **Broadway on Broadway**
Times Square, p116
www.broadwayonbroadway.com
Stars perform for free their Broadway hits and more in Times Square.

Mid **Feast of San Gennaro**
Little Italy, p72
www.sangennaro.org
One-day Italian-American street fair.

Mid **Howl!**
East Village, p85
www.howlfestival.com
Eight days of art events, films, readings and more, in the East Village.

16 September-14 December
Giorgio Morandi
Metropolitan Museum of Art, p141
www.metmuseum.org
A complete overview of Morandi's career, with some 110 works on show.

21 September-4 January 2009
Van Gogh by Night
Museum of Modern Art, p122
www.moma.org

24 September-13 December
Leonard Bernstein
Carnegie Hall, p120
www.carnegiehall.org
A festival in tribute to the legendary conductor/composer.

October 2008

Ongoing Giorgio Morandi (see Sept); Van Gogh by Night (see Sept); Leonard Bernstein (see Sept)

Early-mid **New York Film Festival**
Lincoln Center, p152
www.filmlinc.com

4, 5 **Open House New York**
Various locations
www.ohny.org
Architectural sites that are normally off-limits open their doors for two days.

13 Columbus Day

Winter's magic

The cold weather brings festive lights, dazzling shop-window displays and a chance to go for a glide on the ice. One place to take it all in at once is the **Rock Center Café** (20 W 50th Street, between Fifth & Sixth Avenues, 1-212 332 7620), which looks out on one of the city's most romantic spots, the skating rink at **Rockefeller Center** (p124). Put on some skates and join the mayhem, or just sit back and laugh at the falling tourists. Another rink, behind Fifth Avenue's stately public library, called the **Pond at Bryant Park** (Sixth Avenue, between 40th & 42nd Streets), features ice-skating sessions and festive candy-cane-striped tents filled with gifts and snacks.

If it's Christmas trees you love, check out the **American Museum of Natural History** (p148) where they have a giant evergreen decorated with intricate origami ornaments and crowned with a floating star sculpture. The hundreds of beautifully constructed dragons, dinosaurs and animals on this overwhelming display will take your breath away.

Further uptown, the **Time Warner Center** (p149) offers up a goofy but fun light show featuring three-dimensional stars that change colours in time with music while tiny strobes pop and flash. The show is best viewed from the balconies (or with a drink in one of the third-floor bars), where you'll see reflections in the windows. At **Grand Central Terminal** (p131) children will love the light projections on the famous, celestial ceiling, while the Christmas fair features stacks of presents and candy canes.

In the Bronx, the spirit of the season chugs along at the holiday train exhibit of the **New York Botanical Garden** (p158) amid a striking display of miniature 18th- and 19th-century buildings, including city landmarks, all constructed out of plant materials. Twinkling lights add a dreamy quality to this lush fantasy land.

Last but not least: attention shoppers! From late November to early January, the city's big department stores try to outdo each other with displays that rival the stage sets on Broadway – Barneys (p146), Bergdorf Goodman (p125) and Saks (p127) are especially eye-popping.

16 October-15 February 2009
Alexander Calder: The Paris Years
Whitney Museum of Art, p143
www.whitney.org

21-25 **CMJ Music Marathon & FilmFest**
Various locations
www.cmj.com
Showcase for new musical acts, as well as music-related films.

31 **Village Halloween Parade**
Greenwich Village, p91
www.halloween-nyc.com

November 2008

Ongoing Giorgio Morandi (see Sept); Van Gogh by Night (see Sept); Leonard Bernstein (see Sept); Alexander Calder (see Oct)

Early **Radio City Christmas Spectacular**
Radio City Music Hall, p123
www.radiocity.com
The Rockettes' holiday show.

Early **New York City Marathon**
Various locations
www.nycmarathon.org
Starting on Staten Island, the course runs through Brooklyn and Queens before finishing in Central Park.

2 November-12 January 2009
Joan Miró
Museum of Modern Art, p122
www.moma.org

11 **Veterans' Day**

18 November-15 March 2009
Beyond Babylon
Metropolitan Museum of Art, p141
www.metmuseum.org

20 November-6 January 2009
Annual Christmas Tree and Neapolitan Baroque Crèche
Metropolitan Museum of Art, p141
www.metmuseum.org

26-27 **Macy's Thanksgiving Eve Balloon Blowup & Thanksgiving Day Parade**
Various locations
www.macys.com
The stars of this annual parade are the gigantic, inflated balloons.

27 **Thanksgiving Day**

Late-early January 2009
The Nutcracker
Lincoln Center, p152
www.nycballet.com

Late **Christmas Tree Lighting Ceremony**
Rockefeller Center, p124
www.rockefellercenter.com
Marvel at the giant evergreen.

December 2008

Ongoing Giorgio Morandi (see Sept); Van Gogh by Night (see Sept); Leonard Bernstein (see Sept); Alexander Calder (see Oct) Joan Miró (see Nov); Beyond Babylon (see Nov); Annual Christmas Tree & Neapolitan Baroque Crèche (see Nov)

Mid **National Chorale Messiah Sing-In**
Lincoln Center, p152
www.nationalchorale.org
Join a chorus of 3,000 for an evening performance of Handel's *Messiah*.

25 **Christmas Day**

31 **New Year's Eve Ball Drop**
Times Square, p116
www.timessquarebid.org
See the giant illuminated ball descend.

31 **New Year's Eve Fireworks**
Central Park, p135
www.centralparknyc.org
The fireworks explode at midnight.

31 **New Year's Eve Midnight Run**
Central Park, p135
www.nyrrc.org
Start the new year as you mean to go on – with a four-mile jog.

January 2009

Ongoing Van Gogh by Night (see Sept); Alexander Calder (see Oct) Joan Miró (see Nov); Beyond Babylon (see Nov); Annual Christmas Tree and Neapolitan Baroque Crèche (see Dec); *The Nutcracker* (see Nov)

1 **New Year's Day**

1 **New Year's Day Marathon Poetry Reading**

Gay & Lesbian Pride March p41

East Village, p85
www.poetryproject.com
Big-name bohos step up to the mic in this free spoken-word spectacle.

19 Martin Luther King, Jr Day

Mid-late **Winter Antiques Show**
Midtown East, p130
www.winterantiquesshow.com
One of the world's most prestigious antiques shows.

Late **Winter Restaurant Week**
Various locations
www.nycvisit.com
An opportunity to sample gourmet food at low prices in the last two weeks of January (weekdays only).

26 Chinese New Year
Chinatown, p72
www.explorechinatown.com
Festivals and fun during the two weeks of the Lunar New Year.

February 2009

Ongoing Alexander Calder (see Oct); Beyond Babylon (see Nov)

16 Presidents' Day

Late **The Art Show**
Seventh Regiment Armory

www.artdealers.org
Serious collectors and casual art fans peruse this vast fair.

March 2009

Ongoing Beyond Babylon
(see Nov)

4-23 March **Honor! African American Cultural Legacy**
Carnegie Hall, p120
www.carnegiehall.org
A Jesse Norman curated festival in honour of African American music and performers. See box p155.

4-8 **The Armory Show**
Pier 94, Midtown West, p127
www.thearmoryshow.com
A huge contemporary art mart.

12 **Easter Parade**
Fifth Avenue, p121
Admire the myriad creative Easter bonnets on show at this one-day event.

17 **St Patrick's Day Parade**
Fifth Avenue, p121
www.saintpatricksdayparade.com
The traditional huge march of green-clad merrymakers.

Late **Ringling Bros and Barnum & Bailey Circus Animal Parade**
Midtown

www.ringling.com
Elephants, horses and zebras march through Manhattan.

24 March-8 June **Photography and the American West**
Museum of Modern Art, p122
www.moma.org

April 2009

Ongoing Photography and the American West (see Mar)

Early **New York Antiquarian Book Fair**
Park Avenue Armory, Upper East Side, p140
www.sanfordsmith.com
Book dealers showcase all manner of rare and antique tomes over three days of heaven for bibliophiles.

10-19 **New York International Auto Show**
Jacob Javitz Convention Center, Midtown West, p127
www.autoshowny.com
More than 1,000 autos and futuristic concept cars on display.

Late **Tribeca Film Festival**
Tribeca, p64
www.tribecafilmfestival.org
Two-week Robert De Niro-organised festival of independent films.

May 2009

Ongoing Photography and the American West (see Mar)

5 May-28 July **Aernout Mik**
Museum of Modern Art, p122
www.moma.org

Early **Global Marijuana March**
Downtown
www.globalmarijuanamarch.com
Meet and greet local stoners and learn about marijuana-related issues.

Early **Bike New York: The Great Five Boro Bike Tour**
www.bikenewyork.org
Thousands of cyclists take part in a 42-mile Tour de New York.

Mid **Fleet Week**
Midtown West, p127
www.intrepidmuseum.org
Ahoy there! New York's streets teem with sailors for a week.

Late **Lower East Side Festival of the Arts**
Lower East Side, p76
www.theaterforthenewcity.net
Theatre, poetry readings, films and family-friendly programming, over three days.

25 Memorial Day

Late May-August **Bryant Park Free Summer Season**
Bryant Park, Midtown, p123
www.bryantpark.org
Alfresco movies on Monday nights, Broadway numbers and more.

Late **Ninth Avenue International Food Festival**
Midtown West, p127
www.hellskitchennyc.com
Excellent two-day food festival in, appropriately enough, Hell's Kitchen.

Late May-September **Washington Square Outdoor Art Exhibit**
Washington Square Park, p91
www.washingtonsquareoutdoorart exhibit.org
One-of-a-kind arts and crafts.

June 2009

Ongoing Photography and the American West (see Mar); Aernout Mik (see May); Bryant Park Free Summer Season (see May); Washington Square Outdoor Art Exhibit (see May)

Early-August **Met in the Parks**
Central Park, p135
www.metopera.org
The Metropolitan Opera stages free performances.

Early-August **Central Park SummerStage**
Central Park, p135
www.summerstage.org
Rockers, symphonies, authors and dance companies take over the stage.

Early-August **Shakespeare in the Park**
Delacorte Theater, Central Park, p135
www.publictheater.org
Celebrities pull on their tights and take a whack at the Bard.

Early **SOFA New York**
Park Avenue Armory, Upper East Side, p140
www.sofaexpo.com
Giant three-day show of Sculptural Objects and Functional Art.

Mid **National Puerto Rican Day Parade**
Fifth Avenue, p121
www.nationalpuertoricandayparade.org
Celebrate the city's largest Hispanic community, and its culture.

Mid **Museum Mile Festival**
Various locations, Fifth Avenue, p121
www.museummilefestival.org
Nine major museums are free of charge to the public for one day every year.

Independence Day p41

Mid **Broadway Bares**
Roseland Ballroom, Midtown
www.broadwaycares.org
This one-day charity fundraiser features Broadway's hottest bodies sans their normal costumes.

Mid **JVC Jazz Festival**
Various locations
www.festivalproductions.net
This two-week jazz bash is now a New York City institution.

27 **Mermaid Parade**
Coney Island, Brooklyn
www.coneyisland.com
Decked-out, made-up mermaids share the parade route with elaborate, kitschy floats.

28 **Gay & Lesbian Pride March**
Greenwich Village, p91
www.hopinc.org
Downtown is a sea of rainbow flags.

Late June-July **Midsummer Night Swing**
Lincoln Center Plaza, p152
www.lincolncenter.org
Dance under the stars to salsa, Cajun, swing and other music, over three blissful evenings.

July 2009

Ongoing Aernout Mik (see May); Bryant Park Free Summer Season (see May); Washington Square Outdoor Art Exhibit (see May); Met in the Parks (see June); Central Park SummerStage (see June); Shakespeare in the Park (see June)

4 **Independence Day**

4 **Nathan's Famous July 4 Hot Dog Eating Contest**
Coney Island, Brooklyn
www.nathansfamous.com

4 **Macy's Fireworks Display**
East River
www.macys.com
World-famous annual display.

Mid **New York Philharmonic Concerts in the Parks**
Central Park and various locations
www.newyorkphilharmonic.org
Classical music programme in many of the city's larger parks, over the course of a week. Often sublime.

Turkey day guide

The Thanksgiving Day parade is a time honoured tradition. Here are a few tips for taking in the fun. **The night before** Go witness the final preparations and get a behind the scenes peek. There's two parts: 1. Balloon inflation, 3-10pm. Watch Snoopy and his inflatable chums come to life on Thanksgiving Eve near the American Museum of Natural History. 2. Float assembly, midnight-8am (Thursday morning). Laugh in the face of the wee hours and wait for the floats to emerge from the Lincoln Tunnel in disassembled form. The convoy will advance up Amsterdam Avenue to Central Park West around 11.45pm. At midnight, the Macy's team assembles the fragments on the streets. For the best views head to Central Park West at 81st Street. **Parade Day basics** The route, unchanged for years, starts at 77th Street and Central Park West and meanders south to Macy's at Herald Square. Though the first massive balloon doesn't cross the starting line until 9am, parade officials recommend that you pick your viewing spot by 7am. A map of the route and suggested viewing locations are available at the Macy's website. **The useless facts you want to know** Macy's is the world's second-largest consumer of helium. The parade is put together by a small team of Macy's employees and 4,000 volunteers who work year-round in a studio in Hoboken.
■ www.macys.com

Late **Mostly Mozart Festival**
Lincoln Center, p152
www.lincolncenter.org
Four weeks of works by Mozart and his contemporaries.

Late **Summer Restaurant Week**
Various locations
www.nycvisit.com
An opportunity to sample gourmet food at low prices in the last two weeks of July (weekdays only).

August 2009

Ongoing Washington Square Outdoor Art Exhibit (see May); Met in the Parks (see June); Central Park SummerStage (see June); Shakespeare in the Park (see June); Mostly Mozart (see July)

Early **Central Park Zoo Chillout Weekend**
Central Park, p135
www.wcs.org
This freeze-fest features penguin and polar-bear talent shows, games and more, over a weekend.

Early-September **Lincoln Center Out of Doors Festival**
Lincoln Center, p152
www.lincolncenter.org
Month-long free family-friendly festival of classic and contemporary works.

Early-mid **New York International Fringe Festival**
Various locations
www.fringenyc.org
Wacky, weird and sometimes great. Hundreds of different performances over 16 days.

Harlem Week
Harlem, p154
www.harlemdiscover.com
Massive August street fair serving up live music, art and food.

September 2009

7 Labor Day

Early **Broadway on Broadway**
See above Sept 2008.

Mid **Feast of San Gennaro**
See above Sept 2008.

Mid **Howl!**
See above Sept 2008.

October 2009

Early **Intrepid Museum Re-opens**
Midtown West, p127
www.intrepidmuseum.com

Early-mid **New York Film Festival**
See above Oct 2008.

Early **Open House New York**
See above Oct 2008.

13 Columbus Day

Late **CMJ Music Marathon & FilmFest**
See above Oct 2008.

31 Village Halloween Parade
See above Oct 2008.

November 2009

Early **Radio City Christmas Spectacular**
See above Nov 2008.

Early **New York City Marathon**
See above Nov 2008.

11 Veterans' Day

25-26 Macy's Thanksgiving Eve Balloon Blowup & Thanksgiving Day Parade
See above Nov 2008.

26 Thanksgiving Day

Late **The Nutcracker**
See above Nov 2008.

Late **Christmas Tree Lighting**
See above Nov 2008.

December 2009

Mid **National Chorale Messiah Sing-In**
See above Dec 2008.

25 Christmas Day

31 New Year's Eve Ball Drop
See above Dec 2008.

31 New Year's Eve Fireworks
See above Dec 2008.

31 New Year's Eve Midnight Run
See above Dec 2008.

Itineraries

Surf2Live Surfing School

Surf City

While New York will never be mistaken for a premier surfing destination, that doesn't mean you can't find some gnarly waves here. Whether you want to follow this weekend itinerary or tailor it for a day trip – you'll be surprised how much Surfing USA there is in NYC.

'I caught my first tube today, sir.' Thus spoke Special Agent Johnny Utah to his irate commanding officer in the 1991 Keanu Reeves classic, *Point Break*. Most of what we city-dwellers know about surfing comes from this schlocky – yet strangely captivating – film. Fortunately, you don't have to go to the South Pacific to experience surfing: there are plenty of tubes to be caught right here.

First thing's first: where's the surf? Hop on the LIRR (p184) to Long Beach. After disembarking, cross West Park Avenue to **Bi-Wise Drugs** (26 W Park Avenue, 516-432-7131) to purchase a beach day pass before dropping your stuff off at **Jackson by the Beach Hotel** (405 E Broadway, 516 431 3700; from $99), one of the few places in town to spend the night.

Before diving in, start things with a low-key bike ride. Catch the N33 bus and head to West Beech Street, where you can rent some wheels at **Buddy's Bikes Etc** (907 W Beech Street, 1-516 431 0804), then cruise around the bar and restaurant-laden west end of Long Beach. Take your time and scope out the waves and the bodies. After you return your rental, cross the street to the **Beach House** (906 W Beech Street, no phone),

Buddy's Bikes Etc

an open-air bar that has live music and tasty crab cakes. Later, turn to the **Inn** (943 W Beech Street, 1-516 432 9220) for an evening of sweaty dance-and-grope.

If you require caffeine to get your nerve up for a day of surfing, the Jackson is conveniently situated a few blocks from the **Coffee Nut Café** (250 E Park Avenue, 1-516 897 6616), where the wide variety of java flavours will help you recover from the night before.

But before hitting the waves be sure to adorn yourself with the latest summer styles. Stock up on beach gear at **Unsound Surf** (359 E Park Avenue, 1-516 889 1112) and sign up for lessons with Elliot Zuckerman at **Surf2Live Surfing School** (1-516 432 9211, www.surf2live.com, from $65).

'Listen, you're the quarter-back jock. It's all balance and coordination. How hard can it be?' Well, Utah, pretty hard as it turns

out. Thank God, then, for the group surfing lessons at Long Beach. These last around 90 minutes and the staff – all young and tanned – will teach you how to stand up properly. Later, they give you push-starts into the waves so you're not just floundering around on your board. Plus, the school provides all of the equipment.

Having been disabused of the idea that you'll be a natural at surfing, grab a bite to eat at **Corbin & Reynolds** (20 W Park Avenue, 1-516 431 4600). The burgers come in at around $10.

If you're not too humiliated (or bloodied), continue your surf odyssey in Far Rockaway, a ten-minute cab ride from Long Beach, but note: the wave-heavy beaches here have a tendency to get crowded on the weekends (go early in the morning). Also, most locals don't take kindly to neophytes who get in the way. Those who want to stay on the path of Johnny Utah should consider making friends with a local who actually knows what he or she is doing. This will help prevent disaster, whether it's in the form of a bad wipeout or just getting your ass kicked for being stupid. Overcrowded surf beaches can bring out the worst in people. If you're unsure of where to go or how to comport yourself, ask around at the **Rockaway Beach Surf Shop** (177 Beach 116th Street, 1-718 474 9345).

When you've had your fill of surf and sand, head back to Manhattan and strike the right note by hitting **Bondi Road** (153 Rivington Street, between Clinton & Suffolk Streets, 1-212 253 5311), a bar named after that most famous of Sydney beaches. It has a $15 all-you-can-drink brunch (add $5 for the Queen Adelaide or Barrier Reef Benedict), which will put you in to an appropriate state of mind for the coma-inducing Lomi Lomi Hawaiian Luau Massage at **Just Calm Down** (32 W 22nd Street, between Fifth & Sixth Avenues, 1-212 337 0032). Your aching muscles will appreciate the care and attention of native Hawaiian Kawai Anakalea.

Vaya con dios, dude!

Mo Bay

Harlem, Salsero-style

Opportunities for eating and dancing, not to mention worshipping, abound Uptown – head to Harlem and you'll experience a side of New York that most tourists never see. We've devised this itinerary so you can pick and choose as you go: visit the neighbourhood for an evening or explore it for several days. Either way, you won't be bored.

Set the tone with a lunch of fried chicken, collard greens, macaroni cheese and red velvet cake at **Miss Maude's Spoonbread Too** (547 Lenox Avenue, between 137th & 138th Streets, 1-212 690 3100).

Work off your midday meal with a turn through the visual arts gallery at **Schomburg Center for Research in Black Culture** (p157), one of the country's premier centers for research in to African-American culture, before heading over to the **African Mart** (116th Street, between Fifth & Lenox Avenues), where you can score earrings from Mali, batik cloths and loads of beads.

The after-work scene at **Mo Bay** (17 W 125th Street, between Fifth Avenue & Malcolm X Boulevard, 1-212 876 9300) is always entertaining and they serve Caribbean fare, like shrimp with savoury cabbage.

Now for some dancing. Old-school salseros have been keeping mambo alive Uptown since Eddie Torres, the 'Mambo King', popularised the 'New York on 2' Palladium dance-club style in 1965 (he was also the driving force behind the '80s resurgence of what used to be called 'Latin' dance).

Les Ambassades

Boulevards, 1-212 281 4100) – conveniently located next to the succulent steamed vegetables and soy burgers served up at **Café Veg** (2291 Adam Clayton Powell Jr. Boulevard, between 134th & 135th Streetss, 1-212 491 3223).

If dancing isn't your thing, pass the afternoon with **Harlem Is Home Tours** (1-212 658 9160), whose guides will speed you around various neighbourhoods of architectural interest, including Strivers Row, with its wrought-iron appointed facades. Afterwards, dig into Senegalese-inspired seafood at **Les Ambassades** (2200 Frederick Douglass Boulevard, at 118th Street, 1-212 666 0078), where Marcus Samuelsson, Aquavit's famous chef, has been known to drop by for takeout.

Follow dinner with jazz and cheap drinks on 'Sugar Hill' at **St. Nick's Pub** (773 St Nicholas Avenue, between 149th & 150th Streets, 1-212 283 9728) – late-night snacks, such as crispy fried shrimp and potatoes, can be procured from **Devin's Fish & Chips** (747 St Nicholas Avenue, at 147th Street, 1-212 491 5518). If you like organ-based jazz and stiff martinis, hit **Showman's** (375 W 125th Street, at Morningside Avenue, 1-212 864 8941) and **Minton's Playhouse** (210 W 118th Street, between Adam Clayton Powell Jr. Boulevard & St Nicholas Avenue, 1-212 864 8346) before heading for bed.

Churches abound in Harlem. The lines to get into the Abyssinian and Convent Avenue Baptist churches are notoriously long, so try one off the beaten track. Check out the praise dancing at the **Bethel Gospel Assembly** (2-26 E 120th Street, between Mt Morris Park West & Fifth Avenue, 1-212 860 1510), or hear the thunderous sounds of the McCollough Sons, a spectacular brass band that serves

Most Fridays, they'll be dancing on the third floor of the **Harlem State Office Building** (163 W 125th Street, at Adam Clayton Powell Jr. Boulevard, 1-212 961 4471) to everything from Eddie Palmieri to the Spanish Harlem Orchestra.

In the outdoor sculpture garden at the **Studio Museum** (144 W 125th Street, between Malcolm X & Adam Clayton Powell Jr. Boulevards, 1-212 864 0014), Harlem's leading art institution, you'll find single buppies grooving to R&B. Seven short blocks north on Adam Clayton Powell Jr. Boulevard stands Harlem's newest small club, the **Shrine** (2271 Adam Clayton Powell Jr. Boulevard, between 133rd & 134th Streets, 1-212 690 7807). Drop in for finger food, drinks and live music.

If you think you need some help with your dancing, don't sweat. Jessie Hamilton offers an excellent salsa class from 9am to noon on Saturdays at the **Harlem YMCA** (180 W 135th Street, between Adam Clayton Powell Jr. & Malcolm X

Camaradas el Barrio

as the music ministry at the **United House of Prayer for All People** (2320 Frederick Douglass Boulevard, between 124th & 125th Streets, 1-212 864 8795).

Traditional dinner-breakfast combinations like chicken with waffles began when ladies were 'broads' and men were 'Macs' back at the now-defunct Wells, which was frequented by numbers runners, street pharmacists and show girls in need of a substantial breakfast before passing out after a hard night. Staying true to that tradition is **Amy Ruth's** (113 W 116th Street, between Malcolm X & Adam Clayton Powell Jr. Boulevards, 1-212 280 8779), which serves the waffles warm, the grits creamy and the shrimp crisp.

Work off the calories at a dance lesson at **Santo Rico** (2403 Second Avenue, between 123rd & 124th Streets, 1-212 289 1302). The 'Ladies Style' class teaches the subtleties of the upper body (head, arms, hands, torso and hips), which give salsa its sexy look.

Dine on new-wave Puerto Rican cuisine, complete with musical accompaniment, at **Camaradas el Barrio Bar & Restaurant** (2241 First Avenue, at 115th Street, 1-212 248 2703), a renovated workers' public house. Try the *mofongo* (garlic-flavoured, fried plantains).

Finally, don't miss the **Cotton Club** (666 W 125th Street, between Broadway & Riverside Drive, 1-212 663 7980), a stuccoed building underneath the Henry Hudson Parkway. On Monday nights ($15), you and your partner can swing on a 600-square-foot mahogany dance floor to the sounds of trumpet player Al Pazant, formerly of Count Basie's orchestra. The restaurant, which serves Southern cuisine, is designed to evoke memories of the Prohibition era.

Devotees come from all over to dance here in retro outfits to the 13-piece band. You'll see everything from poodle skirts and fishnet stockings to zoot suits and spectator shoes, though beginners are welcome too.

Our Town

Whether it's your first or tenth visit to New York, here's a chance to bag some essential NYC spots in a single weekend.

Friday

Contemplate the city's rural beginnings during a late afternoon visit to the roof garden (open between May and October) atop the **Metropolitan Museum of Art** (p141). Here, the sculptures of renowned contemporary artists (or old masters) compete for your attention with the most jaw-dropping view of Central Park, Fifth Avenue and Central Park West. There's a beer and wine bar (open until 8.30pm) to help put you in a New York state of mind while you take in the stellar panorama. If the weather is inclement, check out the indoor aesthetics, which are just as breathtaking. Bone up on some of New York's most esteemed artists in the American Wing of Painting and Sculpture, including members of the famed Hudson River School.

When dinner calls, walk west to the **Central Park Boathouse Restaurant** (midpark, at 75th Street, 1-212 517 2233), where a contemporary seafood-oriented menu awaits (or opt for an informal snack on the terrace).

After your meal, it's time for the requisite New York jazz experience. The **Village Vanguard** (p94), Downtown, has been hosting hepcats for 73 years, and it's still a vibrant spot. This basement club was the venue for legendary sets from the likes of Sonny Rollins, John Coltrane and Wynton Marsalis and boasts over 100 'Live From the Village Vanguard' recordings. To get there, walk east to Fifth Avenue and hail a cab.

Lower East Side Tenement Museum

Saturday

Enjoy a leisurely brunch at
Pershing Square (90 E 42nd Street,
at Park Avenue, 1-212 286 9600),
located beneath the Park Avenue
viaduct and across the street from
the sublime Beaux Arts beauty,
Grand Central Terminal
(p131). After you've had your
fill of pancakes and coffee, head
across the street to Grand Central.
Be sure to peek into the main
concourse and, for God's sake, look
up! The astronomical ceiling with
its twinkling constellations was
designed in the 1930s (and restored
in 1998). Then board an eastbound
7 train to Willets Point, the stop
nearest the **Queens Museum of
Art** (p164), your next destination.
The main attraction here is the
Panorama of the City of New York,
a 9,335-square-foot model of NYC
that has been wowing generations
of New Yorkers since it was
commissioned for the 1964 World's
Fair in Queens. In early 2007 the
Panorama underwent a long-
overdue upgrade. An updated
lighting system now mimics the arc
of the sun as it passes over NYC,
while a new 13-minute multimedia
presentation explores the
Panorama's construction and
spotlights various NYC attractions.

When you've finished here, take
the 7 back towards Manhattan and
get off at the 45th Road-Courthouse
Square stop. Exit on to Jackson
Avenue and walk right one block
to 46th Avenue. Welcome to **P.S.1
Contemporary Art Center**
(p164). Take in some of the best
contemporary art shows the city
has to offer. If it's summer (July to
early September), you're in luck:
the world-renowned Warm Up
party will be in full swing.

Sunday

Today's schedule starts at the
**Lower East Side Tenement
Museum** (p76). Walk through the
doors and see where the huddled
masses yearning to breathe free did
their huddling. More than 7,000
immigrants lived in this single

tenement between 1863 and 1935 and, in one remarkable afternoon, the experiences of four of those families are brought to life in a guided tour of the apartments. These are meticulously restored to show what they would have looked like when the families lived there. For lunch, you're going to **Katz's Delicatessen**. (Walk to Delancey Street and head east one block to Ludlow Street. Now go three blocks north to Houston.) At this old neon-lit sentinel at the corner of Ludlow and Houston, the wieners are crisp and the pastrami peerless. The service is old-fashioned, fun even – diners grab tickets, then line up by a long counter to place orders for huge sandwiches, knishes, beer and pickles. Katz's slogan, a patriotic redoubt visited by scores of politicians and luminaries over the years, is 'Send a salami to your boy in the army'. It dates back to World War II, which suddenly doesn't seem so long ago or far away.

Time to check off another New York icon: catch the Downtown 6 train at the corner of Bleecker Street and Lafayette Street (stroll west on Houston about ten blocks to Lafayette and go one block north to Bleecker). Get off the train at the Brooklyn Bridge-City Hall stop. Standing in City Hall Park, just outside the subway entrance, face east towards **Brooklyn Bridge** (p55). As you cross over Centre Street, to the bridge's walkway, say goodbye to Manhattan. The 3,460-foot suspension bridge was the first to use steel for its web of cable wires, and was the longest suspension bridge in the world back on the day it opened – 24 May 1883. That day, more than 150,000 people paid a cent to stroll across the bridge and marvel at the Gothic towers that rise out of the East River. As you stroll, be sure to take a few minutes to read the panels that tell about the bridge's construction. Turn back when you reach the middle of the bridge. You can catch your breath on a bench in City Hall Park and, while you're at it, pat yourself on the back – with all the ground you've covered, you're practically a New Yorker.

Metropolitan Museum of Art p50

New York by Area

City Hall from under Brooklyn Bridge

Downtown

Welcome to the birthplace of New York City. It can be hard to believe that what started so humbly on a tree-lined waterfront evolved into the thriving metropolis we know and love today. Still, much of the old times remains: below 14th Street the roads are (rather charmingly) crooked and, for the most part, have names, not numbers. A wonderful way to while away the day is to take a stroll among the posh shops of Soho and the Meatpacking District. Revel in the punk's-not-dead spirit of the East Village, sip espresso in Greenwich Village or people-watch in Washington Square Park. The real estate boom may not have loosened its grip – some of the costliest rents can be found here – but plenty of bohemian charm remains.

Financial District

The southern tip of Manhattan is generally known as the Financial District because, in the days before telecommunications, banking institutions established their headquarters here to be near the city's active port. Down here, Atlantic Ocean breezes remind you that millions of people once travelled to the city on creaking, overcrowded sailing ships. You can trace the final stretch of their journey past the golden torch of the Statue of Liberty, through the immigration and quarantine centres of Ellis Island and, finally, to the statue-dotted Battery Park promenade. Nearby is the boarding place for the famous Staten Island Ferry.

While this area is bisected vertically by the ever-bustling

Broadway, it's that east-west thoroughfare **Wall Street** that is synonymous with the world's greatest den of capitalism.

Over on the eastern shore of lower Manhattan is the **South Street Seaport**, which was redeveloped in the mid 1980s and is now lined with reclaimed and renovated buildings that have been converted into shops, restaurants, bars and a museum. Check out the fine views of the **Brooklyn Bridge**.

Sights & museums

African Burial Ground

Duane Street, between Broadway & Centre Streets, behind 290 Broadway (www.africanburialground.com). Subway W, R, N, Q to Canal Street; J, M, Z to Chambers Street; 4, 5, 6 to Brooklyn Bridge-City Hall. **Open** 9am-4pm Mon-Fri. **Admission** free. **Map** p56 C2 ❶
A major archaeological discovery, the African Burial Ground is a small remnant of a five-and-a-half-acre cemetery where somewhere between 10,000 and 20,000 African men, women and children were buried. The cemetery closed in 1794, but was unearthed during construction of a federal office building in 1991 and later designated a National Historic Landmark.

Brooklyn Bridge

Subway A, C to High Street; J, M, Z to Chambers Street; 4, 5, 6 to Brooklyn Bridge-City Hall. **Map** p57 D3 ❷
The extraordinary views and awe-inspiring web of steel cables will take your breath away. As you walk, bicycle or rollerblade along its wood-planked promenade, keep an eye out for plaques detailing the story of the bridge's construction.

City Hall

City Hall Park, from Vesey to Chambers Streets, between Broadway & Park Row (1-212 788 3000/www.nyc.gov). Subway J, M, Z to Chambers Street; 2, 3 to Park Place; 4, 5, 6 to Brooklyn Bridge-City Hall. **Map** p56 C2 ❸

Battery Park

NEW YORK BY AREA

Downtown 1

E 26TH ST

E 24TH ST
THIRD AVE

E 23RD ST

22ND ST

GRAMERCY
PARK

Peter Cooper
Village

E 20TH ST

FRANKLIN D ROOSEVELT DR

Manhattan
Marina
70

1

mercy
Park
ational
's Club

ASSER LEVY PL

SECOND AVE

FIRST AVE

E 14TH PL

RUTHERFORD PL

NATHAN D
PERLMAN PL

Stuyvesant
Square

Stuyvesant
Town

E 18TH ST

E 16TH ST

E 15TH ST

6TH ST

M L

E 14TH ST

2

119

111

E 13TH ST

E 12TH ST

112

E 12TH ST

105

E 11TH ST

SZOLD PL

E 12TH ST

St. Mark's Church
in-the-Bowery

25

115

Grace
Church

113

109

E 10TH ST

E 9TH ST

118

129

PL

117

131

ST MARKS PLACE

Tompkins
Square

E 8TH ST

E 7TH ST

AVENUE A

AVENUE B

AVENUE C

FOURTH
AVE

22

30

107

110 114

106 124

108

109

E 6TH ST

E 5TH ST

AVENUE D

3

104
GREAT
ONES ST

128

116

EAST VILLAGE

E 4TH ST

E 3RD ST

E 2ND ST

123

BOND ST

M BLEECKER
ST 127
120

New Museum of
Contemporary Art

64

65

102

100

E HOUSTON ST

M
F.V

87

81

88

98 95

66

83

NORFOLK ST

71

East
River
Park

STANTON ST

99

SUFFOLK ST

CLINTON ST

ATTORNEY ST

RIDGE ST

PITT ST

COLUMBIA ST

72
92

FREEMAN
ALLEY

101

85

86 96

97

90 93

MULBERRY

MOTT ST

ELIZABETH

RIVINGTON ST

89 81

82

77

DELANCEY ST NORTH

WILLIAMSBURG BRIDGE

4

60

91

Lower East Side
Tenement Museum

M J.M.Z

94

LOWER EAST
SIDE

DELANCEY ST SOUTH

BIALYSTOKER PL

ABRAHAM E
KAZAN ST

LEWIS ST

KENMARE ST

CENTRE
MARKET PL

BAXTER

LITTLE
ITALY

THE BOWERY

60

M

S

84

72

GRAND ST

ATTORNEY ST

HESTER ST

CHRYSTIE ST

ALLEN ST

ORCHARD ST

FORSYTH ST

ELDRIDGE ST

LUDLOW ST

ESSEX ST

EAST BROADWAY

HENRY ST

MADISON ST

GOUVERNEUR ST

JACKSON ST

CHERRY ST

WATER ST

D ROOSEVELT DR

Seward
Park

Museum of
hinese in the
Americas

53

Eldridge St.
Synagogue

M

F. JEFFERSON ST

69

CLINTON ST

RUTGERS ST

MONTGOMERY ST

CHERRY ST

5

BAYARD ST

HESTER ST

Confucius
Plaza

FORSYTH ST

DIVISION ST

FRANKLIN
D
ROOSEVELT DR

WN

PELL ST

Columbus
Park

MOSCO ST

MADISON ST

See
p57

OW

HENRY ST

MAR

City Hall p55

City Hall is open for group tours only. For these it is necessary to call two weeks in advance.

Federal Reserve Bank

33 Liberty Street, between Nassau & William Streets (1-212 720 6130/www. newyorkfed.org). Subway 2, 3, 4, 5 to Wall Street. **Open** 9.30-11.30am, 1.30-2.30pm Mon-Fri. Tours every hour on the half hour. Tours must be arranged at least 1 week in advance; tickets are sent by mail. **Admission** free. **Map** p56 C3 ④

A block north on Liberty Street is an imposing structure built in Florentine style. It holds the nation's largest store of gold – just over 9,000 tons – in a vault five storeys below street level (advance reservations required). This is your chance to commune with the world's most famous metal.

Fraunces Tavern Museum

54 Pearl Street, at Broad Street (1-212 425 1778/www.frauncestavernmuseum. org). Subway J, M, Z to Broad Street; 4, 5 to Bowling Green. **Open** noon-5pm Tue-Fri; 10am-5pm Sat. **Admission** $4; free-$3 reductions. No credit cards. **Map** p56 C4 ⑤

This 18th-century tavern was George Washington's watering hole and the site of his famous farewell to the troops at the Revolution's close. During the mid to late 1780s, the building housed the fledgling nation's departments of war, foreign affairs and treasury. In 1904 Fraunces became a repository for artefacts collected by the Sons of the Revolution in the State of New York. Ongoing exhibits include 'George Washington: Down the Stream of Life'. The tavern and restaurant serve hearty fare, Monday to Saturday.

Ground Zero

Subway 1, 2, 3 to Chambers Street; R, W to Cortlandt Street. **Map** p56 B3 ⑥

The streets around Ground Zero, the former site of the World Trade Center, have been drawing crowds since the terrorist attacks of 2001. People come in droves to pay their respects to the nearly 2,800 people who lost their lives on 9/11. The area is currently surrounded by a high fence on which pictures of the devastation are hung alongside historical photos of the area.

Museum of American Finance

NEW *48 Wall Street, at William Street (1-212 908 4110/www.financial history.org). Subway 2, 3, 4, 5 to Wall Street; 1 to Rector Street.* **Open** 10am-4pm Tue-Sat. **Admission** $8; $5 reductions. **Map** p56 C4 ⑦

The newly renovated Bank of New York makes an excellent place to learn about all things money. Trace the development of Wall Street and America's financial markets, see the ticker tape from the morning of the big crash of 29 October 1929, an 1867 stock ticker and the earliest known photograph of Wall Street. The permanent exhibit 'Money: A History' has broad appeal. Because the New York Stock Exchange has been closed to the public since 9/11, the museum also serves as the de facto visitor's centre for the market, offering videos of the Exchange Floor and exhibits.

National Museum of the American Indian

George Gustav Heye Center, Alexander Hamilton Custom House, 1 Bowling Green, between State & Whitehall Streets (1-212 514 3700/www.nmai. si.edu). Subway R, W to Whitehall Street; 1 to South Ferry; 4, 5 to Bowling Green. **Open** 10am-5pm Mon-Wed, Fri-Sun; 10am-8pm Thur. **Admission** free. **Map** p56 C4 ❽

This branch of the Smithsonian Institution displays its collection around the grand rotunda of the 1907 Custom House, at the bottom of Broadway (which, many moons ago, was an Indian trail). The lives and cultures of Native Americans are here presented in rotating exhibitions – from intricately woven fibre Pomo baskets to beaded buckskin shirts – along with contemporary artwork.

New York Stock Exchange

11 Wall Street, between Broad & New Streets. Subway 2, 3, 4, 5 to Wall Street. **Map** p56 C4 ❾

The nerve centre of the US economy is the New York Stock Exchange. For security reasons, the Exchange is no longer open to the public, but the street outside offers an endless pageant of brokers, traders and their minions.

South Street Seaport Museum

Visitors' Center, 12 Fulton Street, at South Street (1-212 748 8600/www. southstseaport.org). Subway A, C to Broadway-Nassau Street; J, M, Z, 2, 3, 4, 5 to Fulton Street. **Open** *Apr-Oct* 10am-6pm Tue-Sun. *Nov-Mar* 10am-6pm Fri-Sun. **Admission** $8; free-$6 reductions. **Map** p57 D3 ❿

Occupying 11 blocks along the East River, the museum is an amalgam of galleries, historic ships, 19th-century buildings and a visitors' centre. Wander around the rebuilt streets and pop in to see an exhibition on marine life and history before climbing aboard

New York Stock Exchange

the four-masted 1911 sailing ship *Peking*. The seaport is generally thick with tourists, but it's still a lively place to spend an afternoon, especially for families with children, who are likely to enjoy the atmosphere and intriguing seafaring memorabilia.

Sports Museum of America

NEW *26 Broadway, at Beaver Street (1-212 747 0900/www.the sportsmuseum.com). Subway 4, 5 to Bowling Green; R, W to Whitehall Street; 2, 3 to Wall Street.* **Open** 9am-7pm Mon-Fri; 9am-9pm Sat, Sun. **Admission** $27; free-$24 reductions. **Map** p56 C4 ⓫

Occupying 45,000 square feet this newcomer to the Downtown museum scene has lofty goals: one stop for all your sporting enthusiasm. A whopping 19 galleries represent dozens of sports each with a smattering of mechanical and computer interactive exhibits. See trophies, photos and artefacts from many a game day here.

Staten Island Ferry

Staten Island Ferry

Battery Park, South Street, at Whitehall Street (1-718 727 2508/www.siferry. com). Subway 1 to South Ferry; 4, 5 to Bowling Green. **Open** 24hrs daily. Tickets free. **Map** p56 C5 ⑫

During this commuter barge's 25-minute crossing, you'll get stunning panoramas of lower Manhattan and the Statue of Liberty. Boats depart South Ferry at Battery Park.

Statue of Liberty & Ellis Island Immigration Museum

Statue of Liberty (1-212 363 3200/ www.nps.gov/stli). Travel: R, W to Whitehall Street; 1 to South Ferry; 4, 5 to Bowling Green; then take the Statue of Liberty ferry (1-866 782 8834/ www.statuecruises.com), departing every 25 mins from gangway 4 or 5 in southernmost Battery Park. **Open** Ferry runs 9.30am-4.30pm daily. Purchase tickets at Castle Clinton in Battery Park. **Admission** $12; free-$10 reductions. **Map** p56 B5 ⑬

Frédéric-Auguste Bartholdi's *Liberty Enlightening the World*, a gift to America from the people of France,

was unveiled in 1886. After security concerns placed the statue off-limits for nearly three years, its pedestal reopened for guided tours in summer 2004 (you still can't climb up to the crown, and backpacks and luggage are not permitted on the island). There's ample room to absorb the 1883 Emma Lazarus poem that includes the renowned lines 'Give me your tired, your poor/Your huddled masses yearning to breathe free'. On the way back to Manhattan, the ferry stops at the Immigration Museum on Ellis Island, through which more than 12 million entered the country between 1892 and 1954. The $6 audio tour is inspiring.

Eating & drinking

Adrienne's Pizza Bar

54 Stone Street, between Mill Street & Coenties Alley (1-212 248 3838). Subway A, C, E to Canal Street. **Open** 11am-11pm Mon-Thur; 11am-midnight Fri; 10.30am-midnight Sat, Sun. **$$**. **Italian**. **Map** p56 C4 ⑭

A bright, modern pizzeria on a quaint, cobbled pedestrian street. You can get your pizza by the slice or thin-crust pie, and wolf it down at the standing-room bar, or take your time in the sit-down dining area. Dinner guests will find an extended menu of small plates and entrées, and plenty of outdoor seating.

Bin No. 220

220 Front Street, between Beekman Street & Peck Slip (1-212 374 9463). Subway A, C to Broadway-Nassau Street; J, M, Z, 2, 3, 4, 5 to Fulton Street. **Open** 4pm-midnight Mon-Sat; 4-11pm Sun. **$**. **Wine bar**. Map p57 D3

The continuing residential influx in to the neighbourhood is well represented by Calli Lerner and Sandy Tedesco, the two female owners of this swanky Italian wine bar, both of whom live in the area. Their oenological choices are quite personal, evidenced by the division of the mostly Italian wine list into 'Calli' and 'Sandy' picks.

Bridge Café

279 Water Street, at Dover Street (1-212 227 3344). Subway A, C to Broadway-Nassau Street; J, M, Z, 2, 3, 4, 5 to Fulton Street. **Open** 11.45am-10pm Mon, Sun; 11.45am-11pm Tue-Thur; 11.45am-midnight Fri; 5pm-midnight Sat. **$$**. **American creative**. Map p57 D3 16

This 1794 building did time as a 'disorderly house' long ago, and its romantic tin-ceilinged dining room can still inspire some old-fashioned hankypanky. Slip into the hideaway, in the shadow of the Brooklyn Bridge, and dine on pine nut-crusted chicken with artichoke caper lemon confit or softshell crabs with spicy potatoes.

Heartland Brewery

93 South Street, at Fulton Street (1-646 572 2742). Subway A, C to Broadway-Nassau Street; 2, 3, 4, 5 to Fulton Street. **Open** 11am-10pm daily. **Bar**. Map p57 D3 17

All of the microbrews on offer come from a Fort Greene brewery, so there's always a little touch of Brooklyn here.

Jack's Stir Brew Coffee

222 Front Street, between Beekman Street & Peck Slip (1-212 227 7631). Subway A, C to Broadway-Nassau Street. **Open** 6am-7pm daily. **$**. **Café**. Map p57 D3 18

Java fiends rejoiced upon the arrival locally of this offshoot of a popular joint; it's brought organic beans and a homely vibe with it. The coffee is served by chatty, quick-to-grin espresso artisans with a knack for unusual concoctions such as the silky Mountie latte, infused with maple syrup.

Ellis Island Immigration Museum

NEW YORK BY AREA

Trinity Place

*115 Broadway, between Cedar Street &
Trinity Place, entrance on Cedar Street
(1-212 964 0939). Subway 2, 3, 4, 5, J,
M, Z to Wall Street.* **Open** 6am-7pm
daily. **$$. American**. **Map** p56 C3 ⑲
See box p65.

Shopping

Bowne & Co Stationers

*211 Water Street, between Beekman
& Fulton Streets (1-212 748 8651).
Subway A, C to Broadway-Nassau
Street; 2, 3 to Fulton Street.* **Open**
10am-5pm Mon, Tue, Fri-Sun.
Map p57 D3 ⑳

An authentic re-creation of the original
1875 print shop, Bowne & Co. not only
looks the part – with its vintage
gaslights and carved mahogany shelv-
ing – but acts it as well. The printing
presses and type settings that were
manufactured from 1844 to 1901 are
used to churn out fine-art prints, sta-
tionery, and custom-order letterheads
and business cards.

Century 21

*22 Cortland Street, between Broadway
& Church Street (1-212 227 9092/
www.c21stores.com). Subway R, W to
Cortland Street.* **Open** 7.45am-8pm

Mon-Wed, Fri; 7.45am-8.30pm Thur;
10am-8pm Sat; 11am-7pm Sun. **Map**
p56 C3 ㉑

Directly east of Ground Zero, bargain
hunters can sift through the stock at
this enormous discount-designer-duds
vault. The score is rare but intoxicat-
ing; savings are usually between 25%
and 75% off regular retail prices.

Tribeca & Soho

Tribeca throbs with energy, but a
few pockets still appear abandoned
– the cobblestones crumbling and
dirty, the cast-iron buildings
chipped and unpainted. Don't
be fooled; derelict areas like these
are transformed with deluxe
makeovers seemingly overnight.
Fine small-scale cast-iron
architecture still stands along
White Street and the parallel
thoroughfares.

Soho, New York's glamorous
Downtown shopping destination,
was at one time earmarked for
destruction, but, thankfully, its
signature cast-iron warehouses
were saved by the many artists
who then inhabited them. Lots of
chain stores have now moved in to

Bowne & Co Stationers

Downtown deluxe!

Hermès

Based on the description, try to guess where this monument to neo-yuppie residential extravagance is being built: a 52-storey building features a lobby lounge with 1970s-style living-room pit, cocktail service and a billiards table; a private screening room and nightclub with 'cinema beds' for four; a heated 'co-ed' lap pool, basketball courts and gym; a covered outdoor dog park; and a year-round outdoor mineral jacuzzi. South Beach? The OC?

Nope. Try Hanover Street, about a cigarette flick from the 103-year-old New York Stock Exchange.

The William Beaver House, as it's called, is just one of the big-bucks residential construction projects sprouting in Manhattan's least hip neighbourhood.

Make no mistake, the gilding of the tip of Manhattan is in full gilt, starting with, would you believe, the new **Gild Hall Hotel** (p173).

Courting bankers instead of Holly Golightly, **Tiffany's** (37 Wall Street, between William & Nassau Streets, 1-212 514 8015), the famed jewellery company's second Manhattan outpost, is located just half a block from the Stock Exchange. For bullish or bearish markets, its goods skew toward gifts for corporate types, including silver cufflinks, engraved money clips, and the Tiffany Grand Wall Street Watch, an alligator-leather and rose-gold timepiece that was created especially for the store.

Developers, mad for a piece of space below Chambers Street, are converting dozens of offices into luxury condos, hotels and super-rich shops. **Hermès**, the purveyor of fine French luxury goods has landed 15 Broad Street. A new 175-room **Four Seasons** hotel will be part of a 912-foot tower at 99 Church Street.

If it's money you love then head over to the new-ish eatery **Trinity Place** (p64), a great place, we hear, to meet people who make six figures, according to one local. Indeed, the spot, recognisable for its 19th-century, 35-ton bank-vault doors, serves continental fare to a well-heeled crowd of stockbrokers and bond traders. Good luck in your search for the highlife!

the neighbourhood, beside the boutiques and bistros, drawing a shopping-mall-at-Christmas-time crush every weekend.

Sights & museums

New York City Fire Museum

278 Spring Street, between Hudson & Varick Streets (1-212 691 1303/www. nycfiremuseum.org). Subway C, E to Spring Street; 1 to Houston Street. **Open** 10am-5pm Tue-Sat; 10am-4pm Sun. **Admission** suggested donation $5; $1-$2 reductions. **Map** p58 B4 ㉒

An active firehouse from 1904 to 1959, this museum is filled with gadgetry and pageantry, from late 18th-century hand-pumped fire engines to present-day equipment. The museum also houses a permanent exhibit commemorating firefighters' heroism after the attack on the World Trade Center.

Eating & drinking

Balthazar

80 Spring Street, between Broadway & Crosby Street (1-212 965 1414). Subway N, R, W to Prince Street; 6 to Spring Street. **Open** 7.30am-11.30am, noon-5pm, 6pm-1am Mon-Wed; 7.30am-11.30am, noon-5pm, 6pm-1.30am Thur; 7.30am-11.30am, noon-5pm, 6pm-2am Fri; 10am-4pm, 6pm-2am Sat; 10am-4pm, 5.30pm-midnight Sun. **$$**. **French bistro**. **Map** p58 C4 ㉓

This authentic French brasserie is still a scene – especially for weekend brunch, when the room is packed with media executives, rail-thin lookers and trendy boys. A three-tiered seafood platter (a house special) casts the most impressive shadow of any appetiser in town. Frisée aux lardons is exemplary, as is roasted chicken on mashed potatoes for two, and skate with brown butter and capers.

Blue Ribbon

97 Sullivan Street, between Prince & Spring Streets (1-212 274 0404). Subway C, E to Spring Street. **Open** 4pm-4am Tue-Sun. **$$**. **American creative**. **Map** p58 C4 ㉔

Since 1992, this Soho fixture has continuously attracted global foodies and off-the-clock chefs from the neighbourhood, who come for the pristine raw bar, excellent blue-cheese burgers and beef marrow with oxtail marmalade. As it's open until 4am, the restaurant lures the fabulous for a late-night nosh – which usually means oysters and champagne.

Bouley Bakery & Market

130 West Broadway, at Duane Street (1-212 608 5829). Subway A, C, 1, 2, 3 to Chambers Street. **Open** *Bakery* 7.30am-7.30pm daily. *Restaurant* 5.30-11pm Mon-Fri; 11am-3pm, 5.30-11.30pm Sat; 11am-4pm Sun. **$-$$**. **French**. **Map** p56 B2 ㉕

Chef David Bouley's new bakery sells pastries, breads, sandwiches, salads and pizza on the ground floor; a cellar full of fresh seafood, meats and cheeses; and on the first floor, a dining room with a sushi bar and cocktails. Sidewalk seats appear in warm weather.

Fanelli's Café

94 Prince Street, at Mercer Street (1-212 226 9412). Subway N, R, W to Prince Street. **Open** 10am-2.30am Mon-Thur; 10am-3am Fri, Sat; 11am-12.30am Sun. **$**. **American**. **Map** p58 C4 ㉖

Deemed the second-oldest restaurant in New York, Fanelli's has stood at this cobblestoned intersection since 1847, and local artists and worldly tourists pour into the lively landmark for perfectly charred beef patties on toasted onion rolls. The long bar, prints of boxing legends and check tablecloths all add to the charm.

Joe at Alessi

NEW *30 Greene Street, between Houston & Prince Streets (1-212 941 7330). Subway B, D, F, V, 6 to Broadway-Lafayette Street; R, W to Prince Street.* **Open** 7am-7pm Mon-Fri; 8am-7pm Sat; 8am-6pm Sun. **$**. **Café**. **Map** p58 C4 ㉗

In 2007, this burgeoning coffee-lover's chain spawned its sleekest branch to date – complete with a molto authentic espresso bar – inside Soho's Alessi

Tribeca p64

store. Baristas proffer rich, nutty cups of java – with an expert foam for those who want it – from the glorious $14,000 La Marzocco machine.

M1-5
52 Walker Street, between Broadway & Church Street (1-212 965 1701). Subway J, M, Z, N, Q, R, W, 6 to Canal Street. **Open** 4pm-4am daily. **Bar**. Map p56 C1/p58 C5 ㉓
The name of the huge, red-walled hangout refers to Tribeca's zoning ordinance, which permits trendy restaurants to co-exist with warehouses. The mixed-use label also applies to M1-5's crowd: suited brokers shoot pool next to ageing garage-bandmates and youthful indie screenwriters. No velvet rope, no fancy cocktails, just a full, well-stocked bar.

New York City Hot Dog Company
NEW *105 Chambers Street, at Church Street (1-212 240 9550). Subway A, C to Chambers Street.* **Open** 10am-10pm Mon-Fri; 10am-7pm Sat. **$**. **American**. Map p56 C2 ㉙
The theme here is haute-dog: you can have turkey, Kobe, tofu or the classic beef variety. Toppings include a wide spectrum. Blue cheese anyone? Eat in or take your dogs for a walk in nearby City Hall Park.

Pegu Club
77 W Houston Street, between West Broadway & Wooster Street (1-212 473 7348). Subway 6 to Bleecker Street; B, D, F, V to Broadway-Lafayette Street. **Open** 5pm-2am Mon-Wed, Sun; 5pm-4am Thur-Sat. **Bar**. Map p58 C4 ㉚
Located on an unassuming Soho block, this bar is both hidden and welcoming. Upstairs, what greets cocktail connoisseurs is an elegant space with a long maple bar and a faint air of nostalgic colonial glamour. Owner-mixologist Audrey Saunders stubbornly discourages trendy vodkas – gin is the basis for most of the menu.

Shorty's .32
NEW *199 Prince Street, between MacDougal & Sullivan Streets (1-212 375 8275). Subway C, E to Spring*

Street. **Open** 6-11pm Mon-Wed; 6pm-midnight Thur, Fri; 11.30am-3pm, 6pm-midnight Sat; 11.30am-3pm, 6-10.30pm Sun. **$$**. **American**. **Map** p58 C4 ③①
See box p87.

Tailor

NEW *525 Broome Street, between Thompson & Sullivan Streets (1-212 334 5182). Subway C, E to Spring Street*. **Open** 6pm-midnight Tue-Thur, Sun; 6pm-1am Fri, Sat. **$**. **Café**.
Map p58 C4 ③②
Chef Sam Mason brings his brand of molecular gastronomy to a loungey restaurant and subterranean bar in Soho. Mixologist Eben Freeman's cocktail menu manages to outshine the rather interesting food. Try the 'violet fizz' (a frothy mix of gin, citrus, cream, egg whites and violet liqueur).

Tribeca Treats

94 Reade Street, between Church Street & West Broadway (1-212 571 0500). Subway A, C, 1, 2, 3 to Chambers Street. **Open** 10am-7pm Mon-Sat. **$**. **Bakery**. **Map** p56 2B ③③

Tribeca Treats is a sprawling 12,000sq ft bakery and boutique that has has launched a Downtown crusade to save the (now endangered) sweet tooth. The aforementioned sweets are made on the premises and include in their sugary ranks peanut-butter-and-jelly cupcakes and chocolate truffles. Oven mitts and dessert cookbooks are also sold.

VinoVino

211 West Broadway, between Franklin & White Streets (1-212 925 8510/ www.vinovino.net). Subway 1 to Franklin Street. **Open** 5-11pm Tue, Wed; 5pm-1am Thur, Fri; 1pm-1am Sat; 1-8pm Sun. **Wine bar**.
Map p56 B1/p58 C5 ③④
VinoVino is a narrow, 2,200sq ft space in Tribeca that's one part wine shop and one part enoteca. Husband-and-wife team Jay and Ashley Donayre don't want shoppers to be intimidated by their stock of artisanal and rare vintages, so nervous sippers can try wines by the glass at the bar before buying a bottle in the store.

New York City Hot Dog Company p67

Bringing a touch of London's Carnaby Street to Soho, Ben Sherman, the eponymous streetwear brand born of the original swinging '60s mod god, has dropped its first US branch. As a salute to its English roots, the co-ed emporium is peppered with mannequins and an antique settee covered in a Union Jack pattern.

INA

101 Thompson Street, between Prince & Spring Streets (1-212 941 4757). Subway C, E to Spring Street. **Open** noon-7pm Mon-Thur, Sun; noon-8pm Fri, Sat. **Map** p58 C4 **37**

INA has reigned Downtown for more than a decade. The Soho location features drastically reduced couture pieces, while the Nolita shop, on Prince Street, carries trendier clothing.

John Masters Organics

77 Sullivan Street, between Spring & Broome Streets (1-212 343 9590/ www.johnmasters.com). Subway C, E to Spring Street; N, R, W to Prince Street. **Open** 11am-7pm Mon-Sat. **Map** p58 C4 **38**

Organic doesn't get more orgasmic than it is at John Masters' chic apothecary. Blood orange and vanilla body wash and lavender and avocado intensive conditioner are just two of the good-enough-to-eat products.

Madewell

NEW *486 Broadway, at Broome Street (1-212 226 6954). Subway 6 to Spring Street; 6, Q, R, W, to Canal Street.* **Open** 10am-8pm Mon-Sat; noon-7pm Sun. **Map** p58 C4 **39**

In a land of cheap-and-chic behemoths like H&M and Forever 21, J.Crew's trendy, wallet-friendly sibling provides a much-needed alternative to what the masses are donning on the L train.

Marc Jacobs

163 Mercer Street, between Houston & Prince Streets (1-212 343 1490/ www.marcjacobs.com). Subway B, D, F, V to Broadway-Lafayette Street; N, R, W to Prince Street; 6 to Bleecker Street. **Open** 11am-7pm Mon-Sat; noon-6pm Sun. **Map** p58 C4 **40**

Shopping

A Bathing Ape

91 Greene Street, between Prince & Spring Streets (1-212 925 0222). Subway N, R, W to Prince Street. **Open** noon-7pm Mon-Sat; noon-6pm Sun. **Map** p58 C4 **35**

The cult streetwear label created by Japanese designer Nigo planted its first flagship on American soil where else but in Soho. The much-in-demand Nigo, who has collaborated with Adidas and NERD frontman Pharrell Williams, among others, devotes most of his shop to BAPE threads, while an upstairs shoe salon housing BAPEsta kicks has made the city's sneaker-hungry masses go ape.

Ben Sherman

96 Spring Street, at Mercer Street (1-212 680 0160/www.bensherman usa.com). Subway C, E to Spring Street; N, R, W to Prince Street. **Open** 10am-9pm Mon-Sat; 11am-7pm Sun. **Map** p58 C4 **36**

NEW YORK BY AREA

Men and women get fashion parity at Jacobs' Soho boutique. A separate but equal policy rules on the designer's Bleecker Street strip (Nos.403-405 & 385), where a trio of stores – men's, women's and accessories – keeps the West Village well kitted out.

Matter

NEW *405 Broome Street, between Centre & Lafayette Streets (1-212 343 2600/www.mattermatters.com). Subway 6 to Spring Street.* **Open** noon-7pm Mon-Fri; 11am-7pm Sat; 11am-6pm Sun. **Map** p59 D4 **④**

The Soho spin-off of Brooklyn design store Matter offers a similarly excellent selection of housewares, like Loyal Loot Collective log bowls and Iraqi-British architect Zaha Hadid's fresh-from-Milan stools.

Paul Smith

142 Greene Street, between Houston & Prince Streets (1-646 613 3060). Subway 6 to Spring Street; N, R, W to Prince Street. **Open** 11am-7pm Mon-Sat; noon-6pm Sun. **Map** p58 C4 **④**

The English fashion designer's new flagship store in Soho fills the former Pace Gallery with both men's and women's fashions. Female fans can check out all three women's lines here.

Phat Farm

129 Prince Street, between West Broadway & Wooster Street (1-212 533 7428/www.phatfarmstore.com). Subway C, E to Spring Street; N, R, W to Prince Street. **Open** 11am-7pm Mon-Sat; noon-6pm Sun. **Map** p58 C4 **④**

Find Def Jam impresario Russell Simmons's classy, conservative take on hip hop couture: phunky-phresh baggy clothing for guys, and for gals, the curvy Baby Phat line.

Rogan

91 Franklin Street, between Broadway & Church Street (1-646 827 7554). Subway A, C, E to Canal Street. **Open** 11am-7pm daily. **Map** p56 C1/p58 C5 **④**

Ever wonder what it is that really makes enigmatic fashion wunderkind Rogan Gregory tick? A twirl through

Tribeca's Rogan flagship reveals that the designer behind culty labels Rogan, EDUN, Loomstate and A Litl Betr has quite an appreciation for rugged materials, as evidenced by the store's exposed brick, driftwood 'sculptures' and concrete floors.

Stüssy

140 Wooster Street, between Houston & Prince Streets (1-212 995 8787). Subway N, R, W to Prince Street. **Open** noon-7pm Mon-Thur; 11am-7pm Fri, Sat; noon-6pm Sun. **Map** p58 C4 **④**

Tricky isn't the only one who wants to be dressed up in Stüssy. Come here for the collection of skate- and surfwear that made Sean Stüssy famous, as well as more utilitarian bags from the Japanese label Headporter.

Supreme

274 Lafayette Street, between Prince & Houston Streets (1-212 966 7799). Subway B, D, F, V to Broadway-Lafayette Street; N, R, W to Prince Street; 6 to Spring Street. **Open** 11.30am-7pm Mon-Sat; noon-6pm Sun. **Map** p58 D4 **④**

Filled mostly with various well known East Coast brands such as Chocolate, Independent and Zoo York, this skatewear store also stocks its own line of clothing. Look out for pieces by Burton and DC Shoe, which are the favourite labels of skaters such as Colin McKay and Danny Way.

Te Casan

382 West Broadway, between Broome & Spring Streets, (1-212 584 8000). Subway C, E to Spring Street; N, R, W to Prince Street. **Open** 10am-7pm Mon-Sat; 11am-7pm Sun. **Map** p58 C4 **④**

A sprawling 7,500sq ft spot, Te Casan is dedicated to limited edition collections from seven nascent labels. The store boasts a team of talented designers who aren't big names themselves but who have worked for some of the top design houses.

Triple Five Soul

290 Lafayette Street, between Houston & Prince Streets (1-212 431 2404/www.triple5soul.com). Subway B, D, F,

Soho p64

V to Broadway-Lafayette Street;
N, R, W to Prince Street; 6 to Bleecker
Street. **Open** 11am-7pm Mon-Thur,
Sun; 11am-7.30pm Fri, Sat.
Map p58 D4 ❽
Although the funky Triple Five Soul
label is no longer exclusive to New
York, the city can still boast the
brand's sole stores. Find the very nec-
essary hooded sweatshirts and T-
shirts stamped with the Triple Five
logo at this Soho spot.

Nightlife

S.O.B.'s
204 Varick Street, at Houston Street
(1-212 243 4940/www.sobs.com).
Subway 1 to Houston Street. **Open**
times vary; call or check website.
Map p58 B4 ❾
The titular sounds of Brazil are just
some of many global genres that keep
this Tribeca spot hopping. Hip hop,
soul, reggae and Latin beats figure in
the mix, with MIA, Seu Jorge, Leela
James and Yellowman each appearing

of late. Careful at the bar – drinks are
outrageously priced. But the sharp
looking clientele doesn't seem to mind.

Studios
Tribeca Grand Hotel, 2 Sixth
Avenue, between Walker & White
Streets (1-212 519 6677/www.
tribecagrand.com). Subway A, C, E
to Canal Street; 1 to Franklin Street.
Open 9pm-2am daily. **Map** p56 B1/
p58 C5 ❿
When the Tribeca Grand first started
showcasing DJs and live music in its
downstairs, club-like sanctum, it unexpectedly became one of the city's top
spots for underground beats – thanks
mostly to its of-the-moment electro-
clash and nu-rock. Things have calmed
down a little since then, but the place
still rocks at the Saturday night Fixed
affair, where groundbreaking DJs and
live acts – folks like Glasgow's Optimo
and crazed bleep-funk duo Mu – sometimes hold court to the throngs. It's best
to call before visiting as the room is
also used for private functions.

Arts & leisure

Flea Theater

*41 White Street, between Broadway &
Church Street (1-212 226 2407/www.
theflea.org). Subway A, C, E, J, M, N,
Q, R, W, Z, 1, 6 to Canal Street.*
Map p56 C1/p58 C5 ⑤
Founded in 1997, Jim Simpson's cosy,
well-appointed venue has presented
both avant-garde experimentation (the
work of Mac Wellman) and political
satires (mostly by AR Gurney).

HERE

*121 Sixth Avenue, at Broome Street
(1-212 647 0202/Smarttix 1-212 868
4444/www.here.org). Subway C, E to
Spring Street.* **Map** p58 C4 ⑤
Containing three intimate performance
spaces, an art gallery and a chic café,
this lovely Tribeca arts complex, dedicated to non-profit arts enterprise, has
hosted a number of exciting companies. It was the launching pad for such
well-known shows as Eve Ensler's
Vagina Monologues.

Chinatown, Little Italy & Nolita

You won't hear much English
along the crowded streets of
Chinatown, lined by fish-, fruit-
and vegetable-stocked stands.
This is one of the largest Chinese
communities outside Asia. Canal
Street, a bargain hunter's paradise,
is infamous for its (illegal) knockoff
designer handbags, perfumes and
other goods among the numerous
cheap gift shops.

  Little Italy, which once ran
from Canal to Houston Streets
between Lafayette Street and the
Bowery, hardly resembles the
insular community famously
portrayed in Martin Scorsese's
Mean Streets. Italian families
have fled Mott Street and gone
to the suburbs, Chinatown has
crept north, and rising rents have
forced mom-and-pop businesses to

Matter p70

surrender to the stylish boutiques
of **Nolita** – North of Little Italy (a
misnomer, since it technically lies
within Little Italy).

  Chi-chi restaurants and boutiques
have taken over Nolita. Elizabeth,
Mott and Mulberry Streets, between
Houston and Spring Streets in
particular, are now the source
of everything from perfectly cut
jeans to hand-blown glass.

Sights & museums

Eastern States Buddhist Temple of America

*64 Mott Street, between Bayard &
Canal Streets (1-212 966 6229).
Subway J, M, N, Q, R, W, Z, 6 to
Canal Street.* **Open** 9am-6pm daily.
Map p57 D1/p59 D5 ⑤

Museum of Chinese in the Americas

2nd Floor, 70 Mulberry Street, at Bayard Street (1-212 619 4785/www. moca-nyc.org). Subway J, M, N, Q, R, W, Z, 6 to Canal Street. **Open** noon-6pm Tue-Thur, Sat, Sun; noon-7pm Fri. **Admission** suggested donation $3; free-$1 reductions; free Fri. No credit cards. **Map** p57 D1/p59 D5 ❸❹

In the heart of Chinatown, a century-old former schoolhouse holds a two-room museum that focusses on Chinese-American history and the Chinese immigrant experience. Call for details about walking tours of the area.

Eating & drinking

Barmarché

14 Spring Street, at Elizabeth Street (1-212 219 9542). Subway N, R, W to Prince Street; 6 to Spring Street. **Open** 11am-11pm Mon, Sun; 11am-midnight Tue-Thur; 10am-1am Fri, Sat. **$$**. **American. Map** p59 D4 ❺❺

Peer inside this bright, white-on-white brasserie, and you'll be tempted to come in and join the party: the dining room is often filled with lively groups, and the kitchen keeps them happy and well fed. The menu is American in the melting-pot sense, covering all the greatest-hits, no-nonsense dishes from around the world: home-made fettuccine with pesto; thick gazpacho with guacamole; tuna tartare with grated Asian pear and citrus ponzu; croques-monsieur; and a juicy, made-in-the-USA burger.

Café Habana

17 Prince Street, at Elizabeth Street (1-212 625 2001). Subway N, R, W to Prince Street; 6 to Spring Street. **Open** 9am-midnight daily. **$**. **Cuban. Map** p59 D4 ❺❻

Hipsters storm this café day and night for its addictive grilled corn doused in butter and rolled in grated cheese and chilli powder. Other staples include crisp beer-battered catfish tortas with spicy mayo, and juicy marinated skirt steak with yellow rice and black beans. This year the owners opened a second location in Greenpoint, Brooklyn.

Congee Village

100 Allen Street, between Broome & Delancey Streets (1-212 941 1818). Subway F to Delancey Street; J, M, Z to Delancey-Essex Streets. **Open** 10.30am-2am daily. **$**. **Chinese. Map** p59 E4 ❺❼

If you've never indulged in the starchy comfort of congee, this is a good place to rectify the omission. The rice porridge in a clay pot over a slow fire is best early in the day; pick a chunky version such as the treasure-laden seafood or sliced fish. Crab is impeccably fresh, as is the well seasoned whole fish served over glistening Chinese broccoli. It may seem incongruous, but the Congee serves a great pina colada – and it will only cost you $3 during the weekday happy hour (4-7pm).

Doyers Vietnamese Restaurant

11 Doyers Street, between Bowery & Pell Street (1-212 513 1521). Subway J, M, N, Q, R, W, Z, 6 to Canal Street. **Open** 11am-10pm Mon-Thur, Sun; 11am-11pm Fri, Sat. **$**. **Vietnamese. Map** p57 D1/p59 D5 ❺❽

The search to find this restaurant is part of the fun: it's tucked away in a basement on a zigzagging Chinatown alley. The 33 appetisers include balls of grilled minced shrimp wrapped around sugarcane sticks and a delicious Vietnamese crêpe filled with shrimp and pork. Hot-pot soups, served on a tabletop stove, are made with an exceptional fish-broth base. For maximum enjoyment, come carrying a six-pack of Singha beer (the restaurant is BYOB only).

Golden Bridge

50 Bowery, between Bayard & Canal Streets (1-212 227 8831). Subway B, D to Grand Street; J, M, N, Q, R, W, Z, 6 to Canal Street. **Open** 9am-11pm daily. **$**. **Chinese. Map** p57 D1/p59 D5 ❺❾

Dim sum devotees often pick Flushing, Queens, over Manhattan as the best place for serious food, but they should maybe reconsider with this serious Cantonese venue above a Popeye's on the Bowery. An armada of carts offers fresh and flavourful standards like

NEW YORK BY AREA

clams in black bean sauce and pillowy steamed pork buns, plus unusual items such as egg tarts with a soft taro crust. Keep an eye open for the elusive cart bearing a mysterious wooden bucket; it's filled with an irresistible, lightly sweetened tofu.

Lombardi's

32 Spring Street, between Mott & Mulberry Streets (1-212 941 7994). Subway 6 to Spring Street. **Open** 11.30am-11pm Mon-Thur; 11.30am-midnight Fri, Sat; 11.30am-10pm Sun. **$**. No credit cards. **Italian**. Map p59 D4 ⑥⓪

Established in 1905, Lombardi's is the city's oldest pizzeria and offers pizza at its best: made in a coal-fired oven and with a chewy, thin crust. The pepperoni is fantastic, as are the killer meatballs in tomato sauce. The setting is classic pizza-parlour – wooden booths, red-and-white checked tablecloths.

Lovely Day

196 Elizabeth Street, between Prince & Spring Streets (1-212 925 3310). Subway J, M, Z to Bowery; 6 to Spring Street. **Open** noon-11pm Mon-Thur; noon-midnight Fri; 11am-midnight Sat; 11am-11pm Sun. **$**. **Pan-Asian**. Map p59 D4 ⑥①

At Lovely Day tamarind appears in the shrimp summer roll's dressing, and again in the dressing for the flank steak served with rice and vegetables. But the fruit isn't the only asset here: coconut curry noodles and pineapple fried rice are equally good. Slide into a booth and take your cue from the scents wafting from the tiny kitchen. Or come for brunch, which features crisp banana rolls.

Public

210 Elizabeth Street, between Prince & Spring Streets (1-212 343 7011). Subway N, R, W to Prince Street; 6 to Spring Street. **Open** 6-11.30pm Mon-Fri; 6pm-12.30am Sat; 6-10.30pm Sun. **$$**. **Eclectic**. Map p59 D4 ⑥②

This gorgeous industrial space is high on concept – machine-age glass lamps, pre-war office doors and a library card catalogue make sly references to public spaces. Chef Brad Farmerie, from London's acclaimed Providores, has created the menu in tandem with Providores colleagues Anna Hansen and Peter Gordon. Look for a Kiwi influence on many of the dishes, such as grilled kangaroo on coriander falafel and New Zealand venison with pomegranates and truffles. The desserts are equally varied.

Shopping

Classic Kicks

298 Elizabeth Street, between Houston & Bleecker Streets (1-212 979 9514). Subway B, D, F, V to Broadway-Lafayette Street; 6 to Bleecker Street. **Open** noon-7pm Mon-Sat. Map p59 D3 ⑥③

One of the more female-friendly sneaker shops, Classic Kicks stocks mainstream and rare styles of Converse, Lacoste, Puma and Vans, to name but a few, for both boys and girls, along with a decent selection of clothes.

Market NYC

268 Mulberry Street, between Houston & Prince Streets (www.themarket nyc.com). Subway B, D, F, V to Broadway-Lafayette Street; N, R, W to Prince Street; 6 to Bleecker Street. **Open** 11am-7pm Sat, Sun. No credit cards. Map p59 D4 ⑥④

Yes, it's housed in the gymnasium of a church's youth centre, but it's no small shakes. Every Saturday, contemporary fashion and accessory designers hawk their (usually unique) wares here. Open weekends only.

Rebecca Taylor

260 Mott Street, between Houston & Prince Streets (1-212 966 0406/www. rebeccataylor.com). Subway B, D, F, V to Broadway-Lafayette Street; N, R, W to Prince Street; 6 to Bleecker Street. **Open** 11am-7pm daily. Map p59 D4 ⑥⑤

This New Zealand designer's shop is adorned with murals of fairy worlds and butterflies – arguably the source of inspiration for her whimsical, kittenish dresses and jackets.

Chinatown p72

Lower East Side

The Lower East Side was shaped by New York's immigrants, millions of whom poured into the city from the late 19th century onwards. From the 1980s on bars, boutiques and music venues opened in response to an influx of young artists and musicians.

Sights & museums

Lower East Side Tenement Museum

90 Orchard Street, at Broome Street (1-212 431 0233/www.tenement.org). Subway F to Delancey Street; J, M, Z to Delancey-Essex Streets. **Open** Visitors' Center 11am-5.30pm Mon; 11am-6pm Tue-Fri; 10.45am-5.30pm Sat, Sun. **Admission** $12; $10 reductions. **Map** p59 E4 ⑯

Housed in an 1863 tenement building along with a gallery, shop and video room, this fascinating museum is accessible only by guided tour. The tours, which regularly sell out (book ahead), explain the daily life of typical tenement-dwelling immigrant families. (See the website for 360-degree views of the museum's interior.) From April to December, the museum also leads walking tours of the Lower East Side.

New Museum of Contemporary Art

NEW *353 The Bowery, between Prince & Stanton Streets (1-212 219 1222/www.newmuseum.org). Subway F, V to Second Avenue-Lower East Side.* **Admission** $12; reductions free-$8. **Open** noon-6pm Wed, Sat, Sun; noon-10pm Thur, Fri. **Map** p59 D4 ⑰

The seven-storey building, designed by cutting-edge Tokyo architectural firm Sejima + Nishizawa/SANAA, includes a theatre, café, roof terraces and galleries. It's the first art museum constructed from the ground up below 14th Street. The focus is on emerging media and surveys of important but under-recognised artists.

Eating & drinking

Allen & Delancey

NEW *115 Allen Street, between Delancey & Rivington Streets (1-212 253 5400). Subway F to Delancey Street; J, M, Z to Delancey-Essex Streets.* **Open** 6pm-midnight Mon-Sat; 5-11pm Sun. **$$. American**. **Map** p59 D4 ⑱

British chef Neil Ferguson's windowless space feels like a gothic speakeasy, both dark and sumptuous, full of brick and candles, mirrors and velvet, leather-bound books and wooden beams. Main courses stick primarily to hearty meats: lamb, duck, pork and beef. The old-school cocktail list, the wine list and the waitstaff are all smart and straightforward.

Broadway East

NEW *171 East Broadway, between Jefferson & Rutgers Streets (1-212 228 3100). Subway F to East Broadway.* **Open** 5.30-11pm Tue-Sat; 5.30-10.30pm Sun. **$$. Vegetarian**. **Map** p59 E5 ⑲

The omnivore menu includes meatless items such as a golden-beet tartare with shallot-hijiki purée, alongside fish and poultry dishes. The space, designed by owner Ron Castellano, who also worked on the adjacent Forward Building, features a 240sq ft 'living wall' of oxygen-producing plants.

Brown

61 Hester Street, at Ludlow Streets (1-212 477 2427). Subway F to East Broadway. **Open** 9am-11pm Tue-Sat; 9am-6pm Sun. **$. Café**. **Map** p59 E5 ⑳

Owner Alejandro Alcocer opened this small café to compensate for the lack of a decent cup of joe in the 'hood. Not only can you get a mean latte here, but now you can also choose from more than 20 entrées, all based on organic ingredients. Daily specials, scribbled on the front-door glass, usually include a soup, a frittata and a cheese-and-fruit plate. The place recently started serving beer and wine and a dinner menu.

Clinton Street Baking Company

4 Clinton Street, between Houston & Stanton Streets (1-646 602 6263). Subway F to Delancey Street; J, M, Z to Delancey-Essex Streets. **Open** 8am-11pm Mon-Fri; 10am-4pm, 6-11pm Sat; 10am-4pm Sun. **$.** **Café**. **Map** p59 E4 ⓒ

The warm buttermilk biscuits at this popular space are reason enough to face the brunchtime crowd. If you want to avoid the onslaught, however, the homely Lower East Side spot is just as reliable at lunch and dinner, when locals drop in for fish tacos, grilled pizzas and a daily $10 beer-and-burger special. Pssst – to better your odds for getting a table at brunch (the best in town), show up between 9 and 10am, when coffee and pastries are served before the rest of the kitchen opens.

East Side Company Bar

49 Essex Street, between Broome & Grand Streets (1-212 614 7408). Subway F to Delancey Street; J, M, Z to Delancey-Essex Streets. **Open** 7pm-4am daily. No credit cards. **Bar**. **Map** p59 E4 ⓒ

This snug space has a 1940s vibe (leather booths, classic cocktails), as well as a few welcome touches, such as a raw bar and slashed prices.

La Esquina

106 Kenmare Street, between Cleveland Place & Lafayette Street (1-646 613 7100). Subway 6 to Spring Street. **Open** 6pm-midnight daily. **$$.** **Mexican**. **Map** p59 D4 ⓒ

Many first-time visitors to La Esquina stand on the corner of Lafayette and Kenmare Streets staring at the deli sign and wondering if they wrote down the wrong address. After watching dozens of people walk through a door marked 'employees only', it becomes clear that a restaurant does lurk within. Dishes like spicy sirloin with poblano chillies, Mayan shrimp coated in a chipotle glaze and grilled fish with avocado salsa somehow taste better served amid exposed brick, wrought iron and wax-dripping candelabras.

To market

OK, if you're scratching your head, wondering why we're writing about a grocery store, it's probably fair to say that you've not yet been to the **Whole Foods Market** on the Lower East Side, which opened in 2007 at 95 E Houston Street (between Bowery & Chrystie Streets) – or, for that matter, the brand spanking new Tribeca outpost (270 Greenwich Street, between Warren & Murray Streets), which threw open its doors in July 2008.

Gentle reader, these are no mere sellers of foodstuffs. Visitors to the Lower East Side's 71,000-square-foot store can browse the giant eco-boutique, try unheard-of artisanal cheeses in the *fromagerie*, or fill up a container with locally brewed beer and take it to go. The enormous second-floor dining room and lounge not only offers free wifi, it's also a great place to unwind and refuel during a hectic day of sightseeing. Sidle up to the sushi bar and choose expertly prepared sushi from brightly coloured plates that slowly make the rounds on the conveyor belt. The on-site culinary centre offers affordable cooking classes by well-known chefs and cookbook authors.

Don't get too full, however, as you've yet to see the dazzling sit-down dessert bar at the new Tribeca location. If you're on a diet, fear not: you're only a short walk away from Battery Park, where you can walk off your indulgences… or simply savour the views of the harbour and the Statue of Liberty.

■ www.wholefoodsmarket.com

Freemans

2 Freeman Alley, off Rivington Street, between Bowery & Chrystie Street (1-212 420 0012). Subway F, V to Lower East Side-Second Avenue; J, M, Z to Bowery. **Open** 5-11.30pm Mon-Fri; 11am-3.30pm, 6pm-midnight Sat, Sun. **$$$**. **American**. Map p59 D4 ⑦

Once you find this secret restaurant you'll feel as though you've stepped into a ski lodge on a mountaintop in Aspen, Colorado, rather than in Downtown New York. Those in the know feast on affordable dishes like juicy trout, warm artichoke dip, rich wild-boar terrine, and perfect batches of mac and cheese, all served under the gaze of mounted animal heads. Brunch, when the sun streams through the front windows, is rather more tranquil.

Home Sweet Home

131 Chrystie Street, between Broome & Delancey Streets (1-212 226 5708). Subway B, D to Grand Street; J, M, Z to Bowery. **Open** 8pm-4am daily. **$**. **Bar**. Map p59 D4 ⑦

It's homely, we suppose, that is if you usually keep dead animals in your living room. Descend the chandelier-lit stairwell to the signless subterranean den bedecked with stuffed critters – there's a beaver, an eagle, even a jackalope. Sassy bartenders dispense draughts and PBRs from a bar inlaid with cases containing icky knick-knacks, like dental moulds.

Katz's Delicatessen

205 E Houston Street, at Ludlow Street (1-212 254 2246). Subway F, V to Lower East Side-Second Avenue. **Open** 8am-10pm Mon, Tue, Sun; 8am-11pm Wed, Thur; 8am-3am Fri, Sat. **$**. **American deli**. Map p59 E4 ⑦

This capacious, no-frills deli draws queues for its pastrami – some of the best you'll find in New York. (FYI, Meg Ryan's famous 'orgasm' scene in *When Harry Met Sally...* was filmed here.)

Schiller's Liquor Bar

131 Rivington Street, at Norfolk Street (1-212 260 4555). Subway F to Delancey Street; J, M, Z to Delancey-

Essex Streets. **Open** 11am-4am Mon-Fri; 10am-4am Sat, Sun. **$**. **Eclectic**. Map p59 E4 ⑦

A playful all-day bohemian hangout attracting a variety show of a clientele, from suits to drag queens and artfully tousled locals. No dish, except steak, costs more than $16. The menu is a mix of French bistro (steak-frites), British pub (Welsh rarebit) and Louisiana lunch counter (oyster po'boys). Finding your way around the wine list is a cinch – it's a mere six bottles long, designated 'cheap', 'decent' or 'good'.

Spitzers Corner

NEW *101 Rivington Street at Ludlow Street (1-212 228 0027). Subway J, M, Z at Essex Street.* **Open** noon-4am daily. **$**. **Bar**. Map p59 E4 ⑦

Chef Michael Cooperman (Le Bernardin) took over the reins in the kitchen when Top Chef contestant Sam Talbot bailed out on this dress-shop-turned-gastropub. The 95-seat eaterie from the brothers Shamlian (Fat Baby) will feature 50 beers on tap, a raw bar and floor-to-ceiling windows ideal for taking in the LES scene.

Shopping

Alife Rivington Club

158 Rivington Street, between Clinton & Suffolk Streets. Subway F to Delancey Street; J, M, Z to Delancey-Essex Streets. **Open** noon-7pm daily. Map p59 E4 ⑦

'Sneakers' equal 'religion' in this tiny, out-of-the-way shop, which is arguably the city's main hub for hard-to-get shoes. The store, like its wares, has a rather exclusive vibe about it: there's no sign visible, no street number, no indication that the joint even exists from the outside. Look closely and ring the bell to check out the rotating selection of 60 or so styles.

Annie O

105 Rivington Street, between Essex & Ludlow Streets (1-212 475 3490). Subway F to Delancey Street. **Open** 1-11pm Tue-Sat; noon-6pm Sun. Map p59 E4 ⑧

Allfe Rivington Club

Party like a rock star? Now you can shop like one too at Annie O, a music-themed boutique tucked in the Hotel on Rivington. Shop curator Annie Ohayon – a former music publicist for acts such as Pearl Jam and Smashing Pumpkins – handpicks goods spiked with a naughty, rock 'n' roll sensibility.

Doyle & Doyle

189 Orchard Street, between E Houston & Stanton Streets (1-212 677 9991/ www.doyledoyle.com). Subway F, V to Lower East Side-Second Avenue. **Open** 1-7pm Tue, Wed, Fri; 1-8pm Thur; noon-7pm Sat, Sun. **Map** p59 D4 ③①
Whether your taste is more art deco or nouveau, Victorian or Edwardian, gemologist sisters Pam and Elizabeth Doyle, who specialise in estate and antique jewellery, will have that intimate, one-of-a-kind piece you're looking for, including engagement rings and eternity bands.

Edith Machinist

104 Rivington Street, between Essex & Ludlow Streets (1-212 979 9992). Subway F to Delancey Street; J, M, Z
to Delancey-Essex Streets. **Open** 1-8pm Mon-Fri; noon-8pm Sat, Sun. **Map** p59 E4 ③②
Check out one of the city's best collections of (mostly) fine leather bags, not to mention an army of shoes, at this below-street-level shop. There's no trash padding – only the cream of the vintage crop. The front rack displays Edith & Daha's own line of clothes.

Foley & Corinna

114 Stanton Street, between Essex & Ludlow Streets (1-212 529 2338/ www.foleyandcorinna.com). Subway F to Delancey Street; J, M, Z to Delancey-Essex Streets. **Open** noon-8pm Mon-Sat; noon-7pm Sun. **Map** p59 E4 ③③
Vintage-clothing fiends like Liv Tyler and Donna Karan know they can have it both ways: shoppers freely mix old (Anna Corinna's vintage finds) with new (Dana Foley's original creations, including lace tops, leather-belted pants and sheer wool knits) to compose a truly one-of-a-kind look. Encourage the boy in your life to spiff up at the men's store, just around the corner.

Russ & Daughters

Guss' Pickles

85-87 Orchard Street, between Broome & Grand Streets. Subway F to Delancey Street; J, M, Z to Delancey-Essex Streets. **Open** *9.30am-6.30pm Mon-Thur; 9.30am-4pm Fri; 10am-6pm Sun.* **Map** *p59 E4* ㉞

After moving twice in recent years, the Pickle King has settled down in this Lower East Side location, and the complete, delicious array of sours and half-sours, pickled peppers, watermelon rinds and sauerkraut is available to grateful New Yorkers once again.

House de Lux

NEW *147 Orchard Street, between Rivington & Stanton Streets (1-212 477 2035). Subway F to Delancey Street; J, M, Z to Delancey-Essex Streets.* **Open** *1-9pm Tue-Sun.* **Map** *p59 E4* ㉟

Former DJ-turned-fashion-designer S Hamady's funky clothing emporium should please exhibitionists, whether latent or proud. His disco-inspired streetwear line offers jeans sporting gold pockets emblazoned with cheeky statements like 'Free Your Ass'.

Marmalade

172 Ludlow Street, between Houston & Stanton Streets (1-212 473 8070). Subway F, V to Lower East Side-Second Avenue. **Open** *noon-8.30pm Mon-Thur, Sun; noon-9.30pm Fri, Sat.* **Map** *p59 E4* ㊱

Marmalade, one of the cutest vintage-clothing stores on the Lower East Side, has some of the hottest 1970s and '80s threads below Houston Street. That slinky cocktail dress or ruffled blouse is tucked away amid a selection of well-priced items. Accessories, vintage shoes and a small selection of men's clothing are also available.

Russ & Daughters

179 E Houston Street, between Allen & Orchard Streets (1-212 475 4880/ www.russanddaughters.com). Subway F, V to Lower East Side-Second Avenue. **Open** *9am-7pm Mon-Sat; 8am-5.30pm Sun.* **Map** *p59 D4* ㊲

Russ & Daughters, which opened in 1914, sells eight kinds of smoked salmon and many Jewish-inflected Eastern European delectables, along with dried fruits, chocolates and caviar.

TG-170

170 Ludlow Street, between Houston & Stanton Streets (1-212 995 8660/ www.tg170.com). Subway F to Delancey Street; J, M, Z to Delancey-Essex Streets. **Open** noon-8pm daily. **Map** p59 E4 ❸❽

Terri Gillis has an eye for emerging designers: she was the first to carry work from Built by Wendy and Pixie Yates. Nowadays you'll find Jared Gold and Liz Collins pieces hanging in her newly expanded store.

Nightlife

Annex

152 Orchard Street, at Rivington Street (1-212 673 3410). Subway F to Delancey Street. **Open** 9pm-4am Mon-Sat. **Map** p59 E4 ❸❾

This boxy, somewhat anonymous room hosts dance nights as well as (generally third-rate) rock bands. There can be a prescribed hipness to the place, as if they are striving to emulate some Lower East Side stereotype, but kids seem to have fun here.

Arlene's Grocery

95 Stanton Street, between Ludlow & Orchard Streets (1-212 995 1652/ www.arlene-grocery.com). Subway F to Delancey Street; J, M, Z to Delancey-Essex Streets. **Open** 6pm-4am daily. **Map** p59 E4 ❾⓿

A mid-level rung on the local-band ladder, Arlene's Grocery can pack in as many as six rock acts in a single night, often adding afternoon shows on Saturday. Monday night's live-band karaoke is an institution, even if the band that started it all has since moved on. A lively spot.

Bowery Ballroom

6 Delancey Street, between Bowery & Chrystie Street (1-212 533 2111/ www.boweryballroom.com). Subway J, M, Z to Bowery; 6 to Spring Street. **Open** 8pm-late daily. **Map** p59 D4 ❾❶

Probably the best venue in town for seeing indie bands either on the way up or precariously holding their own, the Bowery nonetheless brings in a diverse range of artists from town and around the world, as well as offering a clear view and loud, bright sound from just about any spot in the house. Not into the opening band? The spacious downstairs lounge is a great place to relax and socialise between (or during) sets. Past bookings have included the likes of Black Lips, Kate Nash, Nada Surf and Vampire Weekend.

Box

189 Chrystie Street, at Rivington Street (1-212 982 9301). Subway F, V at Lower East Side-Second Avenue; J, M, Z to Bowery. **Open** Call for hours, showtimes. **Map** p59 D4 ❾❷

This former sign factory was transformed into a 200-seat venue for a diverse list of acts, ranging from sultry torch singers and bawdy burlesque to New Orleans jazz dancers. Celebrity A-listers are known to imbibe here until the wee hours of the morning.

Cake Shop

152 Ludlow Street, between Rivington & Stanton Streets (1-212 253 0036/ www.cake-shop.com). Subway F, V to Lower East Side-Second Avenue. **Open** 8pm-late daily. No credit cards. **Map** p59 E4 ❾❸

This narrow but clean-and-new basement space gets points for much more than its keen indie-rock bookings. For one thing there's the location: it's in the heart of the Lower East Side. What's more, it has pastries and coffee for sale upstairs. Better still (for late-night music junkies, at least) is the brightly lit back room on street level, which sells used vinyl and CDs, as well as a smattering of new releases, DVDs and other record-store ephemera.

Delancey

168 Delancey Street, at Clinton Street (1-212 254 9920/www.thedelancey. com). Subway F to Delancey Street; J, M, Z to Delancey-Essex Streets. **Open** 8pm-late daily. **Cover** $6-$10. No credit cards. **Map** p59 E4 ❾❹

Within spitting distance from the Williamsburg Bridge is the Delancey, which has quickly become one of

Lower art side

New Museum of Contemporary Art

A slew of galleries have left the more expected environs of West Chelsea and started anew in the shadow of the recently opened **New Museum of Contemporary Art** (p76), in an area once considered not even remotely glamorous. Today they number at least 25. 'Of course it's a factor,' says **Envoy Gallery**'s (132 Chrystie Street, 1-212 226 4555) Jimi Dams, of the New Museum's presence. 'Not for me, but for the people planning to be part of a new 'It' area.'

'We were drawn to the Lower East Side in large part because of its character as an art neighbourhood,' says Lisa Phillips, the museum's director. '[It's] a creative centre, home to generations of artists and writers and musicians. Galleries that are opening spaces on the Lower East Side are coming to the area for the same reasons we did.'

The influx isn't limited to neophyte dealers: there are also established galleries relocating from other areas, like **Janos Gat Gallery** (195 Bowery, 1-212 677 3525), formerly of the Upper East Side, and **Feature, Inc.** (276 Bowery, 1-212 675 7772), which used to be in Chelsea. These venues are now on the Bowery, but as both Dams and Philip Grauer of Chinatown's **Canada Gallery** (55 Chrustie Street, 1-212 925 4631) acknowledge, the cool factor isn't the only reason people are moving.

'Leases are up in Chelsea for a lot of places,' notes Grauer. 'It's getting expensive there. I think there's an urgent need for people to relocate.' Miguel Abreu, who has had a gallery on Orchard Street for a couple of years, agrees: 'The problem with art in New York City is that there's no more space to make it in.'

Manhattan's hotter spots on account of its frequent bookings of hyped indie bands (Clap Your Hands Say Yeah, Youth Group) and DJs. But it's not all just flash and style; try going out on the lovely second-floor outdoor patio, which is always mobbed with beautiful young hipsters in the summer, and you'll see why the place is popular.

Element

225 E Houston Street, at Essex Street (1-212 254 2220). Subway F, V to Lower East Side-Second Avenue. **Open** 10pm-4am daily. **Map** p59 E4 ⑨⑤
A former bank, goth hotspot and studio of Jasper Johns, this hulking space offers a massive dancefloor encircled by a perfect-view balcony, a mellow VIP area and a cool underground vault. Watch out for nights dedicated to soul, house and new-wave sounds, plus some Saturday night queer action with a party called, appropriately enough, Bank. It's where you'll find all of the Downtown creatures of the night, from Amanda Lepore to Larry Tee and the gang. Be sure to check out the downstairs lounge, Vault, which features underground sounds of all sorts.

Laugh Lounge nyc

151 Essex Street, between Rivington & Stanton Streets (1-212 614 2500/ www.laughloungenyc.com). Subway F to Delancey Street; J, M, Z to Delancey-Essex Streets. **Shows** 8.30pm Tue-Thur; 8.30pm, 10.30pm Fri, Sat. **Map** p59 E4 ⑨⑥
Although the off-peak nights occasionally offer line-ups as edgy as the Lower East Side location would imply, for the most part you can expect standard club-circuit fare from this newish venue.

Living Room

154 Ludlow Street, between Rivington & Stanton Streets (1-212 533 7235/ www.livingroomny.com). Subway F to Lower East Side-Second Avenue; J, M, Z to Delancey-Essex Streets. **Open** 6pm-4am Mon, Tue; 2pm-4am Wed-Sat; 6pm-2am Sun. No credit cards. **Map** p59 E4 ⑨⑦
Many local clubs lay claim to being the place where Norah Jones got her start, but Living Room really was. Still, that was in the venue's old (and drab) location; since moving to Lower East Side's version of Main Street, the stream of singer-songwriters that fill the schedule here has taken on a bit more gleam,

Cake Shop p81

Element p83

NEW YORK BY AREA

and the warmly lit environs seem to be always bustling. Skillful guitarist Jim Campilongo appears regularly, as do local stalwarts such as Tony Scherr, Chris Lee and Matty Charles.

Mercury Lounge

217 E Houston Street, between Essex & Ludlow Streets (1-212 260 4700/ www.mercuryloungenyc.com). Subway F, V to Lower East Side-Second Avenue. **Open** *Call for showtimes.* **Map** p59 E4 ❾❽

Mercury Lounge is both an old standby and pretty much the No.1 indie-rock club in town, with solid sound and sight lines (and a cramped bar in the front room). With four-band bills almost every night, you can catch plenty of locals and touring bands in the course of just one week.

Pianos

158 Ludlow Street, between Rivington & Stanton Streets (1-212 505 3733). Subway F to Delancey Street; J, M, Z to Delancey-Essex Streets. **Shows** *start around 8pm.* **Map** p59 E4 ❾❾

When it opened a few years ago, this small club seemed like the ground zero for New York hip. That's no longer the case, as a lot of the cooler bookings have moved either to Brooklyn or to venues such as Cake Shop. Still, while the sound is often lousy and the room mobbed, there are always good reasons to go back. And the emerging talent booked in the charming, free upstairs lounge is often a good bet.

Sapphire

249 Eldridge Street, between Houston & Stanton Streets (1-212 777 5153/ www.sapphirenyc.com). Subway F, V to Lower East Side-Second Avenue. **Open** *7pm-4am daily.* **Map** p59 D4 ❶❿❿

Monday to Wednesday the music here falls somewhere along the techno-house-disco continuum, and local heroes E-man and Melvin Moore are joined by the occasional big name. Hip hop and funk rule from Thursday to Saturday with beloved veteran DJ Jazzy Nice often running things. A word of warning: weekends can be brutally crowded, so dress to sweat.

Slipper Room

*167 Orchard Street, at Stanton Street
(1-212 253 7246/www.slipperroom.
com). Subway F, V to Lower East Side-
Second Avenue.* **Open** 8pm-4am Tue-
Sat. **Map** p59 D4 **101**

New York has a healthy neo-burlesque
scene, and the petite Slipper Room is,
if not at that scene's nexus, then pretty darn near it. Many of the Victorian
looking venue's happenings, notably
Friday's Hot Box hoedown, feature
plenty of bump-and-grind action, with
DJs spinning the appropriate beats; the
occasional band completes the picture.

Arts & leisure

Landmark's Sunshine Cinema

*143 E Houston Street, between First &
Second Avenues (1-212 330 8182/777
3456). Subway F, V to Lower East
Side-Second Avenue.* **Open** Call for
showtimes. **Map** p59 D4 **102**

A beautifully restored 1898 Yiddish
theatre has become one of New York's
snazziest art house cinemas, presenting some of the finest new independent
films in air-conditioned and stadium-
seated luxury.

East Village

Scruffier than its genteel western
counterpart, the East Village has a
long history as a countercultural
hotbed. The area east of Broadway
between Houston and 14th Streets
is less edgy today, but remnants of
its spirited past endure. Check out
the indie record shops, bargain
restaurants, grungy bars, punky
clubs and funky clothing stores.
Curry Row, on 6th Street,
between First & Second Avenues,
is one of several Little Indias in
New York. Roughly two dozen
Indian restaurants sit side by side
and they remain popular with
diners on an extremely tight
budget. **Tompkins Square Park**
is the community park of the East

Village – and it's a place where
Latino bongo beaters, longhairs
strumming their acoustic guitars,
punky squatters, mangy dogs,
yuppie stroller-pushers and the
homeless all mingle.

Eating & drinking

Against the Grain

*620 E 6th Street, at Avenue B (1-212
358 7065). Subway F, V to Lower
East Side-Second Avenue; L to First
Avenue.* **Open** 6pm-1am Mon, Tue,
Sun; 6pm-2am Wed-Sat. **$**. **Bar**.
Map p59 E3 **103**

This closet-size, pretension-free beer
emporium sits adjacent to the wine-cen-
tric Grape & Grain. Join brew aficiona-
dos at the communal table (dubbed 'the
mingler'), which fills the exposed-brick-
and stamped-tin adorned room. Snack
on spiced nuts and listen carefully while
bartenders explain the globe-spanning
suds menu. Then consider pairing Bear
Republic Racer 5 India Pale Ale with
nibbles like pastry-wrapped chorizo and
beer-steamed shrimp.

Aroma

*36 E 4th Street, between Bowery &
Lafayette Street (1-212 375 0100).
Subway 6 to Astor Place.* **Open** 6pm-
midnight Tue-Thur; 6pm-2am Fri;
12.30am-3.30pm, 6pm-2am Sat;
12.30am-3.30pm, 6pm-midnight Sun.
$$. **Italian**. **Map** p59 D3 **104**

This slender wine bar has been carved
out of a former streetwear boutique,
and the result is enchanting. Chef
Christopher Daly's dishes are careful-
ly conceived: a duck salad is loaded
with lardons, wild chicory and a soft-
poached egg. The excellent 'lamb three
ways' consists of a tower of braised
shoulder, a patty of neck meat, pine
nuts, raisins and capers, and a juicy,
rosemary-rubbed chop.

Cafecito

*185 Avenue C, at 12th Street (1-212
253 9966). Subway L to First Avenue.*
Open 6-10pm Tue, Thur, Sun; 6pm-
2am Fri, Sat. **$**. No credit cards.
Cuban. **Map** p59 E2 **105**

The relaxed outdoor bar is just one of the authentic touches at Cafecito ('tiny coffee'). You can sip a Mojito and nibble green plantain chips as you contemplate the menu: the aborcito de Cuba gives you a taste of each of the small hot appetisers – the best of which are bollos, corn and black-bean fritters. In addition to specials like chargrilled skirt steak with chimichurri sauce, the perfectly pressed Cuban sandwich is spot on.

Death & Co

433 E 6th Street, between First Avenue & Avenue A (1-212 388 0882). Subway F, V to Lower East Side–Second Avenue; L to First Avenue; 6 to Astor Place. **Open** 6pm-1am Mon-Thur, Sun; 6pm-2am Fri, Sat. **$**. **Bar**. Map p59 E3 **106**
Ravi DeRossi and David Kaplan serve cocktails, wine and small plates at this clandestine lounge with 1920s-style decor and a signless exterior.

Degustation

239 E 5th Street, between Second & Third Avenues (1-212 979 1012). Subway 6 to Astor Place. **Open** 6-11pm Mon-Sat. **$**. **Spanish**. Map p59 D3 **107**
This tiny 16-seat eaterie is run by chef Wesley Genovart, a Spaniard who last worked at Jean-Georges Vongerichten's Perry Street. Genovart's small-plates menu blends French and Spanish cuisines in dishes such as slowly poached egg with *jamón serrano* and breadcrumbs, foie gras with tarragon-caramel water and grapefruit, and cod in *salsa verde* with clams and cockles.

EasternBloc

505 E 6th Street, between Avenues A & B (1-212 777 2555). Subway F, V to Lower East Side–Second Avenue; L to First Avenue. **Open** 7pm-4am daily. **Bar**. Map p59 E3 **108**
This cool little space has a red-scare Commie feel – in the sexiest of ways, with TV screens that show Bettie Page films, and Soviet-era posters. Bartenders are cuties, and nightly themes range from Brüt Thursdays, for tough daddies and those who love them, to Outlaw Saturdays, a go-go-stud-laden night of fabulous filth.

Graffiti

NEW *224 E 10th Street, between First & Second Avenues (1-212 464 7743). Subway L to First Avenue.* **Open** 5.30-10.30pm Tue, Sun; 5.30-11.45pm Wed-Sat. **$**. **Global**. Map p59 D2 **109**
A tiny East Village restaurant run by owner Jehangir Mehta and chef Andres Vazquez delivers global fare that's reflected in the decor: a Ganesh bas-relief anchors one wall, and an oversize Buddha the other. Among the tapas on offer, we liked watermelon salad with salty feta and a sweet mint sorbet, and a Chinese-style pork bun fragrant with cinnamon and cloves and served with apricot chutney.

Mermaid Inn

96 Second Avenue, between 5th & 6th Streets (1-212 674 5870). Subway F, V to Lower East Side–Second Avenue. **Open** 5.30-11pm Mon-Thur; 5.30-11.30pm Fri, Sat; 5-10pm Sun. **$$**. **Seafood**. Map p59 D3 **110**
The chefs at the Mermaid dress seafood for New York palates. The menu changes seasonally, but they always have the overstuffed lobster roll and spaghetti with spicy shrimp, scallops and calamares, topped with rocket. Everything tastes even better in summer, when you can sit in the back garden.

Momofuku Ssäm Bar

207 Second Avenue, at 13th Street (1-212 254 3500). Subway L to First, Third Avenues; N, Q, R, W, 4, 5, 6 to 14th Street-Union Square. **Open** 11am-2am daily. **$$**. **Korean**. Map p59 D2 **111**
Momofuku Ssäm Bar chef David Chang's latest feels like two restaurants fused into one: a Korean Chipotle, and a self-aware joint serving designer ham and pricey platters. Waiters hustle to noisy rock music in this 50-seat space. Chefs create concoctions priced to sample, including the wonderfully fatty pork-belly steamed bun with hoisin sauce and cucumbers, and the house ssäm (Korean for 'wrap'), which might be the finest burrito in the city.

Morning glory

New York's newest brunch spots are worth getting out of bed for.

Shorty's .32

Chef Josh Eden fled the fine-dining beat – he was at Jean Georges for 12 years – to open **Shorty's .32** (p67), a cosy neighbourhood eaterie. Legions of mismatched lamps hanging from the ceiling cast a mighty glow over morning coffee (thanks to attentive service, you'll never see an empty mug), and Eden delivers what everyone needs on Sunday morning: fat and starch. We love his sweet-potato hash strewn with bits of short rib over buttered toast and pleasantly cakelike pancakes with the misshapen charm of Mom's. Or forget classic AM victuals altogether and opt for Shorty's excellent burger on a brioche bun, served with house-made pickles.

At **Provence** (38 MacDougal Street, between Houston & Prince Streets, 1-212 475 7500), toile upholstery and a pink powder room ensure that Marc Meyer and Vicki Freeman's French restaurant delivers the romance evoked by its namesake region. The food is almost as dead-on as the look: house-made croissants are tender, flaky and, when treated with Meyer's own quince jam, delicious enough to render any eater momentarily speechless. A tartine, in which sweet figs, honey and crème fraîche intersect on a buttered baguette, has a similarly stultifying effect.

The folks at Peter Hoffman's East Village tavern **Back Forty** (190 Avenue B, at E 12th Street, 1-212 388 1990) understand that there's more that needs coddling at brunch time than the eggs; the lights at the eaterie are kept mercifully dim and the menu is chock-full of hangover killers. Steak and eggs – six nicely charred slices of grass-fed beef with a pair of fried eggs – should fortify any diner, booze-soaked or not. Fried chicken and waffles showcases moist meat soaked in buttermilk for two days and plush waffles. Though the coffee is potent enough, smart diners should put their dollars towards a side of pillowy cider donuts.

Rapture Café & Books

200 Avenue A, between 12th & 13th Streets (1-212 228 1177). Subway L to First Avenue. **Open** 10am-10pm daily. **$. Café. Map** p59 E2 ⑫

This spot hopes to bring a little bit of the old-time East Village back from the dead – a place for artists, writers and musicians (and the people who love them) to hang out and entertain each other. A tiny stage gives ample room for readings, performances and other forms of artistic showing-off.

Rififi

332 E 11th Street, between First & Second Avenues (1-212-677-1027). Subway L to First Avenue; 6 to Astor Place. **Open** 6pm-2am Mon-Thur, Sun; 7pm-4am Fri, Sat. No credit cards. **Bar. Map** p59 D2 ⑬

Hovering between unpretentious and run-down is Rififi, a dive bar with old-world charm. The popular back room screens movies several nights a week; there are also occasional bands and burlesque shows. Rififi (which takes its name from Jules Dassin's heist-film masterpiece) has become a local hang-out with clutches of hipsters engaged in serious conversation.

Spice Cove

326 E 6th Street, between First & Second Avenues (1-212 674 8884). Subway F, V to Lower East Side-Second Avenue. **Open** 11.30am-midnight Mon-Fri; 11.30am-12.30am Sat, Sun. **$. Indian. Map** p59 D3 ⑭

Bright orange walls, stone archways and candles provide a seductive setting; St Germain stands in for sitar music; and in place of an all-you-can-eat buffet is chef Muhammed Ahmed Ali's specialities. Expect properly spiced dishes such as chickpeas stir-fried with coriander, cumin and cinnamon, and fenugreek-scented Atlantic salmon crowned with a delicious tomato masala.

Village Pourhouse

64 Third Avenue, at 11th Street (1-212 979 2337/www.purhousenyc.com). Subway L to Third Avenue; 6 to Astor Place. **Open** 11am-2am Mon-Wed, Sun; 11am-4am Thur-Sat. **Bar. Map** p59 D2 ⑮

Fans of exotic beers – and sports – can sip global finds like Hong Kong's Macau and Kalik, a Bahamian brew, while watching one of the 21 televisions at this East Village A hearty menu, with entrées like chicken madeira, helps soak up the suds.

Shopping

Dave's Quality Meat

7 E 3rd Street, between Bowery & Second Avenue (1-212 505 7551/ www.davesqualitymeat.com). Subway F, V to Lower East Side-Second Avenue. **Open** noon-7pm Mon-Sat; noon-6pm Sun. **Map** p59 D3 ⑯

Dave Ortiz – formerly of the cool urban-threads label Zoo York – and professional skateboarder Chris Keefe stock top-drawer streetwear in their wittily designed shop, the decor complete with meat hooks and mannequins sporting butcher's aprons. Homemade graphic-print T-shirts are wrapped in plastic and carefully displayed in a deli case.

D/L Cerney

13 E 7th Street, between Second & Third Avenues (1-212 673 7033). Subway N, R, W to 8th Street-NYU; 6 to Astor Place. **Open** noon-7.30pm daily. **Map** p59 D3 ⑰

Specialising in timeless, original designs for stylish fellows, this store also carries menswear items from the 1940s to the 1960s. Mint-condition must-haves include hats (with some pristine fedoras), ties and shoes. An adjacent shop carries D/L Cerney's new line in women's clothing.

Fabulous Fanny's

335 E 9th Street, between First & Second Avenues (1-212 533 0637/ www.fabulousfannys.com). Subway L to First Avenue; 6 to Astor Place. **Open** noon-8pm daily. **Map** p59 D2 ⑱

The city's best source of period glasses for more than 17 years, this former booth at the 26th Street flea market now calls the East Village home. It has more

Nublu p90

than 10,000 pairs of spectacles, from World War II aviator goggles to 1970s rhinestone-encrusted Versace shades.

Kiehl's

109 Third Avenue, between 13th & 14th Streets (1-212 677 3171/www. kiehls.com). Subway L to Third Avenue; N, Q, R, W, 4, 5, 6 to 14th Street-Union Square. **Open** 10am-7pm Mon-Sat; noon-6pm Sun. **Map** p59 D2 ⑲

Although it is 154 years old and has recently expanded, this New York institution still gets mobbed. Check out the Motorcycle Room, full of vintage Harleys (the owner's obsession). Try one dab of Kiehl's moisturiser, lip balm or body lotion from the plentiful free samples, and you'll be hooked.

Patricia Field

302 Bowery, between Bleecker & Houston Streets (1-212 966 4066/ www.patriciafield.com). Subway B, D, V, F to Broadway-Lafayette Street. **Open** 11am-8pm Mon-Fri, Sun; 11am-9pm Sat. **Map** p59 D3 ⑳

Patricia Field is a virtuoso at blending eclectic club and street styles (she famously assembled the offbeat costumes for *Sex and the City*). Field recently relocated her idiosyncratic collection of jewellery, make-up and clothes to the East Village.

Nightlife

Ace of Clubs

9 Great Jones Street, at Lafayette Street (1-212 677 6924/www.ace ofclubsnyc.com). Subway B, D, F, V to Broadway-Lafayette Street; 6 to Bleecker Street. **Open** from 7pm daily. No credit cards. **Map** p58 C3 ㉑

All this cosy shoebox of a space had needed in the past was a booker with some taste. Ask and ye shall receive, for as early in 2005 it morphed from the old Under Acme into Ace of Clubs and started bringing in a diverse mix of mostly local rock (the Giraffes), blues (Corey Harris) and progressive jazz (the Jazz Passengers' Bill Ware and his Urban Vibes project).

Joe's Pub

425 Lafayette Street, between Astor Place & E 4th Street (1-212 539 8770/ www.joespub.com) Subway N, R, W to 8th Street-NYU; 6 to Astor Place. **Open** Call for showtimes. **Map** p59 D3 ❷

This plush club and restaurant located within the Public Theater is both hip and elegant, and boasts an extraordinarily varied mix of performers (who are usually booked for just a single night). Among the rock, jazz and world music acts, you will occasionally find a Broadway performer venturing into the world of cabaret.

Nublu

62 Avenue C, between 4th & 5th Streets (1-212 979 9925/www.nublu. net). Subway F, V to Lower East Side-Second Avenue. **Open** 8pm-4am daily. No credit cards. **Map** p59 E3 ❸

Inversely proportional to its size has been Nublu's prominence on the local globalist club scene. A pressure cooker of creativity, the venue gave rise to the Brazilian Girls – who started jamming at one late-night session and haven't stopped yet – as well as starting New York City's romance with the Northern Brazilian style *forró*. Even on weeknight events usually start no earlier than 10pm – but if you show up early (once you've located the unmarked door), you'll find that the bar is well stocked and the staff are as warm as the music.

Pyramid Club

101 Avenue A, between 6th & 7th Streets (1-212 228 4888). Subway F, V to Lower East Side-Second Avenue; L to First Avenue; 6 to Astor Place. **Open** 10pm-4am daily. **Map** p59 E3 ❹

In a clubbing era long gone, this was a cornerstone of forward-thinking queer club culture. In what could be considered a sign of the times, the venue's sole remaining gay soirée is Friday night's non-progressive '80s dancefest, 1984. Otherwise, the charmingly decrepit space features the long-running drum 'n' bass bash Konkrete Jungle, as well as a rotating roster of goth and new wave.

Arts & leisure

Amsterdam Billiards

110 E 11th Street, at 4th Avenue (1-212 496 8180). Subway L to Third Avenue; N, Q, R, W, 4, 5, 6 to 14th Street-Union Square. **Open** noon-3am Mon-Thur, Sun; 11am-4am Fri, Sat. **Map** p59 D2 ❺

This long-time Upper West Side institution transplanted itself Downtown in the early months of 2007. The new set of locals settled in quickly to trying their hand at pool or hanging out in the cosy lounge. There's a full bar and snacks as well, which gives you something to do while you wait for a table to become available.

Blue Man Group

Astor Place Theater, 434 Lafayette Street, between Astor Place & E 4th Street (1-212 254 4370/www.blue man.com). Subway N, R, W to 8th Street-NYU; 6 to Astor Place. **Open** Call for showtimes. **Map** p59 D3 ❻

Three men endowed with extraterrestrial imaginations (and decorated with head-to-toe blue body paint) carry this long-time favourite – a show that is as smart as it is ridiculous. People seated in the front rows are provided with ponchos to protect them from the exuberance of the performers on stage.

Bowery Poetry Club

308 Bowery, at Bleecker Street (1-212 614 0505/www.bowerypoetry.com). Subway B, D, F, V to Broadway-Lafayette Street; 6 to Bleecker Street. **Map** p59 D3 ❼

The name of this colourful joint on the Bowery reveals its roots in the poetry-slam scene, but it's also the truest current iteration of the East Village's legendary creative arts scene: all kinds of jazz, folk, hip hop and improv theatre can be found here on a regular basis. So if you have a taste for the bizarre and think that nothing could possibly offend you, keep eyes peeled for anything from the Jollyship to the Whiz-Bang musical-puppet crew. There is also a range of sandwiches and hot and cold drinks available.

New York Theatre Workshop

*79 E 4th Street, between Bowery &
Second Avenue (1-212 460 5475/
www.nytw.org). Subway F, V to Lower
East Side-Second Avenue; 6 to Astor
Place.* **Map** p59 D3 ⓲

Founded in 1979, NYTW works with
emerging directors eager to take on
challenging pieces. Besides plays by
the likes of Caryl Churchill (*Far Away,
A Number*) and Tony Kushner
(*Homebody/Kabul*), this company also
premièred *Rent*, Jonathan Larson's
Pulitzer Prize-winning musical (still
packing 'em in on Broadway).

Performance Space 122

*150 First Avenue, at E 9th Street
(1-212 477 5288/www.ps122.org).
Subway L to First Avenue; 6 to
Astor Place.* **Map** p59 D2 ⓲

This non-profit arts centre presents
experimental dance, performance art,
music, film and video. Eric Bogosian,
Whoopi Goldberg, John Leguizamo
and others have developed projects
here; of more street-level interest is the
monthly bloggers' night. Australian
trendsetter Vallejo Gantner recently
took over as artistic director, promising to make its programming more
international in flavour.

Public Theater

*425 Lafayette Street, between Astor
Place & E 4th Street (1-212 539
8500/Telecharge 1-212 239 6200/
www.publictheater.org). Subway N, R,
W to 8th Street-NYU; 6 to Astor Place.*
Map p59 D3 ⓲

Founded by the late Joseph Papp and
mainly dedicated to the work of new
American playwrights and performers,
this Astor Place landmark is also well
known for its regular productions of
Shakespeare's plays. The venue is
home to five stages and Joe's Pub (p90).

Stomp

*Orpheum Theater, 126 Second Avenue,
between St Marks Place & E 7th Street
(1-212 477 2477). Subway N, R, W to
8th Street-NYU; 6 to Astor Place.*
Map p59 D3 ⓲

This show is billed as a 'percussion
sensation' because there's no other way
to describe it. Using garbage-can lids,
buckets, brooms, sticks and just about
anything they can get their hands on,
these aerobicised dancer-musicians
make a lovely racket.

Greenwich Village

Stretching from Houston Street
to 14th Street, between Broadway
and Sixth Avenue, Greenwich
Village's leafy streets have inspired
bohemians for almost a century.
Once the dingy but colourful
stomping ground of Beat poets and
folk and jazz musicians, the well-
trafficked strip of Bleecker Street
between La Guardia Place and
Sixth Avenue is now simply an
overcrowded stretch of poster
shops, cheap restaurants and music
venues for the college crowd.

Sights & museums

AIA Center for Architecture

*536 La Guardia Place, between
Bleecker & W 3rd Streets (1-212 683
0023/www.aiany.org). Subway A, B,
C, D, E, F, V to W 4th Street.* **Open**
9am-8pm Mon-Fri; 11am-5pm Sat.
Map p58 C3 ⓲

After five years of planning, the AIA
Center for Architecture opened to
acclaim in autumn 2003. The sweeping, light-filled design is a physical
manifestation of AIA's goal of promot-
ing transparency in its access and programming. Large slabs of flooring
were cut away at the street and basement levels, converting underground
spaces into suitably bright, museum-
quality galleries.

Washington Square Park

*Subway A, B, C, D, E, F, V to
W 4th Street-Washington Square.*
Map p58 C3 ⓲

The hippies who turned up and tuned
out in Washington Square Park, once
a potter's field, are still there in spirit,

Washington Square Park p91

and they often turn up in person: the park positively hums with musicians and street artists. In warmer months this is one of the best places for people-watching to be found in the city.

Eating & drinking

BLT Burger

NEW *470 Sixth Avenue, between 11th & 12th Streets (1-212 243 8226). Subway A, C, E, B, D, F, V to West 4th Street.* **Open** *11.30am-11pm daily.* **$$.**
American. Map p58 B2 **134**
The no-frills house burger – seven ounces of sirloin, short rib, chuck and brisket – not only comes on a cookout-worthy white bun (très américain), it's wrapped in wax paper and served with fries in a plastic basket that evokes hal-cyon drive-in days. Yet more esoteric items, like a spicy patty made of lamb merguez and the $62 Japanese kobe

burger, make it abundantly clear that chef Laurent Tourondel has not forgot-ten the haute that got him here.

Blue Hill

75 Washington Place, between Washington Square West & Sixth Avenue (1-212 539 1776). Subway A, B, C, D, E, F, V to W 4th Street. **Open** *5.30-11pm Mon-Sat; 5.30-10pm Sun.*
$$$. French. Map p58 C3 **135**
This beloved gourmand destination has an uncanny knack for scoring the best local produce throughout the year. Important though that is, it's the not the only reason for chefs Dan Barber and Michael Anthony succeeding so consistently with their dishes. That lies in their solid foundation of classical French cooking. When in season, Blue Hill's strawberries have more berry flavour, and its heirloom tomatoes are juicier, than anyone else's.

La Lanterna di Vittorio

*129 MacDougal Street, between 3rd &
4th Streets (1-212 529 5945). Subway
A, B, C, D, E, F, V to W 4th Street-
Washington Square.* **Open** 10am-3am
Mon-Thur, Sun; 10am-4am Fri, Sat. **$**.
Italian. Map p58 C3 ⓵⒊⒍

Woo your darling by the fire or under
the stars at a romantic Village spot that
has been helping to smooth the course
of true love for the last 28 years. The
200 year old garden was once owned
by Aaron Burr; in wintertime four fireplaces spark your courting. Choose a
bottle from the extensive wine list to go
with light café eats like panini, crosti-
ni, smoked duck breast with salad, or
thin-crust pizza.

Lupa

*170 Thompson Street, between Bleecker
& Houston Streets (1-212 982 5089/
www.luparestaurant.com). Subway
A, B, C, D, E, F, V to W 4th Street.*
Open noon-3pm, 5-11.30pm Mon-Fri;
11.30am-2.30pm, 5-11.30pm Sat, Sun.
$$. **Italian**. Map p58 C3 ⓵⒊⒎

Fans of this 'poor man's Babbo' (celeb-
chef Mario Batali's pricier restaurant
around the corner) keep reclaiming
their seats. Here's the ritual they rec-
ommend: first, a cutting board of fatty-
delicious cured meats. Move on to
sublime pasta. Then choose a meaty
main, like oxtail *alla vaccinara* or a
classic saltimbocca. By the time the
panna cotta with apricot arrives, you'll
be ready to become a regular too.

Peanut Butter & Co

*240 Sullivan Street, between Bleecker
& W 3rd Streets (1-212 677 3995).
Subway A, B, C, D, E, F, V to W 4th
Street.* **Open** 11am-9pm Mon-Thur,
Sun; 11am-10pm Fri, Sat. **$**.
American. Map p58 C3 ⓵⒊⒏

Every day the staff at Peanut Butter &
Co grind out a fresh batch of peanut
butter, which is used to create gooey
mood-pacifiers like the popular Elvis –
the King's infamous grilled favourite
of peanut butter, banana and honey.
Goober-free menu items, like tuna
melts and bologna sandwiches, contin-
ue the brown-bag theme.

Prem-On Thai

*138 W Houston Street, between
Sullivan & MacDougal Streets (1-212
353 2338). Subway C, E to Spring
Street.* **Open** noon-11.30pm Mon-Fri;
noon-midnight Sat, Sun. **$$**. **Thai**.
Map p58 C3 ⓵⒊⒐

In one of several stylish rooms, you'll
watch in awe as dramatically plated
Thai dishes and cocktails are carried
through the dining room. Prem-On
doesn't hold back with the seasoning
either: a whole fried sea bass fillet is
served upright and loaded with basil
and roasted-chilli-paste sauce.

Las Ramblas

*170 W 4th Street, between Cornelia &
Jones Streets (1-646 415 7924). Subway
A, B, C, D, E, F, V to W 4th Street-
Washington Square.* **Open** 4pm-2am
daily. **$**. **Spanish**. Map p58 B3 ⓵⒋⓪

Now that tapas has become the trendy
misnomer for small-plate fare from any
cuisine, it's no wonder you're grateful
when you see the real Spanish deal. The
authenticity of Las Ramblas is appar-
ent in every *centimetro* of the place –
the chef hails from Pamplona; three
flavours of sangria are mixed to order;
and the intimate space actually fosters
social interaction. However, the food
alone provides enough of an incentive
to visit this place: aged serrano ham,
grilled chorizo, *patatas bravas*, *croque-
tas* and a selection of Spanish cheeses.

Stand

*24 E 12th Street, between Fifth Avenue
& University Place (1-212 488 5900).
Subway L, N, Q, R, W, 4, 5, 6 to 14th
Street-Union Square.* **Open** noon-
midnight daily. **$**. **American**.
Map p58 C2 ⓵⒋⒈

This is a thinking person's comfort-
food spot, complete with floor-to-ceil-
ing windows, table service and giant
white plates. Hefty patties with a cook-
out-worthy char come any way except
under a processed cheese single: on
fresh-baked buns, in a three-lettuce
salad or inside a vegetable soup. Fries
are standard, but gooey parmesan
sweet-potato mash serves as a sophis-
ticated substitute.

Yolato

120 MacDougal Street, between Bleecker & W 3rd Streets (1-212 228 6303). Subway A, B, C, D, E, F, V to W 4th Street. **Open** noon-1am Mon-Sat; noon-midnight Sun. **$**. **Dessert**. Map p58 C3 **142**

It's yoghurt, it's gelato – it's yolato, a new fusiony fro-yo shop. Choose from over 100 flavours, such as hazelnut and lychee, as well as crêpes, yoggi (non-flavoured frozen yogurt) and sorbet.

Nightlife

Blue Note

131 W 3rd Street, between MacDougal Street & Sixth Avenue (1-212 475 8592/www.bluenote.net). Subway A, B, C, D, E, F, V to W 4th Street. **Open** 6pm-3am daily. Map p58 C3 **143**

On a bustling, slightly seedy block sits the Blue Note, which prides itself on being 'the jazz capital of the world'. Bona fide musical titans (Cecil Taylor, Charlie Haden) rub up against hot young talents (the Bad Plus) on the calendar, while the tables in the club get patrons rubbing up against each other. The Late Night Groove series and the Sunday brunches are the best bargains.

Smalls

183 W 10th Street, between Seventh Avenue South & W 4th Street (1-212 675 7369). Subway 1 to Christopher Street-Sheridan Square. **Shows** times vary; call for details. Map p58 B3 **144**

The resurrected version of this storied, youth-friendly jazz spot offers one big concession for the grown-ups: A liquor license to go with its fully stocked bar. The same rules apply for the jazz, though. It's still a place to catch the best and brightest up-and-comers as well as moonlighting stars like the Bad Plus's Ethan Iverson or veteran baritone saxist Charles Davis.

Sullivan Room

218 Sullivan Street, between Bleecker & W 3rd Streets (1-212 252 2151/www. sullivanroom.com). Subway A, B, C, D, E, F, V to W 4th Street. **Open** 10pm-4am Wed-Sun. Map p58 C3 **145**

Where's the party? It's right here in this unmarked subterranean space, which hosts some of the best deep house, tech house and breaks bashes the city has to offer. It's an utterly unpretentious club, with little of the glitz that bigger clubs feature – but hell, all you really need are some thumpin' beats and a place to move your feet, right?

Village Vanguard

178 Seventh Avenue South, at Perry Street (1-212 255 4037/www.village vanguard.com). Subway A, C, E, 1, 2, 3 to 14th Street; L to Eighth Avenue. **Open** Showtimes 9pm & 11pm daily. Map p58 B2 **146**

More than 70 years old and still going strong, the Village Vanguard is one of New York's real jazz meccas. History breathes in the very walls that surround you here: John Coltrane, Miles Davis and Bill Evans have all grooved in this hallowed hall, and the walls are lined with photos and artefacts. The big names, old and new, continue to fill the Vanguard's lineup, and the 16-piece Vanguard Jazz Orchestra has been the Monday night regular for almost 40 years. Reservations are strongly recommended, and note that the Vanguard takes only cash or travellers' cheques at the door.

Zinc Bar

90 W Houston Street, between La Guardia Place & Thompson Street (1-212 477 8337/www.zincbar.com). Subway A, B, C, D, E, F, V to W 4th Street. **Open** 6pm-3.30am daily. Map p58 C3 **147**

Located where Greenwich Village meets Soho, Zinc Bar is the place to hoot and holler with die-hard night owls. The after-hours atmosphere is enhanced by the cool mix of African, flamenco, jazz and samba bands.

Arts & leisure

Angelika Film Center

18 W Houston Street, at Mercer Street (1-212 995 2000/www. angelikafilmcenter.com). Subway B, D, F, V to Broadway-Lafayette Street;

N, R, W to Prince Street; 6 to Bleecker Street. **Open** Call for schedule. **Map** p58 C4 **148**

The six-screen Angelika emphasises independent fare, both American and international. The complex is a zoo on weekends, so come extra early or visit the website to buy advance tickets.

West Village & Meatpacking District

The area west of Sixth Avenue to the Hudson River, from 14th Street to Houston Street, still possesses most of the geographical features that moulded the Village's character. Only in this neighbourhood could West 10th Street cross West 4th Street, and Waverly Place cross…Waverly Place. (The West Village's layout follows not the regular grid pattern but the original horse paths that settlers used to navigate it.) Locals and tourists fill the bistros along Seventh Avenue and Hudson Street (aka Eighth Avenue), the neighbourhood's main strips, and patronise the increasingly high-rent shops that line this newly hot end of Bleecker Street. The north-west corner of this area is known as the Meatpacking District; it was primarily a wholesale meat market until the 1990s, when it was also a choice haunt for prostitutes, many of them transsexual.

Eating & drinking

Bar Blanc

NEW *142 W 10th Street, between Greenwich Avenue & Waverly Place (1-212 255 2330). Subway A, C, E, B, D, F, V to W 4th St.* **Open** 5.30-11pm Tue-Sun. **$$**. **French. Map** p58 B3 **149**

A jovial, surprisingly sophisticated West Village spot where random acts of festivity feel completely appropriate. The lively space manages to appear

crowded without jamming folks in, and loud, though not deafening. The food is neither cool nor intimate, but rather rich and classic, full of potent emulsions and hints of Japanese flavor.

Beatrice Inn

285 W 12th Street, between Eighth Avenue & W 4th Street (1-212 243 4626). Subway A, C, E, L to Eighth Avenue. **Open** 10pm-4am daily. **Bar. Map** p58 2B **150**

Paul Sevigny (yes, he's Chloë's brother) has partnered with Employees Only co-owner Matt Bromcheck to open this clandestine hangout (consisting of both bar and restaurant) in a former speakeasy. The retro menu features steaks, Reubens and vodka egg creams.

Buddha Bar

25 Little W 12th Street, between Ninth Avenue & Washington Street (1-212 647 7314). Subway A, C, E, to 14th Street; L to Eighth Avenue. **Open** Call for details. **$$$. Asian. Map** p58 A2 **151**

The irony is obvious to everyone: Buddhism emphasises moderation, whereas Buddha Bar is a temple of excess. Statues line the entrance tunnel. A glass-encased smoking room spares puffers from having to walk outside. As a nightclub party spot, Buddha Bar is successful on many levels: it's visually stimulating, very Vegas, and the lounge scene bustles. Feasting on the Pan-Asian menu, however, requires patience. The entrées come out whenever they are ready.

Commerce

NEW *50 Commerce Street, at Barrow Street (1-212 524 2301). Subway 1 to Christopher Street-Sheridan Square.* **Open** 5.30-11pm daily. **$$$. American. Map** p58 B3 **152**

This homey canteen for the Marc Jacobs-wearing set is pricey but stylish. Desserts outshine the savories: see the silky peanut-butter mousse with celery sorbet and shaved celery salad. Not exactly everyday fare, but appropriately luxurious by the new neighbourhood standards.

NEW YORK BY AREA

Corner Bistro

331 W 4th Street, at Jane Street (1-212 242 9502). Subway A, C, E to 14th Street; L to Eighth Avenue. **Open** 11.30am-4am daily. No credit cards. **Bar**. Map p58 B3 ⑱

There's only one reason to come to this legendary pub: you'll find one of the city's best burgers ($5) – and beer is just $2 a mug (well, that makes two reasons). The patties here are cheap, delish and no-frills, served on a flimsy paper plate. To get your hands on one, you may have to queue for a good hour or so, especially on weekend nights. Fortunately, the game is on the TV and a jukebox covers everything from Calexico to Coltrane.

Employees Only

510 Hudson Street, between Christopher & W 10th Streets (1-212 242 3021). Subway 1 to Christopher Street-Sheridan Square. **Open** 6pm-4am daily. **Bar**. Map p58 B3 ⑲

Walk past the palm reader, sitting under a neon sign in the front window, and you'll find a bar with distinctive 1920s decor and fashionably attired staff – waitresses in custom-designed deco-influenced dresses, bartenders in formal white chef coats. Speciality drinks like the Ginger Smash and the West Side are worth the wait.

Gottino

NEW *52 Greenwich Avenue, between Charles & Perry Streets (1-212 633 2590) Subway 1 to Christopher Street-Sheridan Square.* **Open** 4pm-2am Mon-Fri; 3pm-2am Sat, Sun. **$$**. **Wine bar**. Map p58 B3 ⑮

With it's long marble bar, smattering of tables and menu of choice Italian nibbles to go with the all-Italian wine list, this narrow spot makes a charming enoteca indeed.

Henrietta Hudson

438 Hudson Street, at Morton Street (1-212 924 3347/www.henrietta hudson.com). Subway 1 to Christopher Street-Sheridan Square. **Open** 4pm-4am Mon-Fri; 1pm-4am Sat, Sun. No credit cards. **Bar**. Map p58 B3 ⑯

A long-time, well-loved lesbian bar, Henrietta Hudson used to be more of a grubby pub than glammy lounge. But following a glossy renovation, it's definitely more the latter now. It's still attracting young hottie girls from all over the New York area, especially the nearby 'burbs. Every night's a new DJ party, with Mamacita Sundays and Transcend Tuesdays among the diverse and well-attended line-up.

Merkato 55

NEW *55 Gansevoort Street, between Greenwich & Washington Streets (1-212-255-8555). Subway A, C, E to 14th Street; L to Eighth Avenue.* **Open** 11.30am-midnight Tue, Sun; 11.30am-2am Wed-Sat. **$$**. **Pan-African**. Map p58 B2 ⑰

Ethiopia-born chef Marcus Samuelsson (Aquavit) is behind this eaterie in the Meatpacking District. Samuelsson, whose cookbook *The Soul of a New Cuisine* brought the old continent's cookery into the foreground, offers dishes like lamb rubbed with *berbere* (a spice blend including cardamom, coriander and fenugreek), alongside an infused-rum program.

Plunge

Gansevoort Hotel, 18 Ninth Avenue, at 13th Street (1-212 206 6700). Subway A, C, E to 14th Street; L to Eighth Avenue. **Open** noon-4am daily. **Bar**. Map p58 A2 ⑱

The bar atop the Hotel Gansevoort offers a great aerial view of the Meatpacking District (it trumps Soho House by eight floors), but the experience comes at a premium: drinks are $14 apiece. The stylish executives and banker types who squeeze in here nightly can lounge at tables lining the stone terraces, or venture out to the crowded garden, where low sofas and wooden benches provide additional seating.

P*ONG

150 W 10th Street, at Waverly Place (1-212 929 0898). Subway A, B, C, D, E, F, V to W 4th Street-Washington Square. **Open** 5.30pm-midnight Tue-Sun. **$**. **Dessert**. Map p58 B3 ⑲

Pichet Ong, formerly of Spice Market and 66, has unveiled P*ONG, a dessert-based West Village eaterie where inspiration is taken from the Union Square Greenmarket, which is walking distance from the restaurant. The menu blurs the lines between salty and sweet, and between appetiser, dinner and dessert, even cocktails.

'sNice
45 Eighth Avenue, at 4th Street (1-212 645 0310). Subway A, C, E to 14th Street; L to Eighth Avenue. **Open** 7.30am-10pm Mon-Fri; 8am-10pm Sat, Sun. **$**. No credit cards. **Vegetarian café**. Map p58 B2 ⑯⓪
Someone who hasn't eaten meat for 20 years is bound to know a thing or two about what vegetarians like to eat. Mike Walter opened this sandwich shop as a haven for the herbivorous set and it's a simple, inviting place to spend a few hours reading, snacking or working on a laptop.

Shopping

Chocolate Haven
350 Hudson Street, at King Street (1-212 414 2462). Subway 1 to Houston Street. **Open** 10.30am-7.30pm Mon-Sat; noon-5pm Sun. Map p58 B4 ⑯①
This 8,000sq ft factory serves as the Manhattan hub for the legendary chocolatier Jacques Torres's growing empire. The space features a cocoa-pod shaped café overlooking the candy-making facilities, so visitors can indulge in chocolate treats and watch as cocoa beans are transformed into chocolate bars.

Diane von Furstenberg
874 Washington Street, at W 14th Street (1-646 486 4800/www.dvf.com). Subway A, C, E to 14th Street; L to Eighth Avenue. **Open** 11am-6pm Mon-Wed, Fri; 11am-8pm Thur; 11am-8pm Sat; noon-5pm Sun. Map p58 A2 ⑯②
Indefatigable socialite Diane von Furstenberg's flagship store shows off her classic wrap dress (she sold five million of them in the 1970s) and much more at this enormous space. Whether

'sNice

Diane von Furstenberg p97

you go for ultra-feminine dresses or sporty knits, you'll emerge from the changing room feeling like a princess.

Girlshop

819 Washington Street, between Gansevoort & Little W 12th Streets (1-212 255 4985/www.girlshop.com). Subway L to Eighth Avenue. **Open** 11am-7pm Mon-Wed; 11am-8pm Thur-Sat; noon-7pm Sun. **Map** p58 A2 ⓰

Girlshop.com's bricks-and-mortar sibling offers instant gratification to shoppers who can now try on hot numbers available online by Keanan Dufty, Cigana, or any of the myriad labels.

Jeffrey New York

449 W 14th Street, between Ninth & Tenth Avenues (1-212 206 1272). Subway A, C, E to 14th Street; L to Eighth Avenue. **Open** 10am-8pm Mon-Wed, Fri; 10am-9pm Thur; 10am-7pm Sat; 12.30-6pm Sun. **Map** p58 A2 ⓰

Jeffrey Kalinsky, a former Barneys shoe buyer, was a Meatpacking District pioneer with his namesake store, a branch of the Atlanta original. Designer clothing abounds here – Lang, Versace and YSL among other brands. But the centrepiece is the shoe salon, which features fabulous footwear by Manolo Blahnik, Prada and Robert Clergerie.

Magnolia Bakery

401 Bleecker Street, at 11th Street (1-212 462 2572). Subway 1 to Christopher Street. **Open** noon-11.30pm Mon; 9am-11.30pm Tue-Thur; 9am-12.30am Fri; 10am-12.30am Sat; 10am-11.30pm Sun. **Map** p58 B3 ⓰

Part sweet market, part meet market, Magnolia came to fame thanks to *Sex and the City*. The cupcakes are much vaunted, but you can also pick up a cup of custardy, Southern-style banana pudding (Brits: think trifle) or point yourself out a scoop from the summertime ice-cream cart. Then, sweetmeat in hand, join the other happy eaters clogging nearby apartment stoops.

Tracy Reese

641 Hudson Street, between Gansevoort & Horatio Streets (1-212 807 0505). Subway A, C, E to 14th Street; L to Eighth Avenue. **Open** 11am-7pm Mon-Wed; 11am-8pm Thur-Sat; noon-7pm Sun. **Map** p58 A2 ⓰

With the opening of her eponymous Meatpacking District flagship, apostles of archfeminine designer Tracy Reese now have a house of worship. The 2,200sq ft of curvaceous walls, twinkly chandeliers and fuchsia-cushioned settees pay tribute to all things femme, much like Reese's threads.

Trina Turk

*67 Gansevoort Street, between
Greenwich & Washington Streets
(1-212 206 7383). Subway A, C, E
to 14th Street; L to Eighth Avenue.*
Open 11am-7pm Mon-Sat; noon-6pm
Sun. **Map** p58 A2 **167**

Fans of Left Coast designer Trina
Turk's vintage-inspired pieces are in
luck. In collaboration with chipper
home-design star Jonathan Adler, the
Palm Springs-based couturier has
opened her first NYC outpost, a 2,500sq
ft space that evokes 1970s Big Sur style
with white terracotta tiles, chairs
styled after coral, and a giant wooden
tree sculpture.

Yohji Yamamoto

NEW *1 Gansevoort Street, at W 13th
Street (1-212 966 3615). Subway A,
C, E to 14th St; L to Eighth Avenue.*
Open 11am-7pm Mon-Sat; noon-6pm
Sun. **Map** p58 A2 **168**

Doubling your pleasure, the Japanese
designer's first eponymous New York
City store in 20 years lies just across
the courtyard from the spanking-new
Manhattan shrine to his collaboration
with sports manufacturer Adidas.

Nightlife

APT

*419 W 13th Street, between Ninth
Avenue & Washington Street (1-212
414 4245/www.apt website.com).
Subway A, C, E to 14th Street; L to
Eighth Avenue.* **Open** 7pm-4am daily.
Map p58 A2 **169**

This bi-level boîte is the city's prime
place for hearing cool underground
beats. Everyone from techno deity Carl
Craig to Zulu Nation founder Afrika
Bambaataa has played the platters, in
either the sleek basement bar or the
cosy street-level room. Resident spin-
ners include lounge-kitsch Ursula 1000,
the electrofunky Negroclash crew,
soulful-house guru Neil Aline and
deep-disco master DJ Spun. APT
becomes sardine-packed at weekends
and on guest nights, but at least you're
squeezed in with one of the best-look-
ing crowds in town.

Cielo

*18 Little W 12th Street, between Ninth
Avenue & Washington Street (1-212
645 5700/www.cieloclub.com). Subway
A, C, E to 14th Street; L to Eighth
Avenue.* **Open** 10pm-4am daily.
Map p58 A2 **170**

This is a wonderful little joint – the
urban-ski-lodge decor looks terrific, the
sunken dancefloor is a nice touch, and
the place boasts one of the city's clear-
est sound systems. (Weekends are a
slightly different matter, though, with
all of the tables reserved for those will-
ing to drop a wad for a bottle of hooch.)
The club features top-shelf house from
world-class DJs, with everyone from
Masters at Work's Louie Vega to drum
'n' bass superstar Roni Size having
plied their trade here; every Monday
Cielo is treated to DJ deity François K's
dub-heavy Deep Space session.

Lotus

*409 W 14th Street, between Ninth
Avenue & Washington Street (1-212
243 4420/www.lotusnewyork.com).
Subway A, C, E to 14th Street; L to
Eighth Avenue.* **Open** 10pm-4am daily.
Map p58 A2 **171**

Happily, this venue's trendy patina has
faded, and now Lotus can be fully
appreciated as a well-furnished restaurant, lounge and dance club where DJs
spin a mainstream mix of sounds to an
affluent bridge-and-tunnel crowd.
Friday nights are still the best but getting past the doorman hasn't got sig-
nificantly easier, so make sure you
dress to impress.

Arts & leisure

Film Forum

*209 W Houston Street, between Sixth
Avenue & Varick Street (1-212 727
8110/www.filmforum.com). Subway
1 to Houston Street.* **Map** p58 B4 **172**

Though the seats and sight lines leave
something to be desired, this three-
screen art theatre presents great docu-
mentaries, and new and repertory
films. Viewing them are a cute crowd
of budding NYU auteurs and film
geeks in horn-rimmed glasses.

Empire State Building p122

Midtown

The strip of land roughly between 14th Street and 59th Street, river to river, is the beating heart of the city: high-powered bankers, lawyers and advertising executives pack glass-fronted skyscrapers. The city's crowded middle is where you'll find an endless streams of pedestrians, packed shoulder-to-shoulder, in a hurry to get God knows where. And, here's where Manhattan's best-loved stars reside – the **Empire State Building**, the **Chrysler Building**, **Rockefeller Center**, **Times Square** and **Grand Central Terminal** are all nearby. Culture vultures can take their pick of the **Museum of Modern Art**, **Broadway** and the **Theater District**, **Carnegie Hall** or the **New York Public Library**. If you crave quieter fare, then check out the charming **Union Square Greenmarket** or the quaint tree-lined streets of **Chelsea**, **Tudor City** and **Gramercy Park**.

Chelsea

Chelsea is the center of the city's gay life, but residents of all types inhabit the blocks between 14th and 29th Streets west of Fifth Avenue. There's a generous assortment of bars and restaurants, most of which are clustered along Eighth Avenue. The whole western edge of Chelsea is now the city's hottest art gallery zone.

Sights & museums

Museum of Sex
233 Fifth Avenue, at 27th Street (1-212 689 6337/www.museumofsex.org). Subway N, R, W, 6 to 28th Street.

Midtown 2

Strawberry Fields

Sheep Meadow

Tavern on the Green

Heckscher Playground

Columbus Circle

Museum of Arts & Design

Hearst Tower

Carnegie Hall

CLINTON

De Witt Clinton Park

NYC Official Visitor Info Center

THEATER DISTRICT

Times Square Visitors' Center

TKTS

Times Square

Port Authority Bus Terminal

Madame Tussaud's New York

GARMENT DISTRICT

Intrepid Sea-Air-Space Museum

LINCOLN TUNNEL

Javits Center

Lincoln Center

Time Warner Center

Macy's

See p102

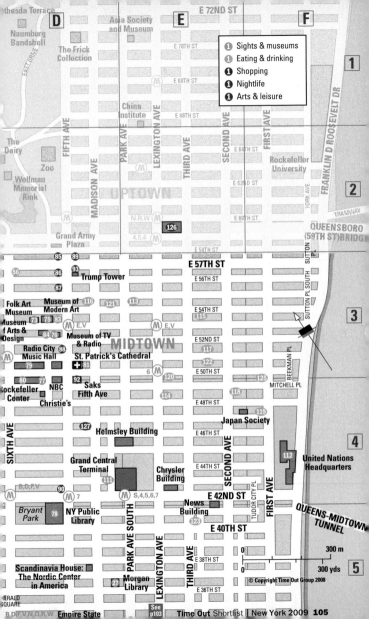

E 72ND ST

D   E   F

1 Sights & museums
1 Eating & drinking
1 Shopping
1 Nightlife
1 Arts & leisure

1

Asia Society and Museum

Naumburg Bandshell

The Frick Collection

E 70TH ST

E 68TH ST

China Institute

E 66TH ST

FIFTH AVE
PARK AVE
MADISON AVE
LEXINGTON AVE
THIRD AVE
SECOND AVE
FIRST AVE

E 64TH ST

Rockefeller University

The Dairy

Zoo

E 62ND ST

YORK AVE

FRANKLIN D ROOSEVELT DR

2

Wollman Memorial Rink

UPTOWN

TRAMWAY

N,R,W

E 60TH ST

4,5,6

126

E 58TH ST

QUEENSBORO (59TH ST) BRIDGE

Grand Army Plaza

E 57TH ST

85 89

3

56 86 93 **Trump Tower**

E 56TH ST

SUTTON PL SOUTH
SUTTON PL

87

Folk Art Museum
Museum of Modern Art 116 121 113

E 54TH ST

115

Museum of Arts & Design
74 75 83

84 76 **Museum of TV & Radio**

E,V

E,V

E 52ND ST

MIDTOWN

117

Radio City Music Hall 88
St. Patrick's Cathedral 81

6

E 50TH ST

122

BEEKMAN PL

120

125

79

80 77

92 Saks Fifth Ave

114

MITCHELL PL

E 48TH ST

Rockefeller Center
NBC
Christie's

118

119

127

Helmsley Building

E 46TH ST

Japan Society

4

SIXTH AVE

B,D,F,V

90

Grand Central Terminal

111

Chrysler Building

E 44TH ST

112

United Nations Headquarters

SECOND AVE

FIRST AVE

M 7

S,4,5,6,7

E 42ND ST

TUDOR CITY PL

QUEENS-MIDTOWN TUNNEL

Bryant Park 78

NY Public Library

News Building 123

PARK AVE SOUTH

E 40TH ST

LEXINGTON AVE
THIRD AVE

E 38TH ST

0   300 m

5

Scandinavia House: The Nordic Center in America

27

Morgan Library

0   300 yds

© Copyright Time Out Group 2008

E 36TH ST

HERALD SQUARE

B,D,F,V,N,Q,R,W **Empire State**

See p103

Chrysler Building p101 ❶

Open 11am-6.30pm Mon-Fri, Sun; 11am-8pm Sat. **Admission** $14.50; $13.50 reductions. No under-18s. **Map** p103 D3 ❶

Despite the subject matter, don't expect too much titillation at this museum. Instead, you'll find presentations of historical documents and items – many of which were too risqué to be made public in their own time – that explore prostitution, burlesque, birth control, obscenity and fetishism. The museum acquired an extensive collection of pornography from a retired Library of Congress curator; the Ralph Whittington Collection features thousands of items, including 8mm films, videos and blow-up dolls.

Eating & drinking

Barracuda
275 W 22nd Street, between Seventh & Eighth Avenues (1-212 645 8613). Subway C, E, 1 to 23rd Street. **Open** 4pm-4am daily. No credit cards. **Bar**. **Map** p102 C4 ❷

While a recent makeover gets high style points, this is still just a friendly little neighbourhood place to have a beer and watch drag shows. A pleasant mix of chilled-out locals converge around the small stand-up tables up front or in the back room, which is full of inviting, get-comfy couches and a pool table. Drinks are always stiff, the crowd is good looking, and DJs keep the place pumping. The divine drag shows take place from Sunday to Thursday.

Blossom
187 Ninth Avenue, between 21st & 22nd Streets (1-212 627 1144). Subway C, E to 23rd Street. **Open** 11.45am-3.30pm, 5-10.30pm Mon-Sat; noon-3.30pm, 5-10pm Sun. **$$**. **Vegetarian/Vegan**. **Map** p102 B4 ❸

Blossom, winner of the 2008 Eating & Drinking award for best vegetarian restaurant, offers a big surprise: all the eggless pastas and mock meats actually taste pretty good. For vegans, it's a candlelit godsend. Try the pan-seared seitan medallions, unusually satisfying mock veal with capers, served with broccoli rabe and buttery-tasting polenta (without butter, of course). The South Asian *lumpia* – a chickpea pancake filled with curried potato – is a spicy starter that would be right at home in a good Indian restaurant.

BRGR
287 Seventh Avenue, between 26th & 27th Streets (1-212 488 7500). Subway 1 to 28th Street. **Open** 11am-11pm daily. **$**. **American**. **Map** p102 C3 ❹

This vowel-challenged restaurant riffs on the fast-food formula while adding gourmet flourishes such as organic beef and inventive shakes. The wood beams and ceiling fans layer honky-tonk texture over a prime do-it-yourself dining experience.

Buddakan
75 Ninth Avenue, between 15th & 16th Streets (1-212 989 6699). Subway A, C, E to 14th Street; L to Eighth Avenue. **Open** 5pm-midnight Mon-Wed, Sun; 5pm-1am Thur-Sat. **$$**. **Chinese**. **Map** p102 B5 ❺

Buddakan

Buddakan relies almost entirely on the shock and awe of 16,000 stunning square feet of space. There's a bustling front bar, dominated by giant square tables, a birdcage filled with taxidermy, Buddha pictures and European tapestries, all leading to a grand staircase that descends into a soaring, golden-hued main room with a 35ft ceiling and a long communal table. The food sounds more fancy, by the descriptions on the menu, than it really is. Noodle and rice dishes offer great bang for the buck.

Cafeteria
119 Seventh Avenue, at 17th Street (1-212 414 1717). Subway 1 to 18th Street. **Open** 24hrs daily. **$$.**
American. Map p102 C4 ⑥
Cocktails and eye candy fuel a non-stop cruising scene in the spare white dining room. Cafeteria feeds the fashionista hordes with nostalgic pleasures, like a gravy-heavy meat loaf mac and cheese, and a juicy charred burger with blue cheese. On a liquid diet? Head straight for the pint-size basement bar.

City Bakery
3 W 18th Street, between Fifth & Sixth Avenues (1-212 366 1414). Subway L, N, Q, R, W, 4, 5, 6 to 14th Street-Union Square. **Open** 7.30am-7pm Mon-Fri; 7.30am-6.30pm Sat; 9am-6pm Sun. **$. American.** Map p103 D4 ⑦
Pastry wiz Maury Rubin has settled nicely into this loft-size space jammed with Chelsea shoppers loading up on unusual salad-bar choices (bean sprouts with smoked tofu). There's also a small selection of soups, pizzas and hot dishes. But to heck with all that: the thick, rich hot chocolate with fat house-made marshmallows is heaven in a cup, and the moist 'melted' chocolate-chip cookies are better than a marked-down pair of Prada pumps.

Craftsteak
85 Tenth Avenue, between 15th & 16th Streets (1-212 400 6699). Subway A, C, E to 14th Street; L to Eighth Avenue. **Open** 5.30-10pm Mon-Thur, Sun; 5.30-11pm Fri, Sat. **$$$.**
Steakhouse. Map p102 B5 ⑧

NEW YORK BY AREA

Tom Colicchio's 10,000sq ft steakhouse is about as open and bright as a beef emporium can be: 16ft high ceilings and giant windows lend it a luxurious airiness. The meat line-up reads like a wine list – diners can select by cattle breed, type of feed, cut and time spent ageing. The Hawaiian grass-fed Angus steak had a clean, herbaceous quality.

Eagle

554 W 28th Street, between Tenth & Eleventh Avenues (1-646 473 1866/ www.eaglenyc.com). Subway C, E to 23rd Street. **Open** 10pm-4am Mon-Sat; 5pm-4am Sun. No credit cards. **Bar. Map** p102 A3 ❾

This classic Levi's-and-leather bar boasts a killer roof deck. Look out for beer blasts, leather soirées and simple nights of pool playing and cruising.

Naka Naka

458 W 17th Street, between Ninth & Tenth Avenues (1-212 929 8544). Subway A, C, E to 14th Street; L to Eighth Avenue. **Open** 6pm-midnight Tue-Sat. **$$. Japanese. Map** p102 ❿

Tasty traditional dishes, starting with spicy lotus root, delicate mixed vegetable tempura and deliciously dense shrimp dumplings. The sushi is neither phenomenal nor disappointing, but considering how difficult it is to find peace and quiet over dinner in this part of town, we can't complain.

Red Cat

227 Tenth Avenue, between 23rd & 24th Streets (1-212 242 1122). Subway C, E to 23rd Street. **Open** 5.30-11pm Mon-Thur; 5.30pm-midnight Fri, Sat; 5-10pm Sun. **$$. American. Map** p102 B4 ⓫

Art-world luminaries and London Terrace residents descend on this comfortable, reliable and handsome eatery, which is done out with red walls and crisp white tablecloths. Do not attempt to eat lightly here. The Red Cat specialises in everything that's hearty: gargantuan pork chops, parmesan-covered french fries, extra-juicy shell steak, and big-time sweets like banana splits.

Tia Pol

205 Tenth Avenue, between 22nd & 23rd Streets (1-212 675 8805). Subway C, E to 23rd Street. **Open** noon-3pm, 5pm-midnight Mon-Thur; noon-3pm, 5pm-1am Fri, Sat; 11am-3pm, 6pm-midnight Sun. **$. Spanish. Map** p102 B4 ⓬

This tiny tapas restaurant keeps things simple with traditional tapas such as sautéed cockles and razor clams. Other dishes showcase some rather unlikely combinations, tomato-covered bread with lima-bean purée, and chorizo and chocolate on bread rounds among them. The all-Spanish wine list is well-priced, with selections that pair well with the eaterie's spicy food.

Shopping

Billy's Bakery

184 Ninth Avenue, between 21st & 22nd Streets (1-212 647 9956/www. billysbakerynyc.com). Subway C, E to 23rd Street. **Open** 9am-11pm Mon-Thur, Sun; 9am-12.30am Fri, Sat. **Map** p102 B4 ⓭

Amid super-sweet retro delights such as coconut cream pie, Hello Dollies and Famous Refrigerator Cake, you'll find friendly service in a setting that will remind you of Grandma's kitchen.

Garage

112 W 25th Street, between Sixth & Seventh Avenues (1-212 647 0707). Subway F, V to 23rd Street. **Open** sunrise-sunset Sat, Sun. No credit cards. **Map** p102 C3 ⓮

Designers (and the occasional dolled-down celebrity) hunt regularly – and early – at this flea market inside an emptied parking garage. This spot specialises in old prints, vintage clothing, silver and linens; there's lots of household paraphernalia too.

Jazz Record Center

Room 804, 236 W 26th Street, between Seventh & Eighth Avenues (1-212 675 4480/www.jazzrecord center.com). Subway C, E to 23rd Street; 1 to 28th Street. **Open** 10am-6pm Mon-Sat. **Map** p102 C3 ⓯

Eagle

The city's best jazz store stocks current and out-of-print records, books, videos and other jazz-related merchandise. Worldwide shipping is available.

Kidding Around
60 W 15th Street, between Fifth & Sixth Avenues (1-212 645 6337). Subway F, V to 14th Street; L to Sixth Avenue. **Open** 10am-7pm Mon-Sat; 11am-6pm Sun. **Map** p102 C5 ⑯
Loyal customers frequent this quaint shop for clothing and learning toys for the brainy baby. A play area will keep your little one occupied while you shop.

Natrona
145 W 20th Street, between Fifth & Sixth Avenues (1-212 404 7649/ www.natrona.com). Subway F, V, 1 to 23rd Street. **Open** 11am-7pm Mon-Sat; noon-6pm Sun. **Map** p102 C4 ⑰
This furniture store, specialising in contemporary and mid-20th century pieces, caters to all household needs.

Nightlife

Highline Ballroom
431 W 16th Street, between 9th & 10th Avenues (1-212 414 5994/ www.highlineballroom.com). Subway A, C, E to 14th Street-Eighth Avenue. **Open** Call for show times. **Map** p102 B5 ⑱

Steven Bensusan, owner of the Highline Ballroom in addition to the Blue Note Jazz Club and BB King Blues Club, kicked off this club's debut with a sold out show featuring Lou Reed. Look out for great things here.

Metropolitan Room
34 W 22nd Street, between Fifth & Sixth Avenues (1-212 206 0440/ www.metropolitanroom.com). Subway F, R, V, W to 23rd Street. **Open** Call for show times. **Map** p103 D4 ⑲
The Metropolitan Room's atmospheric space, which was formerly occupied by the Gotham Comedy Club, is quickly establishing itself as Manhattan's mid-level cabaret venue of choice. The very solid line-up of nightclub and musical theatre performers includes jazz legend Annie Ross and the medley-friendly lounge duo Gashole.

Rush
NEW *579 Sixth Avenue at 16th street (1-212 243 6100). Subway F, V to 14th Street.* **Open** 10pm-4am daily. **Map** p102 C5 ⑳
Young studs pack the place weekly for cheap drinks and three floors of 18-and-over fun and games. Catch go-go boys, rotating drag hostesses and music from DJ Steve Sidewalk. Locals wipe away their work fatigue with a

Metropolitan Room p109

stiff one at this midweek get together, where there'll be drink specials, music by DJ Dimitri and many hunks.

Studio Mezmor

530 W 28th Street, between Tenth & Eleventh Avenues (1-212 629 9000/ www.crobar.com). Subway C, E to 23rd Street. **Open** 5pm-4am Thur; 10pm-7am Fri, Sat. **Map** p102 A3 ❷❶

This splendiferous club, formerly called Crobar, is as close to a full-on superclub as NYC has to offer: it can squeeze 2,750 revellers into its main room and two smaller party dens, and it has a great sound system and a dazzling repertoire of disco lights. Though the beats tend to lean towards the lowest-common-denominator end of the dance-music spectrum, this is a must-see on the city's after-dark circuit.

Arts & leisure

Chelsea Piers

Piers 59-62, W 17th to 23rd Streets, at Eleventh Avenue (1-212 336 6666/ www.chelseapiers.com). Subway C, E to 23rd Street. **Map** p102 A4 ❷❷

This massive sports complex, which occupies a six-block stretch of riverfront real estate, offers just about every popular recreational activity in a bright, clean, well-maintained facility. Would-be Tigers can practise their swings at the Golf Club; bowlers can set up their pins at the AMF Lanes. Or hit the Roller Rink and Skate Park. At the Sports Center gym, classes cover everything from triathlon training to hip hop dance. Hours and fees vary; call or see the website for information.

Joyce Theater

175 Eighth Avenue, at 19th Street (1-212 242 0800/www.joyce.org). Subway A, C, E to 14th Street; 1 to 18th Street; L to Eighth Avenue. **Map** p102 B4 ❷❸

This intimate space, formerly a cinema, is one of the finest theatres in town. Of the 472 seats at the Joyce, there's not a single bad one. Companies and choreographers who present work here, including the Ballet Hispanico, David Parsons and Doug Varone, tend to be more traditional than experimental.

Kitchen

512 W 19th Street, between Tenth & Eleventh Avenues (1-212 255 5793/ www.thekitchen.org). Subway A, C, E to 14th Street; L to Eighth Avenue. **Map** p102 B4 ❷❹

Although the Kitchen is best known as an avant-garde theatre space, it also features experimental dance by inventive, often provocative artists.

Laughing Lotus Yoga Center

3rd Floor, 59 W 19th Street, between Fifth & Sixth Avenues (1-212 414 2903/www.laughinglotus.com). Subway F, V, N, R, W to 23rd Street. **Open** Call or see website for schedule. **Map** p102 C4 ㉕
Roomy yogic community centre offering weekly workshops and classes.

Flatiron District & Union Square

The Flatiron District, which extends from 14th to 29th Streets between Fifth and Park Avenues, gives Downtown a run for its money in terms of cachet and cool. This chic enclave is full of shops as stylish as those below 14th Street, yet often less expensive.

You need a key to enter tranquil **Gramercy Park**, at the bottom of Lexington Avenue (between 20th & 21st Streets). The gated green square is the preserve of those lucky residents of the beautiful townhouses and apartments that ring the park. Anyone, however, can enjoy the charms of the area.

Murray Hill spans 30th to 40th Streets between Third and Fifth Avenues. Townhouses of the rich and powerful were once clustered around Madison and Park Avenues. Sniffen Court (150-158 E 36th Street, between Lexington & Third Avenues) is an unspoiled row of 1864 carriage houses.

Sights & museums

Flatiron Building

175 Fifth Avenue, between 22nd & 23rd Streets (no phone). Subway N, R, W, 6 to 23rd Street. **Map** p103 D4 ㉖

The 22-storey edifice is clad in white terracotta: its light colour was revealed again by cleaning and restoration in the early 1990s. The surrounding neighbourhood was christened in honour of the structure, which was the world's first steel-frame skyscraper.

Morgan Library

E 36th Street, between Madison & Park Avenues (1-212 685 0008/www. morganlibrary.org). Subway 6 to 34th Street. **Open** 10.30am-5pm Tue-Thur; 10.30am-9pm Fri; 10am-6pm Sat; 11am-6pm Sun. **Admission** $12, $8 reductions. **Map** p103 D2/p105 D5 ㉗
After undergoing a dramatic expansion, the library reopened its doors in spring 2006. Serving as both museum and research library, the impressive, light-filled space (glass walls in the main pavilion allow you to see more of the 1906 Charles McKim building and a naturally-lit reading room tops the Madison Avenue structure) has an awe-inspiring collection of rare books, illuminated manuscripts, drawings and prints. Among the treats are etchings and drawings by Rembrandt and da Vinci, Mary Shelley's own copy of Frankenstein and one of the first copies of the Declaration of Independence.

Union Square

Subway L, N, Q, R, W, 4, 5, 6 to Union Square. **Map** p103 D5 ㉘
Union Square (from 14th to 17th Streets, between Union Square East & Union Square West) is the home of the Union Square Greenmarket (p116), which is fast becoming a New York City institution.

Eating & drinking

Craftbar

900 Broadway, at 20th Street (1-212 461 4300). Subway N, R, W, 6 to 23rd Street. **Open** noon-11pm Mon-Thur, Sun; noon-midnight Fri, Sat. **$$**.
American creative. **Map** p103 D4 ㉙
Tom Colicchio's flashy spin-off of his upscale restaurant Craft is in a bigger and brighter space around the corner from the original Craftbar. The dining

room is still positively raucous, and the busy bar is jammed with chatty, wine-swigging groups. Appetisers rate particularly highly, but don't forget to leave some room: desserts like chocolate pot de crème and steamed lemon pudding are sheer heaven.

Eleven Madison Park
11 Madison Avenue, at 24th Street (1-212 889 0905). Subway R, W, 6 to 23rd Street. **Open** 11.30am-2pm, 5.30-11pm Mon-Thur; 11.30am-2pm, 5.30-11pm Fri, Sat; 5.30-10pm Sun. **$$$. American creative.** Map p103 D4 ⑳

A five-course tasting menu here is a bargain at $65. The list might include melt-away sautéed sweetbreads, skate with a grenobloise twist, or flavour-packed côte de boeuf alongside fat, golden onion rings. The dining room, with its park views, soaring ceilings and attentive service, is sufficiently serious for business deals, yet elegant enough for dates.

Encore
757 Sixth Avenue, between 25th & 26th Streets (1-212 414 4696). Subway 1 to 28th Street. **Open** 9pm-4am Tue-Sat. **Bar.** Map p102 C3 ㉛

Karaoke junkies now have an upscale alternative to all those traditional seedy Japanese joints. This space boasts oversize portraits of Axl Rose and Jim Morrison, flat-screen televisions looping 1980s videos and all kinds of speciality shots.

L'Express
249 Park Avenue South, at 20th Street (1-212 254 5858). Subway 6 to 23rd Street. **Open** 24hrs daily. **$. French.** Map p103 D4 ㉜

It's 3am and, if you want to dodge that hangover, you'd better eat something. So why not consider this bustling bistro, which stays open 24 hours a day, seven days a week? The place is as lively in the wee hours as at 8pm and bistro standards like steak au poivre, seared tuna steak, along with monkfish and chorizo brochettes, are satisfying at any hour.

Flatiron Building p111

Flatiron Lounge
37 W 19th Street, between Fifth & Sixth Avenues (1-212 727 7741). Subway F, V, R, W to 23rd Street. **Open** 5pm-2am Mon-Wed, Sun; 5pm-4am Thur-Sat. **Bar.** Map p103 D4 ㉝

To get to the 30ft mahogany bar, built in 1927, follow the arched hallway, warmed by the soft glow of candles. Once inside, you'll find an art deco space filled with red leather booths, round wooden tables, flying-saucer-shaped lamps and an imaginative cocktail menu.

119
119 E 15th Street, between Union Square East & Irving Place (1-212 777 6158). Subway L, N, Q, R, W, 4, 5, 6 to 14th Street-Union Square. **Open** 4pm-4am daily. No credit cards. **Bar.** Map p103 D5 ㉞

This rock 'n' roll bar, one of the few above 14th Street, has a lively after-show scene: bartenders have spotted Trent Reznor and some Strokes after their Irving Plaza performances. DJs, serious pool, and a juke that plays Jane's Addiction and early Nirvana – what else do you need?

Speak

28 E 23rd Street, between Madison Avenue & Park Avenue South (1-212 637 0100). Subway 6 to 23rd Street. **Open** 4pm-4am Tue, Wed; 3pm-4am Thur, Fri; 6pm-2am Sat. **Bar.** **Map** p103 D4 ㉟

This lounge takes its cues from the heyday of Hollywood glamour: vintage wallpaper, oversized oval mirrors, French sconces, curved crimson banquettes and crystal chandeliers. Drink enough Blood Martinis (fresh-squeezed beet and orange juices) and Between the Sheets (passion fruit and lime mixed with rum and cognac), and you'll have a swingin' time indeed.

Tavalon Tea Bar

22 E 14th Street, between Fifth Avenue & University Place (1-212 807 7027/www.tavalon.com). Subway L, N, Q, R, W, 4, 5, 6 to 14th Street-Union Square. **Open** 8am-10pm Mon-Fri; 8am-11pm Sat, Sun. **$.** **Café.** **Map** p103 D5 ㊱

With DJs and an Indian drummer, this Union Square tea salon aims to appeal to younger tea drinkers. You can sample house-blended loose leaf varieties or make it a meal by adding pastries, salads or sandwiches.

Underground

613 Second Avenue, between 33rd & 34th Streets (1-212 683 3000). Subway 6 to 33rd Street. **Open** 4pm-4am daily. **Bar.** **Map** p103 E2 ㊲

About a third of this rather sprawling venue feels like a neighbourhood pub (lined with exposed brick), another section is a swanky, libraryesque lounge dotted with leather couches and low wooden tables, and the backyard functions as a sports bar.

Shopping

ABC Carpet & Home

888 Broadway, at 19th Street (1-212 473 3000/www.abchome.com). Subway L, N, Q, R, W, 4, 5, 6 to 14th Street-

Union Square. **Open** 10am-8pm Mon-Thur; 10am-6.30pm Fri, Sat; noon-6pm Sun. **Map** p103 D4 ㊳

At this shopping landmark, the selection of accessories, linens, rugs, and reproduction and antique furniture (Western and Asian) is unbelievable; so are the mostly steep prices. For bargains, head to ABC's warehouse outlet in the Bronx.

Barnes & Noble Union Square

33 E 17th Street, between Park Avenue S & Broadway (1-212 253 0810/www.barnesandnoble.com). Subway L, N, Q, R, W, 4, 5, 6 to 14th Street-Union Square. **Open** 10am-10pm daily. **Map** p103 D4 ㊴

Miles and miles of books await at this emporium of all things literary. Check out the awesome views of Union Square while you're browsing.

Union Square Greenmarket

From 16th to 17th Streets, between Union Square East & Union Square West (1-212 788 7476). Subway L, N, Q, R, W, 4, 5, 6 to 14th Street-Union Square. **Open** 8am-6pm Mon, Wed, Fri, Sat. **Map** p103 D4 ㊵

Shop with top chefs for all manner of regionally grown culinary pleasures, at this established farmers' market.

Nightlife

Gramercy Theatre

127 E 23rd Street, between Park & Lexington (1-212 777 6800). Subway R, W, 6 to 23rd Street. **Open** Call for show times. **Map** p103 D4 ㊶

This 1930s movie theatre recently got an overhaul by Live Nation (it operates a few other heavy-hitting music venues in town). The 600-seat space features a wide range of acts.

Paddy Reilly's Music Bar

519 Second Avenue, at 29th Street (1-212 686 1210). Subway 6 to 28th Street. **Open** 11am-4am Mon-Sat; 11am-midnight Sun. **Shows** 9.30pm Mon-Fri; 10pm, 11pm Fri, Sat; 4pm Sun. **Map** p103 E3 ㊷

Patrons flock to this Gramercy institution for the silky Guinness (the house's only draught beer) but they stay on until the wee small hours for the lively Irish folk and rock acts that bring the room to life. Popular pub-rockers the Prodigals are regulars on Fridays, while the rest of the weekend features Irish-rock and traditional jam sessions.

Rodeo Bar & Grill

375 Third Avenue, at 27th Street (1-212 683 6500). Subway 6 to 28th Street. **Open** 4pm-4am daily. **Map** p103 E3 🌮

The unpretentious crowd and roadhouse atmosphere – not to mention the lack of a cover charge – make the Rodeo the city's best roots club, with a steady stream of rockabilly, country and related sounds. Rockabilly filly Rosie Flores is a regular, and bluegrass scion Chris Scruggs recently visited, making the trek from Nashville.

Herald Square & Garment District

The epicentre of America's multibillion-dollar clothing industry is New York's Garment District (roughly from 34th to 40th Streets, between Broadway and Eighth Avenue), where platoons of designers – and thousands of workers – create the clothes we'll be wearing next season.

Beginning on 34th Street at Broadway and stretching all the way to Seventh Avenue, **Macy's** is still the biggest – and busiest – department store in the world. Across the street at the junction of Broadway and Sixth Avenue is **Herald Square**, which is named after what is now a long-gone newspaper but still surrounded by a veritable retail wonderland. To the east, the many restaurants and shops of **Koreatown** line 32nd Street, between Broadway and Madison Avenue.

Eating & drinking

Maru

11 W 32nd Street, between Broadway & Fifth Avenue (1-212 273 3413). Subway A, C, E to 34th Street-Penn Station. **Open** 6pm-2am Mon-Wed, Sun; 6pm-3am Thur; 6pm-4am Fri, Sat. **Bar**. **Map** p103 D3 🌮

This chic lounge in Koreatown is almost impossible to find – which somehow adds to the allure. There's a discreet sign outside and you enter via a freight elevator that leads to the bar's third-floor location. When the doors swing open, you're greeted with a spectacular bi-level space, where white walls and soft lighting complement soaring ceilings and modern, wraparound banquettes. The bartenders serve upscale drinks like lychee martinis and vodka mojitos.

Stitch

247 W 37th Street, between Seventh & Eighth Avenues (1-212 852 4826). Subway A, C, E to 34th Street-Penn Station. **Open** 11am-1am Mon-Fri; 2pm-4am Sat. **Bar**. **Map** p102 C2/p104 C5 🌮

The owner of Stitch realised that the Garment District lacked a good postwork drink spot, so he converted a former apparel showroom into a spacious bar and lounge, and made one. The fashion theme is far from subliminal, however: antique sewing machines sit above the bar, and on the cocktail menu you'll find evocatively named drinks such as the Silk Scarf, Cashmere and, our favourite, the Stiletto.

Shopping

Macy's

151 W 34th Street, between Broadway & Seventh Avenue (1-212 695 4400/www.macys.com). Subway B, D, F, N, Q, R, V, W to 34th Street-Herald Square; 1, 2, 3 to 34th Street-Penn Station. **Open** 10am-9pm Mon-Sat; 11am-8pm Sun. **Map** p102 C2/p104 C5 🌮

Behold the real miracle on 34th Street. Macy's has everything you want let

Comedy central

Rob Lathan

For years, we've been predicting that New York is headed towards another comedy boom. It's arrived. It may not look like the chuckle-hut explosion of the get-up stand-up 1980s, but make no mistake: we are currently living in a golden age of comedy.

Famous clubs **Carolines on Broadway** (1626 Broadway, between 49th & 50th Streets, 1-212 757 4100) and **Gotham Comedy Club** (34 W 22nd Street, between Fifth & Sixth Avenues, 1-212 367 9000) continue to attract A-list funny people and pack houses. They've even embraced a new sibling, **Comix** (353 W 14th Street, between Eighth & Ninth Avenues, 1-212 524 2500), the city's third 300-plus-seat theatre devoted to

comedy, which has pulled in Janeane Garofalo, Emo Phillips and *Curb Your Enthusiasm*'s JB Smoove.

Those seeking a more unpredictable style of laugh-making will find it in the city's do-it-yourself rooms; each showcase is typically run by the same host but features a variety of acts, and happens weekly, bi-weekly or monthly in downtown music venues and the back rooms of bars. 'Sweet', which Seth Herzog cohosts with his mum, takes place every Tuesday at the **Slipper Room** (p85), while 'Moonwork' delivers the thinking person's comics on Saturdays at the **Greenwich Village Center Theater** (219 Sullivan Street, between Bleecker & W 3rd Streets, no phone).

In the improv and sketch world, theatres that once struggled to fill their seats now regularly turn audience members away at the door. Head to the **Upright Citizens Brigade Theatre** (307 W 26th Street, between Eighth & Ninth Avenues, 1-212 366 9176) to see Rob Lathan and top improv teams Reuben Williams and the Stepfathers. For sidesplitting sketches, **Peoples Improv Theater** (154 W 29th Street, between Sixth & Seventh Avenues, 2nd floor, 1-212 563 7488) is a good bet.

alone need: designer labels and lower-priced knock-offs, a pet supply shop, a restaurant housed in the Cellar (the housewares section) and even a Metropolitan Museum of Art gift shop. Regular in-store events are also held, like the Jantzen swimwear event with supermodel Carolyn Murphy.

Arts & leisure

Madison Square Garden

Seventh Avenue, between 31st & 33rd Streets (1-212 465 6741/www.thegarden.com). Subway A, C, E, 1, 2, 3 to 34th Street-Penn Station. **Map** p102 C3 ❼

Madison Square Garden, the huge sports and concert complex (known locally as simple 'the Garden'), occupies the site of the old Pennsylvania Station, a McKim, Mead & White Beaux Arts architectural masterpiece that was demolished in the 1960s – an act so soulless, it spurred the creation of the Landmarks Preservation Commission. The railroad terminal, now known as Penn Station, lies beneath the Garden and serves approximately 600,000 people every day. Fortunately, the aesthetic tide has turned. The city has approved a $788 million restoration and development project to move Penn Station across the street, into the General Post Office. The arena is currently also the home of the NBA's New York Knicks.

Broadway & Times Square

Times Square is really just the elongated intersection of Broadway and Seventh Avenue, but it's also the heart of the Theater District. More than 40 stages showcasing extravagant dramatic productions are situated on the streets that cross Broadway. The streets west of Eighth Avenue are filled with eateries catering to theatregoers, especially along Restaurant Row (46th Street, between Eighth &

Ninth Avenues). This stretch is also popular after the theatres let out, when the street's bars host stand-up comedy and campy drag cabaret.

Sights & museums

ABC Television Studios

7 Times Square (1500 Broadway), at 44th Street. Subway A, C, E to 42nd Street-Port Authority; N, Q, R, W, 42nd Street S, 1, 2, 3, 7 to 42nd Street-Times Square. **Map** p102 C1/p104 C4 ❽

The television network's studios draw dozens of early morning risers hoping to catch a glimpse of the *Good Morning America* crew.

Madame Tussaud's New York

234 W 42nd Street, between Seventh & Eighth Avenues (1-800 246 8872/www.nycwax.com). Subway A, C, E to 42nd Street-Port Authority; N, Q, R, W, 42nd Street S, 1, 2, 3, 7 to 42nd Street-Times Square. **Open** 10am-8pm daily. **Map** p102 C1/p104 C4 ❾

If you're a fan of frozen, life-sized celebs, every few months they roll out a new posse of waxed victims.

Times Square Visitors' Center

1560 Broadway, between 46th & 47th Streets, entrance on Seventh Avenue (1-212 869 1890/www.timessquarebid.org). Subway N, R, W to 49th Street; 1 to 50th Street. **Open** 8am-8pm daily. **Map** p102 C1/p104 C4 ❺⓿

TKTS

Duffy Square, 47th Street, at Broadway (1-212 221 0013/www.tdf.org). Subway N, Q, R, W, 42nd Street S, 1, 2, 3, 7 to 42nd Street-Times Square. **Open** 3-8pm Mon-Sat; 11am-7pm Sun. Matinée tickets 10am-2pm Wed, Sat; 11am-2pm Sun. No credit cards. **Map** p102 C1/p104 C4 ❺❶

TKTS has become a New York tradition. Broadway and Off Broadway tickets are sold at discounts of 25%, 35% and 50% for same-day performances; tickets to other highbrow events are also offered. The queue can be long, but tends to move quickly, and it's often worth the wait.

Eating & drinking

Blue Fin

W Times Square Hotel, 1567 Broadway, at 47th Street (1-212 918 1400). Subway N, R, W to 49th Street. **Open** 7-11am, 11.30am-4pm, 5pm-midnight Sun, Mon; 7-11am, 11.30am-4pm, 5pm-12.30am Tue-Thur; 7-11am, 11.30am-4pm, 5pm-1am Fri, Sat. **$$$**. **Seafood**. **Map** p102 C1/p104 C4 ®

This noisy, singles-friendly, packed-to-the-gills bar has probably been the scene of more than a few hookups. Chef Paul Sale cranks out crowd-pleasers such as sesame-crusted bigeye tuna with ginger-soy vinaigrette and pan-seared halibut with green and white asparagus in a vanilla-flavoured brown butter.

Carnegie Club

156 W 56th Street, between Sixth & Seventh Avenues (1-212 957 9676). Subway F, N, Q, R, W to 57th Street. **Open** 4.30pm-2am Mon-Sat; 4.30pm-1am Sun. Fri 2-drink minimum; Sat $30 plus 2-drink minimum. **Bar**. **Map** p104 C3 ®

The low-lit Carnegie Club is classy and quiet. A bartender in pinstripes is on hand to expertly mix classic cocktails, such as the house Carnegie Cocktail (dark rum, Grand Marnier, passion fruit juice and champagne). On Saturdays, a singer does Sinatra covers with an 11-piece orchestra.

Dave & Busters

3rd Floor, 234 W 42nd Street, between Seventh & Eighth Avenues (1-646 495 2015). Subway N, Q, R, S, W, 1, 2, 3 to 42nd Street-Times Square. **Open** 11am-12am Mon-Thur, Sun; 11am-2am Fri, Sat. **$**. **American**. **Map** p102 C1/p104 C4 ®

The latest addition to Times Square's restaurant collection of giant theme-park eateries is this behemoth food-and-entertainment venue, which offers virtual-reality simulators, video games galore and Skee-Ball – plus Philly cheese steaks, salads and burgers.

Heartland Brewery & Chop House

127 W 43rd Street, between Sixth Avenue & Broadway (1-646 366 0235). Subway 42nd Street S, 1, 2, 3, 7 to 42nd Street-Times Square. **Open** 11.30am-midnight Mon-Sat; noon-9pm Sun. **Bar**. **Map** p102 C1/p104 C4 ®

TKTS

Bernstein lives

Carnegie Hall

When the New York Philharmonic presented its groundbreaking concert in Pyongyang, North Korea, in February 2007, the performance included the overture to Leonard Bernstein's *Candide,* played without a conductor. That gesture, a continuing tribute to the legendary composer, pianist, music director and pedagogue who led the orchestra for 11 years, demonstrates the extent to which Bernstein, who died in 1990, continues to hold a dear place in the hearts of New York City's music lovers. In September, to mark what would have been Bernstein's 90th birthday, the Philharmonic joins Carnegie Hall in launching an extensive celebration in his memory – 'Bernstein: The Best of All Possible Worlds.'

Clive Gillinson, artistic and executive director of Carnegie Hall, can attest to Bernstein's powerful attraction firsthand. As a cellist in the London Symphony Orchestra, he played under Bernstein's leadership many times, and when Gillinson became the orchestra's managing director

in 1984, Bernstein accepted his invitation to become the orchestra's president. 'Bernstein was the most extraordinary artist that I've ever worked with in my entire life,' Gillinson says. 'His life was an eternal exploration, and he never stopped seeking answers. And he would never repeat himself – nothing was ever routine.'

Of special interest is a concert entirely devoted to Bernstein's own music, led by the Phil's young music director designate Alan Gilbert, at Carnegie Hall on 14 November – the exact 65th anniversary of Bernstein's first appearance with the New York Philharmonic.

The Bernstein extravaganza will celebrate practically every aspect of his career – including pop songs, jazz and musical theater – in 30 events from 24 September to 13 December. And 'The Bernstein Mass Project' will enlist hundreds of local public school students to celebrate Bernstein in his most spiritually exuberant, personal creation.
■ www.carnegiehall.org/bernstein

All of the microbrews served here come from a Fort Greene brewery, so there's a little touch of Brooklyn at the four Manhattan locations. Each franchise offers the Classic Voyage, a quintet of five-ounce brews including the award-winning Farmer Jon's Oatmeal Stout, a dark-roasted malt.

Rue 57

60 W 57th Street, at Sixth Avenue (1-212 307 5656). Subway F to 57th Street. **Open** 7.30am-midnight Mon; 7.30pm-1am Tue-Fri; 9pm-1am Sat; 9pm-midnight Sun. **$$. French.** **Map** p105 D3 56

Serving steak tartare alongside tuna tataki sounds like the making of a culinary identity crisis. But Rue 57's spacious flower-decked dining room has a pleasing Parisian look, and the red leather banquettes are often full – for the most part with Midtown expensers and tourists.

Spotlight Live

1604 Broadway, between 48th & 49th Streets (1-212 262 1111). Subway 1 to 50th Street. **Open** 11am-2am daily. **$$. American.** **Map** p104 C4 57

American Idol meets American grub at this four-storey Times Square (crossed with a little Las Vegas) karaoke hotspot. There are two stages for amateur performers, but a pro, *Iron Chef* (a cult TV show) champ Kerry Simon, runs the kitchen.

Shopping

Toys 'R' Us Times Square

1514 Broadway, between 44th & 45th Streets (1-800 869 7787). Subway N, Q, R, W, 42nd Street S, 1, 2, 3, 7 to 42nd Street-Times Square. **Open** 9am-10pm Mon-Sat; 11am-6pm Sun. **Map** p102 C1/p104 C4 58

The chain's flagship location is the world's largest toy store – big enough to accommodate a 60ft-high Ferris wheel inside and an animatronic tyrannosaur to greet you at the door. Brands rule here: there's a two-storey Barbie doll's house and a café with its very own sweetshop.

Nightlife

BB King Blues Club & Grill

237 W 42nd Street, between Seventh & Eighth Avenues (1-212 997 4144/ www.bbkingblues.com). Subway A, C, E to 42nd Street-Port Authority; N, Q, R, W, 42nd Street S, 1, 2, 3, 7 to 42nd Street-Times Square. **Open** 11am-midnight daily. **Map** p102 C1/ p104 C4 59

The BB King Blues Club plays host to perhaps the widest variety of music in town: cover bands and soul tributes fill the gaps between big names like Aretha Franklin, the Neville Brothers, Rodney Crowell and Judy Collins. Lately, the club has also proved a viable space for extreme metal bands (Napalm Death, Obituary, Hate Eternal) and neosoul and hip hop acts (Angie Stone, Method Man, Ghostface, and assorted other Wu-Tangers). The best seats are at the dinner tables up front, but menu prices are steep. The Harlem Gospel Choir buffet brunch, on Sundays, raises the roof.

Birdland

315 W 44th Street, between Eighth & Ninth Avenues (1-212 581 3080/ www.birdlandjazz.com). Subway A, C, E to 42nd Street-Port Authority. **Open** 5pm-1am daily. **Map** p102 B1/p104 C4 60

The name means jazz but, perhaps in deference to its Theater District digs, Birdland is also a prime destination for cabaret. The jazz names are unimpeachable (Kurt Elling, Jim Hall, Paquito D'Rivera), the cabaret stars glowing (Christine Andreas, Christine Ebersole). It's fair to say that residencies are among the better ones in town: the Chico O'Farrill Afro-Cuban Jazz Orchestra play on Sundays, with David Ostwald's Louis Armstrong Centennial Band on Tuesdays; on Monday there's cabaret's waggish Jim Caruso and his Cast Party.

Don't Tell Mama

343 W 46th Street, between Eighth & Ninth Avenues (1-212 757 0788/ www.donttellmama.com). Subway

A, C, E to 42nd Street-Port Authority.
Open 9pm-4am daily. **Map** p102
B1/p104 C4 ❻❶

Showbiz pros and piano-bar buffs love this dank but homey Theater District stalwart, where acts range from the strictly amateur to potential stars of tomorrow. The nightly line-up may include pop, jazz or Broadway singers, as well as female impersonators, magicians, comedians or musical revues.

Nokia Theatre Times Square

1515 Broadway, at 44th Street (1-212 930 1950). Subway N, Q, R, W to 42nd Street; S, 1, 2, 3, 7, to 42nd Street-Times Square. **Open** Call for show times. **Map** p102 C1/p104 C4 ❻❷

The Nokia Theatre Times Square may well be the club-going experience NYC music fans have always deserved. And that assessment has relatively little to do with the crowd-pleasing bookings or extensive wiring job in the underground space. The 85ft marquee, plentiful plasma-TV screens, and phone-charging kiosks are all impressive features, for sure. But it's the music room itself that's most striking.

Swing 46

349 W 46th Street, between Eighth & Ninth Avenues (1-212 262 9554/ www.swing46.com). Subway A, C, E to 42nd Street-Port Authority. **Open** 5pm-midnight Mon-Thur; 5pm-1am Fri, Sat; 5-11pm Sun. **Map** p102 B1/p104 C4 ❻❸

Swing isn't just a trend at this supper club – whether peppy or sappy, these cats mean it. Bands (with names like the Flying Neutrinos and the Flipped Fedoras) that jump, jive and wail await you, so be sure to wear your dancin' shoes. Dance lessons are available too.

Arts & leisure

Avenue Q

Golden Theater, 252 W 45th Street, between Broadway & Eighth Avenue (1-212 239 6200/www.avenueq.com). Subway A, C, E to 42nd Street-Port Authority. **Shows** 8pm Tue-Fri; 2pm,

8pm Sat; 2pm, 7pm Sun. **Length** 2hrs 15mins. 1 intermission. **Map** p102 C1/p104 C4 ❻❹

Mixing puppets and live actors with irreverent jokes and snappy songs, this clever, good-hearted musical comedy was a surprise hit. It garnered several 2004 Tonys, including Best Musical.

Billy Elliot

NEW *Imperial Theatre, 249 West 45th Street, between Broadway & 8th Avenue (1-212 239 6200).* **Shows** 8pm Tue-Fri; 2pm, 8pm Sat; 2pm, 7pm Sun. **Length** 2hrs 30 mins. 1 intermission. **Map** p104 C4 ❻❺

Celebrate the journey of one boy's dream. The movie-cum-musical made a splash on the London stage and is sure to capture the hearts of New Yorkers.

Carnegie Hall

154 W 57th Street, at Seventh Avenue (1-212 247 7800/www.carnegiehall. org). Subway N, Q, R, W to 57th Street. **Map** p104 C3 ❻❻

The stars – both soloists and orchestras – in the classical music firmament continue to shine most brightly in the venerable Isaac Stern Auditorium, inside this renowned concert hall. Still, it's the spunky upstart Zankel Hall that has generated the most buzz; the below-street-level space offers a mix of classical, contemporary, jazz, pop and world music. Next door, Weill Recital Hall hosts chamber music programmes.

City Center

131 W 55th Street, between Sixth & Seventh Avenues (1-212 581 7907/ www.nycitycenter.org). Subway B, D, E to Seventh Avenue; F, N, Q, R, W to 57th Street. **Map** p104 C3 ❻❼

Before the creation of Lincoln Center changed the city's cultural geography, this was the home of the American Ballet Theatre, the Joffrey Ballet and the New York City Ballet. The City Center's lavish decor is golden – as are the companies that pass through here.

Levitate Yoga

780 Eighth Avenue, between 47th & 48th Streets (1-212 974 2288/www. levitateyoga.com). Subway C, E to 50th

Street. **Open** Call or check website for schedule & prices. **Map** p102 C1/p104 C4 **68**

This modern-looking studio caters to beginners, tourists and casts and crews performing at nearby theatres. In the warm months, special classes are held on the 2,000sq ft rooftop terrace.

Manhattan Theatre Club

City Center, 131 W 55th Street, between Sixth & Seventh Avenues (1-212 581 1212/Telecharge 1-212 239 6200/www.mtc-nyc.org). Subway B, D, E to Seventh Avenue. **Map** p104 C3 **69**

Manhattan Theatre Club has a history of sending young playwrights to Broadway, as seen with such successes as David Auburn's *Proof* and John Patrick Shanley's *Doubt*. The club's two theatres are in the basement of City Center. The 275-seat Stage I Theater features four plays a year; the Stage II Theater offers works-in-progress, workshops and staged readings, as well as full-length productions.

Mary Poppins

Amsterdam Theatre, 214 West 42nd Street, between Seventh & Eighth Avenues (1-212 307 4747). Subway A, C, E to 42nd Street-Port Authority; N, Q, R, W, 42nd Street, S, 1, 2, 3, 7 to 42nd Street-Times Square. **Shows** 8pm Tue; 2pm, 8pm Wed, Sat; 8pm Thur, Fri; 3pm Sun. **Length** 2hrs 45mins. 1 intermission. **Map** p102 C1/p104 C4 **70**

This drolly understated yet spectacular treat is a new beast for Uncle Walt's musical menagerie: a genuine book musical that adults can enjoy. Based on the famed 1964 movie and PL Travers's original, darker novel, the story is familiar: overworked parents hire an efficient but odd nanny to tame beastly brats. Children should be enraptured by the flying effects and Bob Crowley's eye-popping sets.

Monty Python's Spamalot

Shubert Theatre, 225 W 44th Street, between Broadway & Eighth Avenue (1-212 239 6200). Subway A, C, E to 42nd Street-Port Authority; N, Q, R, W, 42nd Street, S, 1, 2, 3, 7 to 42nd Street-Times Square. **Shows** 7pm Tue; 2pm, 8pm Wed, Sat; 8pm Thur, Fri; 3pm Sun. **Length** 2hrs 15mins. One intermission. **Map** p102 C1/p104 C4 **71**

Monty Python founder Eric Idle is behind this 'lovingly ripped-off' musical adaptation of *Monty Python and the Holy Grail*. Veteran director Mike Nichols stages the mélange of greatest-hits laughs and Broadway-spoofing novelty. Winner of the 2005 Tony Award for Best Musical.

Wicked

Gershwin Theatre, 222 W 51st Street, between Broadway & Eighth Avenue (1-212 307 4100). Subway C, E, 1 to 50th Street. **Shows** 7pm Tue; 2, 8pm Wed, Sat; 8pm Thur, Fri; 3pm Sun. **Length** 2hrs 45 mins. 1 intermission. **Map** p104 C3 **72**

Based on novelist Gregory Maguire's 1995 riff on *The Wizard of Oz* mythology, *Wicked* provides a witty prequel to the classic children's book and movie. At press time, Joe Mantello's sumptuous production starred Megan Hilty and Shoshana Bean as young versions of Glinda the Good Witch and the Wicked Witch of the West.

Fifth Avenue

Synonymous with the chic and moneyed, Fifth Avenue caters to the elite; it's also the main route for the city's many ethnic (and inclusive) parades: National Puerto Rican Day, St Patrick's Day, Gay and Lesbian Pride, and many more. The well-heeled still shop here, but mall stores are nudging in. Whatever your pleasure, the gaggle of landmarks and first-rate museums never disappoints.

Sights & museums

American Folk Art Museum

45 W 53rd Street, between Fifth & Sixth Avenues (1-212 265 1040/ www.folkartmuseum.org). Subway E, V to Fifth Avenue-53rd Street. **Open**

10.30am-5.30pm Tue-Thur, Sat, Sun; 10.30am-7.30pm Fri. **Admission** $9; free-$7 reductions. Free to all 5.30-7.30pm Fri. **Map** p105 D3 🅰

Celebrating traditional craft-based work is the American Folk Art Museum (formerly the Museum of American Folk Art). Designed by architects Billie Tsien and Tod Williams, the architecturally stunning eight-floor building is four times larger than the original Lincoln Center location (which is now a branch of the museum) and includes a café.

Empire State Building

350 Fifth Avenue, between 33rd & 34th Streets (1-212 736 3100/www. esbnyc.com). Subway B, D, F, N, Q, R, V, W to 34th Street-Herald Square. **Open** 8am-2am daily (closed during extreme weather). Last elevator up 1.15am. **Admission** $18; reductions free-$16. **Map** p103 D2 🅰

Located smack-bang in the centre of Midtown Manhattan, this magnificent building is visible from most parts of the city and beyond. At night, it's illuminated in showy colours to celebrate a holiday or special event (the lights turn off at the stroke of midnight). To say they don't build 'em like they used to is an understatement. The Empire State Building was financed as a speculative venture by General Motors executive John J Raskob; builders broke the ground in 1930. It sprang up in 14 months with amazing speed, and was completed more than a month ahead of schedule and $5 million under budget. The 1,250ft tower snatched the title of world's tallest building from under the nose of the months-old, 1,046ft Chrysler Building, thus conveniently showing up Raskob's Detroit rival Walter P Chrysler.

Museum of Modern Art (MoMA)

11 W 53rd Street, between Fifth & Sixth Avenues (1-212 708 9400/ www.moma.org). Subway E, V to Fifth Avenue-53rd Street. **Open** 10.30am-5.30pm Mon, Wed, Thur, Sat, Sun; 10.30am-8pm Fri. **Admission**

(includes film programmes) $20; free-$16 reductions. Free to all 4-8pm Fri. **Map** p105 D3 🅰

MoMA contains the world's finest and most comprehensive holdings of 20th-century art and, thanks to a sweeping redesign by architect Yoshio Taniguchi completed in 2004, it is now able to show off much more of its immense permanent collection in serene, high-ceilinged galleries that almost outshine the art on display. Inside, the soaring five-storey atrium is the central artery from which six curatorial departments – Architecture and Design, Drawings, Photography, Painting and Sculpture, Prints and Illustrated Books, and Film and Media – display works that include the best of Matisse, Picasso, Van Gogh, Giacometti, Pollock, Rothko and Warhol, among many others. Outside, Philip Johnson's sculpture garden has been restored to its original, larger plan from 1953, and its powerful minimalist sculptures and sheer matt black granite and glass wall are overlooked by the sleek high-end restaurant and bar the Modern, run by Midas-touch restaurateur Danny Meyer. The museum's eclectic exhibition of design objects is a must-see, with examples of art nouveau, the Bauhaus and the Vienna Secession lining up alongside a vintage 1946 Ferrari and architectural drawings and models from the likes of Rem Koolhaas and Mies van der Rohe.

Event highlights Van Gogh by Night (21 September-4 January 2009): this exhibition will explore Van Gogh's depictions of night landscapes and interior scenes. Joan Miró: Painting and Anti-Painting 1927–1937 (2 November-12 January 2009): taking Miró's notorious declaration of 1927 – 'I want to assassinate painting' – as its starting point, the exhibition showcases creations that highlight acidic colors, grotesque disfigurement and other 'tactics of aggression'. Aernout Mik (5 May-28 July 2009): the contemporary Dutch born artists displays a host of artworks. Photography and the American West (24 March-8 June 2009).

Museum of Modern Art (MoMA)

Museum of Television & Radio

25 W 52nd Street, between Fifth & Sixth Avenues (1-212 621 6800/ www.mtr.org). Subway B, D, F, V to 47th-50th Streets-Rockefeller Center; E, V to Fifth Avenue-53rd Street. **Open** noon-6pm Tue-Sun; noon-8pm Thur. **Admission** $10; $5-$8 reductions. No credit cards. **Map** p105 D3 ⑦

This nirvana for boob-tube addicts and pop-culture junkies contains an archive of more than 100,000 radio and TV programmes. Head to the fourth-floor library to search the computerised system for your favourite *Star Trek* or *I Love Lucy* episodes, then walk down one flight to take a seat at your assigned console. (The radio listening room operates the same way.) Screenings of modern cartoons, public seminars and special presentations are offered.

NBC

30 Rockefeller Plaza, 49th Street, between Fifth & Sixth Avenues (1-212 664 3700/www.nbc.com/Footer/ Tickets). Subway B, D, F, V to 47-50th Streets-Rockefeller Center. **Map** p105 D3/D4 ⑦

Peer through the *Today* show's studio window or pay admission (at the NBC Experience Store, www.shopnbc.com) for a guided tour of the studios. The tours are led by pages, many of whom (such as Ted Koppel, Kate Jackson and Michael Eisner) have gone on to bigger and better things in showbiz.

New York Public Library

455 Fifth Avenue, at 42nd Street (1-212 930 0830/www.nypl.org). Subway B, D, F, V to 42nd Street-Bryant Park; 7 to Fifth Avenue. **Open** 11am-7.30pm Tue, Wed; 10am-6pm Thur-Sat. **Admission** free. **Map** p103 D1/p105 D5 ⑦

When people mention 'the New York Public Library,' most are referring to this imposing Beaux Arts building. Two massive stone lions, dubbed Patience and Fortitude by former mayor Fiorello La Guardia, flank the main portal. Free guided tours (at 11am and 2pm) stop at the beautifully renovated Rose Main Reading Room and the Bill Blass Public Catalog Room, which offers free internet access. Lectures, author readings and exhibitions are worth checking out. Behind the library is Bryant Park, a well-cultivated green space that hosts a dizzying schedule of free entertainment during the summer, when it also attracts outdoor internet users with its free wireless service. In the winter it becomes an ice-skating rink.

Radio City Music Hall

1260 Sixth Avenue, at 50th Street (1-212 247 4777/www.radiocity.com). Subway B, D, F, V to 47-50th Streets-Rockefeller Center. **Map** p105 D3 ⑦

Few rooms scream 'New York City!' more than this gilded hall, which has drawn Wilco, Alanis Morissette and Carole King as headliners. The greatest challenge for any performer is not to get upstaged by the awe-inspiring art deco surroundings. Radio City was the world's largest cinema when it was built in 1932 (the backstage tour is one of the best in town).

Rockefeller Center

From 48th to 51st Streets, between Fifth & Sixth Avenues (1-212 632 3975/tickets 1-212 664 7174/www. rockefellercenter.com). Subway B, D, F, V to 47-50th Streets-Rockefeller Center. **Map** p105 D3/D4 ⁶⁰

Veer off Fifth Avenue into the 19 buildings of Rockefeller Center and you'll see why this interlacing of public and private space is so lavishly praised. The centre is filled with murals, sculptures, mosaics and other artwork. On weekday mornings, a crowd of (mainly) tourists gathers at NBC television network's glass-walled, ground-level studio (where the *Today* show is shot), at the south-west corner of Rockefeller Plaza and 49th Street. Exploring the centre is free. For guided tours in and around the buildings, however, advance tickets are necessary and available by phone, online or at the NBC Experience Store. The recently opened Top of the Rock (1-212 698 2000, www.topoftherocknyc.com), an observation deck at 30 Rockefeller Center, offers jaw-dropping views.

St Patrick's Cathedral

Fifth Avenue, between 50th & 51st Streets (1-212 753 2261). Subway B, D, F to 47-50th Streets-Rockefeller Center; E, V to Fifth Avenue-53rd Street. **Open** 6.30am-8.45pm daily. **Admission** free. **Map** p105 D3 ⁶¹

St Patrick's adds Gothic grace to Fifth Avenue. The diocese of New York bought the land for an orphanage in 1810, but then in 1858 it switched gears and began construction on what would become the country's largest Catholic church. Today, the white marble spires are dwarfed by Rockefeller Center, but inside the vaulted ceilings, stained-glass windows from Chartres and altars by Tiffany & Co are still stunning.

Eating & drinking

Le Bernardin

155 W 51st Street, between Sixth & Seventh Avenues (1-212 489 1515). Subway B, D, F, V to 47th-50th Streets-Rockefeller Center; N, R, W to 49th Street. **Open** noon-2.30pm, 5.30-10.30pm Mon-Thur; noon-2.30pm, 5.30-11pm Fri; 5.30-11pm Sat. **$$$$**. **Seafood**. **Map** p104 C3 ⁶²

Eric Ripert's shrine to seafood is, by nearly all measures, the most consistently acclaimed restaurant to be found in New York City. A true Frenchman, Ripert rarely lets a bite go sauceless, drizzling plates with rich truffle-butter vinaigrette, black pepper and brandy butter sauce or pungent sweet garlic sauce with chorizo essence.

Modern

9 W 53rd Street, between Fifth & Sixth Avenues (1-212 333 1220) Subway E, V to Fifth Avenue-53rd Street. **Open** noon-2.15pm, 6-9.30pm Mon-Thur; noon-2.15pm, 5.30-10.30pm Fri; 5.30-10.30pm Sat. **$$$**. **American creative**. **Map** p105 D3 ⁶³

From the moment he was tapped to run the renovated Museum of Modern Art's flagship restaurant, chef Gabriel Kreuther set about creating a modern culinary art of his own. Here you'll find inspired dishes that would do justice to any setting, even a dining room overlooking the museum's famed sculpture garden, filled as it is with priceless works of art. Every element of the Modern (slickly dressed servers, Christofle silverware, flower displays) shows attention to detail.

'21' Club

21 W 52nd Street, between Fifth & Sixth Avenues (1-212 582 7200). Subway B, D, F, V to 47-50th Streets-Rockefeller Center; E, V to Fifth Avenue-53rd Street. **Open** noon-10pm Mon-Thur; noon-11pm Fri; 5.30-11pm Sat. **$$$$**. **American**. **Map** p105 D3 ⁶⁴

After 75 years this clubby sanctum for the rich and powerful remains true to its past while continuing to thrive in the 21st century. In addition to ever-changing seasonal fare, the menu lists '21 Classics', such as steak Diane, flambéed tableside, which was on the restaurant's first menu. The famous house burger mixes lean ground meats with duck fat – for just $29!

Rockefeller Center

Shopping

Bergdorf Goodman

754 Fifth Avenue, at 57th Street (1-212 753 7300/www.bergdorfgoodman.com). Subway E, V to Fifth Avenue-53rd Street; N, R, W to Fifth Avenue-59th Street. **Open** 10am-7pm Mon-Wed, Fri, Sat; 10am-8pm Thur; noon-6pm Sun. **Map** p105 D3

Bergdorf is dedicated to an elegant, understated clientele that has plenty of disposable income. Luxury clothes, accessories and even stationery are found here, along with an over-the-top Beauty Level. The famed men's store is across the street (745 Fifth Avenue).

Bulgari

730 Fifth Avenue, at 57th Street (1-212 315 9000/www.bulgari.com). Subway E, V Fifth Avenue-53rd Street. **Open** 10am-6pm Mon-Sat, noon-5pm Sun. **Map** p105 D3

The luxury brand has reinvented its formerly stoic temple of jewellery on Fifth Avenue, creating a chic and contemporary look. A new line of pricey handbags and sunglasses compliments all those baubles.

Henri Bendel

712 Fifth Avenue, at 56th Street (1-212 247 1100/www.henribendel.com). Subway E, V to Fifth Avenue-53rd Street; N, R, W to Fifth Avenue-59th Street. **Open** 10am-8pm Mon-Sat; noon-7pm Sun. **Map** p105 D3

Bendel's lavish quarters resemble an opulently appointed townhouse. Naturally, there are elevators – no one expects you to walk, this is Fifth Avenue – but it's nicer to saunter up the elegant, winding staircase. Prices are comparable with those of other upscale stores, but the merchandise somehow seems more desirable here – we guess it must be those darling brown-striped shopping bags.

Jimmy Choo

645 Fifth Avenue, at 51st Street (1-212 593 0800/www.jimmychoo.com). Subway E, V to Fifth Avenue-53rd Street. **Open** 10am-6pm Mon-Wed, Fri, Sat; 10am-7pm Thur; noon-5pm Sun. **Map** p105 D3

The British luxury footwear label has conquered America with this six-year-old emporium, showcasing chic boots, sexy stilettos, curvaceous pumps and kittenish flats. Prices start at $450.

Louis Vuitton

1 E 57th Street, at Fifth Avenue (1-212 758 8877/www.vuitton.com). Subway F to 57th Street; N, R, W to Fifth Avenue-59th Street. **Open** 10am-7pm Mon-Wed, Fri, Sat; 10am-8pm Thur; noon-6pm Sun. **Map** p105 D3

Sweet relief

Food-based beauty treatments are gaining popularity at high-end spas around the city, and *Time Out New York* decided to weigh in on these yummy indulgences.

Technically, there's no bubbly involved in the champagne facial at **Faina European Day Spa** (315 W 57th Street, between Eighth & Ninth Avenues, suite 402, 1-212 245 6557), but it's probably better that way, since alcohol would only dry you out (your skin, that is). Owner Faina Shafir named this treatment after the sparkling elixir because of its copious use of grapeseed oil and extract, which hydrates and exfoliates the skin. Starting off with a pineapple and papaya enzyme treatment with grapeseeds, layers of dead skin are sloughed off. The final touch is a relaxing face, neck and shoulder massage with grapeseed oil, which leaves skin dewy and soft.

While the spa menu at **Just Calm Down** (32 W 22nd Street, between Fifth & Sixth Avenues, 1-212 337 0032) can read like an overplayed gimmick (virtually everything, from the 'Grape Gatsby' manicure to the 'Just Knocked Up' massage, is a pun), the treatments at this Flatiron space have real substance. As the name implies, the 'Marriage of Figaro' massage employs fig oil, 'married' to chocolate oil. A rubdown with this concoction will have your tight muscles softening in no time. It's a deliciously cosy hour-long extravaganza.

At **Haven Spa** (150 Mercer Street, between E Houston & Prince Streets, 1-212 343 3515), a hot chocolate body wrap is designed to detoxify and energise dull, flaky skin, but it's also ideal for any cocoa lover. While you lounge on the comfy treatment bed, the aroma of chocolate fills the room. You'll be vigorously scrubbed with a warm exfoliating salt to stimulate circulation. Next, get ready for the good stuff: a gooey paste of cocoa powder (chocolate is known for its antioxidant properties) and goat's and cow's milk – all to soften and moisturise your body. A final topping of Serendipity 3 Frrrozen Hot Chocolate Body Icing, a decadent lotion redolent of its namesake treat, leaves you shimmering and hydrated… not to mention hungry.

The four-storey, glass-encased retail cathedral certainly gives cause for jubilation: crane your neck to view the three-floor-high LED wall screen and antique Vuitton trunks suspended from the ceiling. The much-coveted bags and ready-to-wear collection are here as well.

Nat Sherman

500 Fifth Avenue, at 42nd Street (1-212 764 5000/www.natsherman. com). Subway B, D, F, V to 42nd Street-Bryant Park; 7 to Fifth Avenue. **Open** 10am-8pm Mon-Fri; 10am-7pm Sat; 11am-5pm Sun. **Map** p103 D1/ p105 D4 ⑨⓪

Just across the street from the New York Public Library, Nat Sherman offers its own brand of slow-burning cigarettes, as well as cigars and related accoutrements. Flick your Bic in the upstairs smoking room.

Otto Tootsi Plohound

137 Fifth Avenue, between 20th & 21st Streets (1-212 460 8650). Subway N, R, W to 23rd Street. **Open** 11.30am-8pm Mon-Fri; 11am-8pm Sat; noon-7pm Sun. **Map** p103 D4 ⑨①

One of the best places to head if you're looking for the latest shoe styles, Otto Tootsi Plohound has a wide selection of trendy, and slightly overpriced, imports for both women and men.

Saks Fifth Avenue

611 Fifth Avenue, at 50th Street (1-212 753 4000). Subway E, V to Fifth Avenue-53rd Street. **Open** 10am-7pm Mon-Wed, Fri, Sat; 10am-8pm Thur; noon-6pm Sun. **Map** p105 D3 ⑨②

The store features all the big names in women's fashion, from Armani to Yves St Laurent, plus an excellent menswear department and a children's section. There are also fine household linens, La Prairie skincare and attentive customer service. New management is exploring the possibility of an overhaul; at press time, Frank Gehry's name had made the rumour mill as the architect.

Tiffany & Co

727 Fifth Avenue, at 57th Street (1-212 755 8000/www.tiffany.com). Subway E, V to Fifth Avenue-53rd
Street; F to 57th Street; N, R, W to Fifth Avenue-59th Street. **Open** 10am-7pm Mon-Fri; 10am-6pm Sat; noon-5pm Sun. **Map** p105 D3 ⑨③

The heyday of Tiffany's was at the turn of the 19th century, when Louis Comfort Tiffany, the son of founder Charles Lewis Tiffany, took the reins and began to create sensational art nouveau jewellery. Today the design stars are the no less august Paloma Picasso and Elsa Peretti. Three floors are stacked with precious jewels, silver, watches, porcelain and the classic Tiffany engagement rings. FYI: breakfast is not served.

Midtown West

West of Times Square, in the vicinity of the Port Authority Bus Terminal (on Eighth Avenue) and the Lincoln Tunnel's traffic-knotted entrance, is an area historically known as Hell's Kitchen, where a gang- and crime-ridden Irish community scraped by in the 19th century. Italians, Greeks, Puerto Ricans, Dominicans and other ethnic groups followed. The neighbourhood maintained its tough reputation into the 1970s, when, in an effort to precipitate gentrification, local activists renamed it Clinton, after the one-time mayor (and governor) DeWitt Clinton.

Sights & museums

Circle Line Cruises

Pier 83, 42nd Street, at the Hudson River (1-212 563 3200/www.circleline. com). Subway A, C, E to 42nd Street-Port Authority. **Tours** Call or visit website for schedule. **Tickets** $29.50; $17-$25 reductions. **Map** p102 A1/ p104 A4 ⑨④

Circle Line's famous three-hour, guided circumnavigation of Manhattan is one of the best ways to take in the city's sights. Themed tours, such as the New Year's Eve cruise or autumn foliage trip to the Hudson Valley, are also offered.

Intrepid Sea-Air-Space Museum

NEW *From Nov 2008. USS Intrepid, Pier 86, 46th Street, at the Hudson River (1-212 245 0072/www.intrepid museum.org). Subway A, C, E to 42nd Street-Port Authority, then M42 bus to Twelfth Avenue.* **Open** *Apr-Oct* 10am-5pm Mon-Fri; 10am-6pm Sat, Sun. *Nov-Mar* 10am-5pm Tue-Sun **Admission** call to check. **Map** p102 A1/p104 A4 **95**

This is a major stop for both naval and air enthusiasts. The retired aircraft carrier returns from undergoing major renovation, and reopens on November 11, 2008. Many new interactive exhibits join a collection that spans World War II bombers to modern supersonic jet fighters.

Eating & drinking

El Centro

824 Ninth Avenue, at 54th Street (1-646 763 6585). Subway C, E to 50th Street. **Open** 5-11pm Mon, Tue, Sun; 5pm-midnight Wed-Sat. **$**. **Mexican**. **Map** p104 B3 **96**

To start the party on the right note, indulge in one of El Centro's fine frozen margaritas, available with guava and raspberry. The menu's tried-and-true offerings – tacos, burritos, enchiladas, fajitas and so on – are all solid. We especially liked a quesadilla made with fat chunks of shrimp and melted monterey jack cheese, and a tostada appetiser consisting of black beans, lettuce, tomato, sour cream and thick, juicy slices of grilled skirt steak.

Gordon Ramsay at the London

151 W 54th Street, at Seventh Avenue (1-212 468 8888). Subway B, D, E at Seventh Avenue; N, Q, R, W at 57th Street. **Open** noon-2pm, 5.30-10.30pm daily. **$$$$**. **French**. **Map** p104 C3 **97**

The 12 tables that occupy the dining room of the first stateside restaurant from the famously foul mouthed, celebrity chef Gordon Ramsay are almost as well known locally for being particularly difficult to score a place at. The menu hews close to that of Ramsay's eponymous three-star flagship in London: French cuisine with international influences, served as either a three-course or seven-course prix fixe meal – with extra amuse-bouches and palate cleansers. Ramsay has delivered on the promises of his perfectionist TV alter ego.

Kemia Bar

630 Ninth Avenue, at 44th Street (1-212 582 3200). Subway A, C, E to 42nd Street-Port Authority. **Open** 6pm-2am Tue-Sat. **Bar**. **Map** p102 B1/p104 B4 **98**

Descending into this lush Middle Eastern oasis is like penetrating the fourth wall of a brilliant stage set. Gossamer fabric billows from the ceiling, ottomans are clustered around low tables and dark-wood floors are strewn with rose petals. The libations are equally luscious.

Kyotofu

705 Ninth Avenue, between 48th & 49th Streets (1-212-974-6012). Subway C, E at 50th Street. **Open** noon-12.30am Tue, Wed, Sun; noon-1.30am Thur-Sat. **$**. **Dessert**. **Map** p104 B4 **99**

Ritsuko Yamaguchi (Daniel) combines French technique with Japanese ingredients, swapping out milk and cream for a preponderance of tofu, in dishes like a large shot glass filled with black sugar syrup and silky tofu – the perfect eggless crème caramel. While most diners pop in only for a sugary fix (and a glass of saké perhaps), it is possible to cobble together a full-blown meal from the selection of small, appetiser-like selections.

Russian Tea Room

150 W 57th Street, between Sixth & Seventh Avenues (1-212 581 7100). Subway F, N, Q, R, W to 57th Street. **Open** 11.30am-3.30pm, 5-11.30pm Mon-Fri; 11am-3pm, 5-11.30pm Sat, Sun. **$$$**. **Russian**. **Map** p104 C3 **100**

See box p133.

Sortie

329 W 51st Street, between Eighth & Ninth Avenues (1-212 265 0650). *Subway C, E to 50th Street.* **Open** 5pm-4am Tue-Sat. **Bar**. Map p104 C3 **101**

The owners of this sultry bordello-like bar have done their level best to make sure their subterranean space could never be accused of being boring. They painted the walls a deep red and added velvet banquettes and studded black-leather café tables. They also hired flamenco dancers and serious guest DJs, and came up with a menu that specialises in tapas, cocktails and 30 artisanal beers.

Vlada Lounge

331 W 51st Street, between Fifth & Sixth Avenues (1-212 974 8030/ www.vladabar.com). Subway C, E to 50th Street. **Open** 4pm-4am daily. **Bar**. Map p104 C3 **102**

This super-chic and sleek bar attracts a mostly gay crowd looking to chill out and indulge in one of the 15 special infused vodkas.

Xai Xai Wine Bar

NEW *365 W 51st Street at Ninth Avenue (1-212 541 9241). Subway C, E to 50th Street.* **Open** 6pm-1am Mon-Thur; 4pm-2am Fri-Sun. **Bar**. Map p104 B3 **103**

Owners Brett Curtin and Tanya Hira named this 50-seat wine bar (pronounced 'shai shai') for a beach town in Mozambique. The 100-rich vino list features selections culled exclusively from South Africa and emphasizing pinotage, a smoky varietal which is unique to that country. Then nibble traditional snacks such as biltong, a spiced dried meat similar to jerky, and boerewors, sausage seasoned with coriander and nutmeg.

Shopping

Amy's Bread

672 Ninth Avenue, between 46th & 47th Streets (1-212 977 2670/ www.amysbread.com). Subway C, E to 50th Street; N, R, W to 49th Street.

Open 7.30am-11pm Mon-Fri; 8am-11pm Sat; 9am-6pm Sun. No credit cards. **Map** p102 B1/p104 B4 **104**

Whether you want sweet (chocolate-chubbie cookies) or savoury (semolina-fennel bread, hefty French sourdough boules), this wonderful bakery-kitchen never disappoints. Coffee and sandwiches are served on the premises.

B&H Photo

420 Ninth Avenue, at 34th Street (1-212 444 5040/www.bhphotovideo.com). Subway A, C, E to 34th Street-Penn Station. **Open** 9am-7pm Mon-Thur; 9am-2pm Fri; 10am-5pm Sun. **Map** p102 B2 **105**

B&H is the ultimate one-stop shop for all your photographic, video and audio needs – stock includes professional audio equipment and discounted Bang & Olufsen products. Note that the store is closed Friday after 2pm, all day Saturday and on Jewish holidays.

Hell's Kitchen Flea Market

39th Street, between Ninth & Tenth Avenues (1-212 243 5343). Subway A, C, E to 34th Street-Penn Station. **Open** sunrise-sunset Sat, Sun. No credit cards. **Map** p102 B2/p104 B5 **106**

The once-expansive Annex Antiques Fair & Flea Market on 26th Street lost its lease to a property developer, so many of the vendors packed up and moved to this stretch of road in Hell's Kitchen. Anyone familiar with the mind-boggling array of goods on offer at the former site is likely to feel a bit cheated in the new space, but there are treasures to be found and momentum is still growing.

London Sole

Suite 2501, 110 W 40th Street, between Broadway & Sixth Avenue (1-212 719 3001). Subway B, D, F, V to 42nd Street-Bryant Park; 7 to Fifth Avenue. **Open** 10am-5.30pm Mon-Thur. **Map** p102 C2/p104 C5 **107**

In a modern midtown space, this London-based boutique offers faux-crocodile driving shoes, gold-ribboned flats and more – all a stiletto-free step in the right direction.

Vlada Lounge p129

Nightlife

Copacabana

*560 W 34th Street, between Tenth &
Eleventh Avenues (1-212 239 2672/
www.copacabanany.com). Subway A,
C, E to 34th Street-Penn Station.*
Cover $10-$40, $30 at tables.
Map p102 A2
The city's most iconic destination for
Latin music has now become a fully
fledged party palace. It's still a prime
stop for salsa, cumbia and merengue,
but in addition to booking world-
renowned stars (Ruben Blades, El Gran
Combo, and Tito Nieves with Conjunto
Clasico), the Copa now has an alternative nook called the House Room,
where dancers can spin to disco, house
and Latin freestyle.

Pacha

*618 W 46th Street, between Eleventh
& Twelfth Avenues (1-212 209 7500/
www.pachanyc.com). Subway C, E to
50th Street.* **Open** 10pm-4am daily.
Map p102 A1/p104 A4
The worldwide glam-clubbing chain
Pacha, with famous outposts in
nightlife hotspots such as Ibiza,
London and Buenos Aires, has finally
hit the American market with a
swanky space helmed by superstar
spinner Erick Morillo.

Terminal 5

NEW *610 W 56th St at 11th Ave (1-
212 260 4700/www.terminal5nyc.com).
Subway A, C, B, D, 1 to 59th St-
Columbus Circle.* **Open** Call for show
times. **Map** p104 A3
Terminal 5 is an enormous room
booked by Bowery Presents that takes
up three floors of Far West Side real
estate. In a former life, it was a dance
club, and even a performance by, say,
Ween, can feel oddly rave-like. It's a
schlep from the subway but plays host
to a good assortment of top-tier acts,
from M.I.A. to Boredoms.

Midtown East

The area east of Fifth Avenue may
seem less appealing to visitors than
Times Square or Rockefeller Center.
Although the neighbourhood is
home to some of the city's most
recognisable landmarks – the
United Nations, Grand Central
Terminal and the distinctive art
deco Chrysler Building – the grid
of busy streets is lined with large,
imposing buildings, and the
bustling sidewalks are all business.
The area is a little thin on plazas
and street-level attractions, but it
compensates with a dizzying array

of world-class architecture including the MetLife Building, Waldorf-Astoria, Lever House and the Seagram Building.

Sights & museums

Grand Central Terminal

From 42nd to 44th Streets, between Vanderbilt & Lexington Avenues. Subway 42nd Street S, 4, 5, 6, 7 to 42nd Street-Grand Central. **Tours** Call 1-212 697 1245 for information. **Map** p103 D1/p105 D4 ⑪

The 1913 Beaux Arts train station is the city's most spectacular point of arrival. Grand Central played an important role in the nation's historic preservation movement, after a series of legal battles that culminated in the 1978 Supreme Court decision affirmed NYC's landmark laws. Since its 1998 renovation, the terminal itself has become a destination, with classy restaurants and bars, such as the Campbell Apartment cocktail lounge (off the West Balcony, 1-212 953 0409), the expert Grand Central Oyster Bar & Restaurant (Lower Concourse, 1-212 490 6650) and star chef Charlie Palmer's Métrazur (East Balcony, 1-212 687 4600). The Lower Concourse food court spans the globe with its fairly priced lunch options. One notable oddity: the constellations on the Main Concourse ceiling are drawn in reverse, as if seen from outer space.

United Nations Headquarters

UN Plaza, First Avenue, between 42nd & 48th Streets (tours 1-212 963 8687/ www.un.org/tours). Subway 42nd Street S, 4, 5, 6, 7 to 42nd Street-Grand Central. **Admission** $13.50; $9 seniors, students; $7.50 5-14s. Under-5s not admitted. **Open** 9.30am-4.45pm Mon-Fri. **Map** p103 F1/p105 ⑫

Although you don't need a passport, you will technically be leaving US soil when you enter the UN complex – it's designated as an international zone, and the vast buffet at the Delegates Dining Room (fourth floor, 1-212 963

7626) literally puts cultural diversity on the table. The grounds and the Peace Garden along the East River are strictly off-limits for security reasons. Unless you pay for a 45-minute guided tour, the only accessible attractions are the exhibitions in the lobby and the bookstore and gift shop on the lower level.

Eating & drinking

Adour Alain Ducasse

NEW *2 E 55th Street, at Fifth Avenue in the St. Regis Hotel (1-212 710 2277). Subway E, V to Fifth Avenue-53rd Street; F to 57th Street.* **Open** 5-10.30pm Mon-Thur, Sun; 5-11pm Fri, Sat. **$$$$**. **French**. **Map** p105 D3 ⑬

Here, wine is the muse (the list includes 70 under-$50 selections among its 1,800-strong list), and chef Tony Esnault's menu is equally geared towards the best. Entrées, such as a sumptuous tenderloin and short ribs anointed with foie gras-truffle jus, are rich without being heavy. Ditto on the desserts, which include a could-soon-be-legendary chocolate sorbet.

Avra

141 E 48th Street, between Lexington & Third Avenues (1-212 759 8550). Subway E, V to Lexington Avenue-53rd Street; 6 to 51st Street. **Open** noon-4pm, 5pm-midnight Mon-Fri; 11am-4pm, 5pm-midnight Sat; 11am-4pm, 5-11pm Sun. **$$$**. **Seafood**. **Map** p103 E1/p105 E4 ⑭

Arched doorways and a limestone floor evoke an Ionian seaside village; fabric draped like sails over wooden ceiling beams adds to the breezy feel. Starters such as grilled whole sardines and feta-and-tomato-stuffed squid whet the appetite for the main attraction: impeccably fresh fish, priced by the pound and served on a bed of ice. Whole fish, a flaky royal dorado, for example, is charcoal grilled and dressed with lemon juice, olive oil and oregano.

Branch

226 E 54th Street, between Second & Third Avenues (1-212 688 5577). Subway E, V to Lexington Avenue-53rd

Street; 6 to 51st Street. **Open** 6pm-4am Thur; 10.30pm-4am Fri, Sat. **Admission** $10. **Bar**. Map p105 E3
Branch is an elegant lounge-club that caters to local lawyer and banker types and out-of-towners who have come in for a little weekend fun.

Caviar Russe

538 Madison Avenue, between 54th & 55th Streets (1-212 980 5908). Subway E, V to Fifth Avenue-53rd Street. **Open** noon-10pm Mon-Sat. **Caviar bar**. Map p105 D3
See box p133.

CB Six

252 E 51st Street, between Second & Third Avenues (1-212 888 2453). Subway E, V to Lexington Avenue-53rd Street; 6 to 51st Street. **Open** 11am-4am daily. **Bar**. Map p105 E3
For the sports fan whose taste has developed beyond Coors Light, this midtown spot has fancy beers – more than 80 bottled brews and 16 on tap – in addition to standard-issue pub grub and plasma-screen TVs.

2nd Ave Deli p134

Manchester Pub

920 Second Avenue, at 49th Street (1-212 935 8901). Subway E, V to Lexington Avenue-53rd Street; 6 to 51st Street. **Open** 11am-4pm daily. **Bar**. Map p105 E4
A little bit of Northern English grit near the United Nations, this prototypical pub offers all the amenities (Boddingtons and Guinness on tap, greasy pub food and grungy bathrooms) to make a Mancunian homesick.

Megu Midtown

845 UN Plaza, Trump World Tower, First Avenue, at 47th Street (1-212 964 7777). Subway E, V to Lexington Street; 6 to 51st Street. **Open** 5.30-10.30pm Mon-Wed; 5.30-11.30pm Thur-Sat $$$$. **Japanese**. Map p103 E1/p105 F4
The 115-seat dining room has 24ft ceilings, 16ft-long lampshades, black wood panelling, a monumental mural of tigers poised to pounce and, like the original, a Buddha ice sculpture. Inside the open kitchen, an army of chefs produces pristine sushi and meat dishes (kobe beef, lamb, foie gras) the likes of which you won't find elsewhere.

Mint

150 E 50th Street, between Lexington & Third Avenues (1-212 644 8888). Subway E, V to Lexington Avenue-53rd Street; 6 to 51st Street. **Open** 11.30am-3pm, 5-11pm daily. $$. **Indian**. Map p105 E3
At this Indian eaterie, chefs pull all sorts of traditional baked goods out of the fiery clay oven – fluffy nan, roti and kulcha – but the best is the *aloo paratha*: warm, chewy and slightly charred rounds with a layer of soft, spicy potato in the middle. The secret is in the seasoning and the precisely heated oven.

Monkey Bar

NEW *Hotel Elysée, 60 E 54th Street between Madison & Park Avenues (1-212 838 2600). Subway E, V to Lexington Ave-53rd Street; 6 to 51st Street.* **Open** 11am-4am daily. **Bar**. Map p105 E3
The Monkey Bar is defined by its past. The mischievous, 72-year-old simian

Moscow on the Hudson

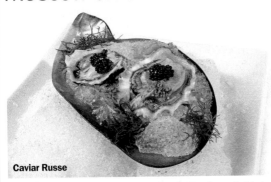

Caviar Russe

Who knew that vodka and caviar were alive and well here in little ol' New York City? Go on, make Boris and Natasha proud.

Caviar Russe (p132) takes its fish eggs seriously. At the seven-seat caviar bar facing the open kitchen, every detail has been designed for an experience that's refined but not fussy. Ask the bartender for a pairing recommendation, then order a 'taste' – two oysters with beluga and chilled saké, or a lobster and caviar profiterole accompanied by vodka, champagne or a glass of white wine. Za Vas!

The frenetic **Russian Vodka Room** (265 W 52nd Street, between Broadway & Eighth Avenue, 1-212 307 5835) is no Moscow memory lane – it lives for today. The vast horseshoe-shaped bar is always packed with a mix of young Russian and American rowdies with roving eyes. In the bright dining room, inebriated patrons feast on gravadlax with potato pancakes and cabbage pie. Entrées like chicken tabaka are unabashed greasy goodness.

And while there's much debate about the authenticity of certain flavours of Russian infused vodka, the horseradish shot packs a punch that goes well with the food and the flirting.

The recently reborn **Russian Tea Room** (p128) has never looked or tasted better. Nostalgia buffs will be happy to hear that nothing's happened to the gilded-bird friezes or the famously tacky crystal bear-shaped aquarium. But the food, thankfully, hasn't been frozen in time. Chef Gary Robins has modernised the menu and he makes the best borscht in the city.

Named for Michel Fokine's 1910 ballet, the opulent **FireBird** (365 W 46th Street, between Eighth & Ninth Avenues, 1-212 586 0244) transports you to pre-revolutionary Russia. The walls are a collage of Ballets Russes costumes and Léon Bakst reproductions, and golden eggs dangle from a gilded tree. Start with delicate beluga caviar folded with sour cream and bits of egg into a buttery blini. A feast should follow, but desserts yield to French influence.

NEW YORK BY AREA

murals that give this Hotel Elysée den its name, the glamorous icons from the last century who frequented its stools – Joe DiMaggio, Tennessee Williams, Marlon Brando – created multiple layers of lore. These days, the soigné celebs have been replaced by expense-accounting executives during the week and wide-eyed tourists on the weekend.

Montparnasse

230 E 51st Street, between Second & Third Avenues (1-212 758 6633). Subway E, V to Lexington Avenue-53rd Street; 6 to 51st Street. **Open** noon-3pm, 5-11pm Mon, Sun; noon-3pm, 5pm-midnight Tue-Fri; 5pm-midnight Sat. **$$**. **French**. **Map** p105 E3 ⓶

Both decor and menu are bistro standard, but the food at Montparnasse is fresher, prettier and tastier than what's on offer at many French joints. Top dishes include the seared hanger steak with red-wine sauce, and bouillabaisse; the saffron-accented broth has an abundant tumble of seafood.

Phoenix Garden

242 E 40th Street, between Second & Third Avenues (1-212 983 6666). Subway 42nd Street S, 4, 5, 6, 7 to 42nd Street-Grand Central. **Open** 11.30am-9.45pm Mon-Fri; noon-9.45pm Sat, Sun. **$**. No credit cards. **Chinese**. **Map** p103 E2/p105 E5 ⓶

Here's proof that you don't have to go to Chinatown to get the good stuff. Everything here tastes incredible, especially dumplings stuffed with chives and crisp sea bass with shredded pork and black mushrooms.

2nd Ave Deli

NEW *162 E 33rd Street between Lexington & Third Avenue (1-212 689 9069). Subway 6 to 33rd Street.* **Open** 24hrs daily. **$**. **Jewish deli**. **Map** p103 E2 ⓶

Two years after the original's close, the deli reopened at this misleading address. Though the kitchen has some difficulty executing staples, some things are as good as ever: schmaltz-laden chopped liver is whipped to a mousselike consistency, and the meats,

including juicy pastrami and corned beef, straddle the line between fatty and lean. Good news for aficionados: the decor, from the Hebraic logo to the blue-white-and-brown tiles and celeb headshots made the trip uptown too.

Top of the Tower

Beekman Tower, 3 Mitchell Place, at First Avenue (1-212 980 4796). Subway E, V to Lexington Avenue-53rd Street; 6 to 51st Street. **Open** 5pm-1am Mon-Thur, Sun; 5pm-2am Fri, Sat. **Bar**. **Map** p105 F3/F4 ⓶

Sweeping views of Midtown and the East River are not the only draws at this swanky lounge with two small outdoor terraces, perched on the 26th floor of the art deco landmark Beekman Tower Hotel. There's also live jazz piano (Thur-Sat) and good cocktails.

Shopping

Bloomingdale's

1000 Third Avenue, at 59th Street (1-212 705 2000/www.bloomingdales. com). Subway N, R, W to Lexington Avenue-59th Street; 4, 5, 6 to 59th Street. **Open** 10am-8.30pm Mon-Fri; 10am-7pm Sat; 11am-7pm Sun. **Map** p105 E2 ⓶

Bloomies is a gigantic, glitzy department store offering everything from handbags and cosmetics to furniture and designer clothes. Brace yourself for the crowds – this store ranks among the city's most popular tourist attractions, right up there with the Empire State Building. Check out the cool newer little-sister branch in Soho.

J. Press

NEW *380 Madison Avenue between 46th & 47th Streets (1-212 687 7642/ www.jpress.com). Subway 4, 5, 6, 7, S at Grand Central-42nd Street.* **Open** 9am-7pm Mon-Sat. **Map** p103 D1 ⓶

Go on, what are you afraid of? Embrace your inner preppie and head straight to the recently opened flagship of J. Press. If patchwork Madras aren't your thing no problem: they'll deck you out in classic collegiate faster than you can say Skull & Bones.

Bethesda Fountain p140

Uptown

This is where you'll find **Lincoln Center**, the **Metropolitan Museum of Art**, the **American Museum of Natural History** and the **Guggenheim**, to name just a few. If you really are hankering to cool your heels, you can't go wrong in **Central Park**. Once you've caught your breath, we guarantee a walk up Fifth Avenue will leave you breathless, but in a good way. The very northern tip of Manhattan not only provides glorious views of the Hudson River, it also offers a look back in time: the medieval castle of the **Cloisters** sits majestically in Fort Tryon Park.

Central Park

Two and a half miles long and half a mile wide, this patch of the great outdoors was the first man-made public park in the US. In 1853, the newly formed Central Park Commission chose landscape designer Frederick Law Olmsted and architect Calvert Vaux to turn this vast tract of rocky swampland into a rambling oasis of greenery. In 2003, the park celebrated its 150th anniversary, and it has never looked better, thanks to the Central Park Conservancy, a private non-profit civic group formed in 1980 that has been instrumental in its restoration and maintenance.

The park is dotted with landmarks. **Strawberry Fields**, near the West 72nd Street entrance, commemorates John Lennon, who lived in the nearby Dakota Building. The statue of Balto, a heroic Siberian husky (East Drive, at 67th Street), is a favourite sight for tots. Slightly older children appreciate the statue of Alice in Wonderland, just north of the

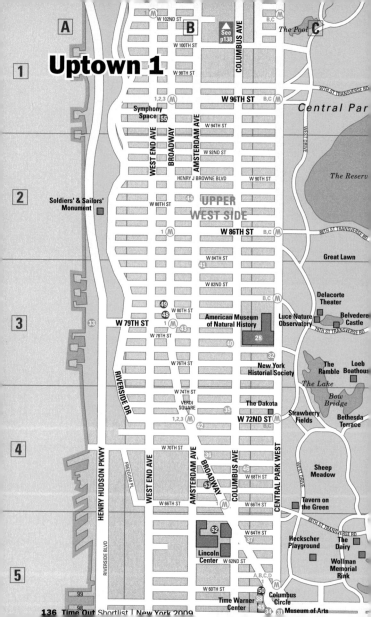

W 102ND ST
W 100TH ST
W 98TH ST
COLUMBUS AVE
B, C
The Pool
C

1,2,3 Ⓜ
W 96TH ST
B, C Ⓜ

Symphony Space 55
W 94TH ST
W 92ND ST

AMSTERDAM AVE
WEST END AVE
BROADWAY

HENRY J BROWNE BLVD
W 90TH ST

Central Par

97TH ST TRANSVERSE RD

WEST DRIVE

The Reserv

2

Soldiers' & Sailors' Monument
W 88TH ST
44
UPPER WEST SIDE

1 Ⓜ
W 86TH ST
B, C Ⓜ
86TH ST TRANSVERSE RD

Great Lawn

W 84TH ST
41
W 82ND ST

B, C Ⓜ

Delacorte Theater

3

49
48
W 80TH ST

W 79TH ST
1 Ⓜ
43
W 78TH ST

American Museum of Natural History
28

40
32

Luce Nature Observatory
79TH ST TRANSVERSE RD

Belvedere Castle

New York Historical Society
The Ramble

Loeb Boathous

33

RIVERSIDE DR

W 76TH ST

W 74TH ST
VERDI SQUARE

The Lake

Bow Bridge

Bethesda Terrace

The Dakota
1,2,3 Ⓜ
42
35
W 72ND ST
B, C Ⓜ

Strawberry Fields

4

W 70TH ST
36

HENRY HUDSON PKWY

FREEDOM PL

WEST END AVE

AMSTERDAM AVE

BROADWAY

COLUMBUS AVE

46
W 68TH ST

53
W 66TH ST

CENTRAL PARK WEST

Sheep Meadow

Tavern on the Green

WEST DRIVE

Ⓜ

52
W 64TH ST

37

Heckscher Playground
The Dairy

85TH ST TRANSVERSE RD

RIVERSIDE BLVD

Lincoln Center
W 62ND ST

Wollman Memorial Rink

5

W 60TH ST

A, B, C, D
1 Ⓜ
Columbus Circle

99
98

Time Warner Center
38
45
34
Museum of Arts

31

E 102ND ST

See p139

FIFTH AVE
MADISON AVE
PARK AVE
LEXINGTON AVE
THIRD AVE
SECOND AVE
FIRST AVE

E 100TH ST

1

① Sights & museums
① Eating & drinking
① Shopping
① Nightlife
① Arts & leisure

E 98TH ST

E 96TH ST Ⓜ 6

E 94TH ST

E 92ND ST

FRANKLIN D ROOSEVELT DR

4 Jewish Museum

E 90TH ST

1 Cooper-Hewitt National Design Museum **24**

9 Guggenheim Museum

E 88TH ST

2

3 Gracie Mansion

EAST END AVE

Carl Schutz Park

Neue Galerie

8

12 E 86TH ST Ⓜ 4,5,6

YORKVILLE

E 84TH ST

11

Goethe House **17**

E 82ND ST

UPPER EAST SIDE

Metropolitan Museum of Art

E 80TH ST

5

E 79TH ST

3

25

E 78TH ST

19

Ⓜ 6

E 76TH ST

John Jay Park

Conservatory Water

Whitney Museum **10** of American Art

E 74TH ST

16

Naumburg Bandshell

Roosevelt Island

E 72ND ST

2

Asia Society and Museum

E 70TH ST

The Frick Collection

4

26 23

Ⓜ 6

E 68TH ST

China Institute

Rockefeller University

FIFTH AVE
PARK AVE
LEXINGTON AVE
THIRD AVE
SECOND AVE
FIRST AVE

E 66TH ST

27

E 64TH ST

FRANKLIN D ROOSEVELT DR

Zoo

21

Ⓜ

15

E 62ND ST

20

N,R,W

18

E 60TH ST

22

YORK AVE

Ⓜ N,R,W

Bloomingdales

QUEENSBORO (59TH ST) BRIDGE

Grand Army Plaza

14

4,5,6

E 58TH ST

0   300 m
0   300 yds

© Copyright Time Out Group 2008

1

W 145TH ST

M A,C,B,D

E 145TH ST

PED BR

Riverside Park

W 143RD ST

HAMILTON HEIGHTS

W 143RD ST

North River Water Pollution Control Plant & Riverbank State Park

HENRY HUDSON PKWY

W 141ST ST

HAMILTON PLACE

W 141ST ST

EDGECOMBE AVE

W 141ST ST

BROADWAY

AMSTERDAM AVE

CLAYTON POWELL JR BLVD

MALCOLM X BLVD (LENOX AVE)

W 139TH ST

RIVERSIDE DR

TWELFTH AVE

W 139TH ST

Abyssinian Baptist Church

56

PED BR

W 137TH ST

M 1

CONVENT AVE

W 137TH ST

56

Schomburg Center

67

ADAM

2,3

RIVERSIDE DR

W 135TH ST

City College of New York

St Nicholas Park

M B,C

2

TWELFTH AVE

W 133RD ST

W 133RD ST

W 131ST ST

CONVENT AVE

ST NICHOLAS TER

ST CLAIR PL

OLD BROADWAY

W 129TH ST

HARLEM

MARTIN

W 128TH ST

W 127TH ST

TIEMANN PL

59

LUTHER

Apollo Theater

64

RIVERSIDE DR EAST

RIVERSIDE DR WEST

LA SALLE ST

KING

M A,C,B,D

W 125TH ST

2,3

3

30

General Grant National Memorial

58

JR

62

57

W 123RD ST

BLVD

Studio Museum in Harlem

Riverside Church

CLAREMONT AVE

W 121ST ST

FREDERICK DOUGLASS BLVD

REINHOLD NIEBUHR PL

W 119TH ST

Columbia University

Morningside Park

ADAM CLAYTON POWELL JR BLVD

MALCOLM X BLVD

Barnard College

66

4

M 1 54

W 116TH ST

MANHATTAN AVE

63

M B,C

2,3

W 115TH ST

MORNINGSIDE DRIVE

ST NICHOLAS AVE

W 113TH ST

39

Cathedral of St. John the Divine

29

W 111TH ST

Cathedral Close

CATHEDRAL PARKWAY

M B,C

CENTRAL PARK NORTH

2,3

W 109TH ST

Riverside Park

WEST DRIVE

Harler

5

W 107TH ST

WEST END AVE

51

57

DUKE ELLINGTON BLVD

W 106TH ST

AMSTERDAM AVE

W 105TH ST

COLUMBUS AVE

See p136

Central Park

M 1

W 103RD ST

M

B,C

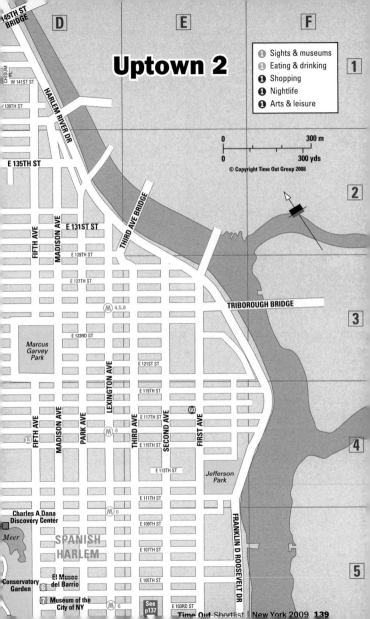

Uptown 2

1 Sights & museums
2 Eating & drinking
3 Shopping
4 Nightlife
5 Arts & leisure

D | E | F

1

45TH ST BRIDGE

CHISUM PL

W 141ST ST

139TH ST

HARLEM RIVER DR

E 135TH ST

2

THIRD AVE BRIDGE

0   300 m
0   300 yds

© Copyright Time Out Group 2008

FIFTH AVE

MADISON AVE

E 131ST ST

E 129TH ST

E 127TH ST

TRIBOROUGH BRIDGE

(M) 4,5,6

E 123RD ST

3

Marcus Garvey Park

E 121ST ST

LEXINGTON AVE

E 119TH ST

E 117TH ST

60

SECOND AVE

FIRST AVE

FIFTH AVE

MADISON AVE

PARK AVE

THIRD AVE

(M) 6

E 115TH ST

13

E 113TH ST

4

Jefferson Park

E 111TH ST

(M) 6

E 109TH ST

Charles A Dana Discovery Center

Meer

SPANISH HARLEM

E 107TH ST

FRANKLIN D ROOSEVELT DR

E 105TH ST

Conservatory Garden

6

El Museo del Barrio

5

7 Museum of the City of NY

(M) 6

See p137

E 103RD ST

popular meeting places in the park is the grand **Bethesda Fountain and Terrace**, near the midpoint of the 72nd Street Transverse Road. North of it is the **Loeb Boathouse** (midpark, at 75th Street), where you can rent a rowing boat or gondola to take out on the lake, which is crossed by the elegant Bow Bridge. The bucolic park views enjoyed by diners at the nearby **Central Park Boathouse Restaurant** (midpark, at 75th Street, 1-212 517 2233) make it a lovely place for brunch or drinks, with an outdoor terrace and bar that are idyllic in summer. The **Great Lawn** (midpark, between 79th and 85th Streets) is a sprawling stretch of grass that doubles as a rally point for political protests and a concert spot for just about any act that can rally a six-figure audience, as well as free shows courtesy of the Metropolitan Opera and the New York Philharmonic in summer.

Central Park

Conservatory Water at the East 74th Street park entrance.

In winter, ice-skaters lace up at **Wollman Rink**, where the skating comes with a picture-postcard view of the fancy hotels surrounding the park. A short stroll to about 64th Street brings you to the **Friedsam Memorial Carousel**, still a bargain at $1.50 per ride.

Come summer, kites, frisbees and soccer balls fly every which way across **Sheep Meadow**, the designated quiet zone that begins at 66th Street. East of Sheep Meadow, between 66th and 72nd Streets, is the **Mall**, where you'll find volleyball courts and plenty of in-line skaters. East of the Mall's **Naumburg Bandshell** is **Rumsey Playfield** – site of the annual Central Park SummerStage series, an eclectic roster of free and benefit concerts held from Memorial Day weekend to Labor Day weekend. One of the most

Upper East Side

A stroll along Fifth, Madison and Park Avenues, from 61st to 81st Streets, will take you past the great old mansions, many of which are now consulates. The structure at 820 Fifth Avenue (at 64th Street) was one of the earliest luxury-apartment buildings on the avenue. Philanthropic gestures made by the moneyed class over the past 130 years have helped to create a cluster of art collections, museums and cultural institutions. In fact, Fifth Avenue from 82nd to 104th Streets is known as Museum Mile.

Sights & museums

Cooper-Hewitt, National Design Museum
2 E 91st Street, at Fifth Avenue (1-212 849 8400/www.cooperhewitt.org). Subway 4, 5, 6 to 86th Street. **Open**

10am-5pm Tue-Thur; 10am-9pm Fri; 10am-6pm Sat; noon-6pm Sun. **Admission** $10; free-$7 reductions. **Map** p137 D2 ①

The Smithsonian's National Design Museum was once the home of industrialist Andrew Carnegie (there is still a lovely lawn behind the building). Now it's the only museum in the US dedicated to domestic and industrial design, and it boasts a fascinating roster of temporary exhibitions.

Frick Collection

1 E 70th Street, between Fifth & Madison Avenues (1-212 288 0700/ www.frick.org). Subway 6 to 68th Street-Hunter College. **Open** 10am-6pm Tue-Sat; 1-6pm Sun. **Admission** $12; $5-$8 reductions; Under-10s not admitted. **Map** p137 D4 ②

The opulent 1914 residence that houses this private collection of great masters (from the 14th to the 19th centuries) was originally built for industrialist Henry Clay Frick, with a beautiful interior court and reflecting pool. The collection boasts world-class paintings, sculpture and furniture by the likes of Rembrandt, Vermeer and Renoir.

Gracie Mansion Conservancy

Carl Schurz Park, 88th Street, at East End Avenue (1-212 570 4751). Subway 4, 5, 6 to 86th Street. **Tours** *Mar-mid Nov* 10am, 11am, 1pm, 2pm Wed; tours last 45mins. **Admission** $7; free-$4 reductions; reservations required, same-day reservations not permitted. No credit cards. **Map** p137 F2 ③

At the eastern end of 88th Street is the only Federal-style mansion in Manhattan, and it's been New York's official mayoral residence since 1942; the current mayor, billionaire Michael Bloomberg, famously eschewed this traditional address in favour of his own Beaux Arts mansion at 17 East 79th Street (between Fifth & Madison Avenues). The green-shuttered yellow edifice, built in 1799 by Scottish merchant Archibald Gracie, was originally constructed as a country house for the wealthy businessman.

Jewish Museum

1109 Fifth Avenue, at 92nd Street (1-212 423 3200/www.thejewish museum.org). Subway 4, 5 to 86th Street; 6 to 96th Street. **Open** 11am-5.45pm Mon-Wed, Sun; 11am-9pm Thur; 11am-3pm Fri. Closed Jewish holidays. **Admission** $10; free-$7.50 reductions; donation 5-8pm Thur. **Map** p137 D2 ④

The Jewish Museum, in the 1908 Warburg Mansion, contains a fascinating collection of more than 28,000 works of art, artefacts and media installations. A two-floor permanent exhibition, 'Culture and Continuity: The Jewish Journey', examines the survival of Judaism and the essence of Jewish identity. The Museum's Café Weissman features a menu of contemporary kosher fare.

Metropolitan Museum of Art

1000 Fifth Avenue, at 82nd Street (1-212 535 7710/www.metmuseum. org). Subway 4, 5, 6 to 86th Street. **Open** 9.30am-5.30pm Tue-Thur, Sun; 9.30am-9pm Fri, Sat. No strollers Sun. **Admission** suggested donation (incl same-day admission to the Cloisters) $12; free-$7 reductions. **Map** p137 D3 ⑤

It could take weeks to cover the Met's two million square feet of gallery space, so it's best to be selective when you visit. Besides the enthralling temporary exhibitions, there are excellent collections of African, Oceanic and Islamic art, along with more than 3,000 European paintings from the Middle Ages right up through to the fin de siècle period, including major works by Titian, Brueghel, Rembrandt, Vermeer, Goya and Degas. Egyptology fans should head straight for the glass-walled atrium housing the Temple of Dendur. The Greek and Roman halls have recently received a graceful makeover, and the incomparable collection of medieval armour – a huge favourite with adults and children alike – was recently enriched by gifts of European, North American, Japanese and Islamic armaments.

Whitney Museum of American Art

The museum has also made significant additions to its modern-art galleries, including major works by American artist Eric Fischl and Chilean surrealist Roberto Matta. Contemporary sculptures are displayed each year in the Iris and B Gerald Cantor Roof Garden (May to late autumn, weather permitting). **Event highlights** Giorgio Morandi (16 September-14 December 2008); and 'Beyond Babylon: Art, Trade & Diplomacy in the Second Millennium BC' (18 November 2008-15 March 2009), showcasing the spectacular Near Eastern royal treasures of the period (see box p145).

El Museo del Barrio

1230 Fifth Avenue, between 104th & 105th Streets (1-212 831 7272/ www.elmuseo.org). Subway 6 to 103rd Street. **Open** 11am-5pm Wed-Sun. **Admission** $6; free-$4 reductions. Seniors free Thur. **Map** p139 D5 ⑥
Located in Spanish Harlem (aka El Barrio), El Museo del Barrio is, not surprisingly, dedicated to the work of Latino artists who reside in the United States as well as various Latin American masters. The 8,000-piece collection ranges from pre-Columbian artefacts to contemporary installations.

Museum of the City of New York

1220 Fifth Avenue, between 103rd & 104th Streets (1-212 534 1672/ www.mcny.org). Subway 6 to 103rd Street. **Open** 10am-5pm Tue-Sun. **Admission** suggested donation $7; $5 seniors, students, children; $15 families. **Map** p139 D5 ⑦
This institution contains a wealth of city history and includes paintings, sculptures, photographs, military and naval uniforms, theatre memorabilia, manuscripts, ship models and rare books. The toy collection, full of New Yorkers' playthings dating from the colonial era to the present day, is especially well loved.

Neue Galerie

1048 Fifth Avenue, at 86th Street (1-212 628 6200/www.neuegalerie.org). Subway 4, 5, 6 to 86th Street. **Open** 11am-6pm Mon, Sat, Sun; 11am-9pm Fri. **Admission** $10; $7 reductions; under-12s not admitted. **Map** p137 D2 ⑧
This elegant museum is devoted in its entirety to late 19th- and early 20th-century German and Austrian fine and decorative arts. The creation of the late art dealer Serge Sabarsky and cosmetics mogul Ronald S Lauder, the Neue

Gallerie has the largest concentration of works by Gustav Klimt and Egon Schiele anywhere outside Vienna.

Solomon R Guggenheim Museum

1071 Fifth Avenue, at 89th Street (1-212 423 3500/www.guggenheim.org). Subway 4, 5, 6 to 86th Street. **Open** 10am-5.45pm Mon-Wed, Sat, Sun; 10am-8pm Fri. **Admission** $15; free-$10 reductions; half-price 5-8pm Fri. **Map** p137 D2 ❾

Even if your schedule doesn't allow time to view the collections, you must get a glimpse (if only from the outside) of this dramatic spiral building, designed by Frank Lloyd Wright. In addition to works by Manet, Kandinsky, Picasso, Chagall and Louise Bourgeois, the museum owns Peggy Guggenheim's haul of cubist, surrealist and abstract expressionist works, along with the Panza di Biumo Collection of American minimalist and conceptual art from the 1960s and '70s. A ten-storey tower provides space for a sculpture gallery (with views of Central Park), an auditorium and a café.
Event highlights 'Catherine Opie: American Photographer' (26 September 2008-5 January 2009); 'theanyspacewhatever' (24 October 2008-5 January 2009), a selection of site-specific works created by a group of artists who have claimed the exhibition as their medium; and a major show examining the impact of Asian art and concepts on American art from 1900 to the present (30 January-19 April 2009).

Whitney Museum of American Art

945 Madison Avenue, at 75th Street (1-212 570 3676/1-800 944 8639/ www.whitney.org). Subway 6 to 77th Street. **Open** 11am-6pm Wed, Thur, Sat, Sun; 1-9pm Fri. **Admission** $12; free-$9.50 reductions; donation 6-9pm Fri. **Map** p137 D3 ❿

Like the Guggenheim, the Whitney Museum is set apart by its architecture: it's a Marcel Breuer-designed gray granite cube with an all-seeing upper-storey 'eye' window. When Gertrude

Vanderbilt Whitney, a sculptor and art patron, opened the museum in 1931, she dedicated it to living American artists. Today, the Whitney holds about 15,000 pieces by nearly 2,000 artists, including Alexander Calder, Willem de Kooning, Edward Hopper (the museum holds his entire estate), Jasper Johns, Louise Nevelson, Georgia O'Keeffe and Claes Oldenburg. Still, the museum's reputation rests mainly on its temporary shows, particularly the exhibition everyone loves to hate, the Whitney Biennial. Held in even-numbered years, the Biennial remains the most prestigious (and controversial) assessment of contemporary art in America.
Event highlights 'Alexander Calder: The Paris Years' (16 October 2008-15 February 2009), a collaboration with the Centre Pompidou in Paris.

Eating & drinking

Big Daddy's Diner

NEW *1596 Second Avenue, at 83rd Street (1-212 717 2020). Subway 4, 5, 6 to 86th Street.* **Open** 7am-midnight Mon-Thur, Sun; 24hrs Fri, Sat. **$. Café. Map** p137 E3 ⓫

Blue-plate specials are the best way to go: you'll find yourself elbow-deep in heaps of crisp fries, fat grilled sandwiches and pancakes so big they hang over the side of the plate (breakfast is available anytime). Plus, Big Daddy serves great fried chicken.

Centolire

1167 Madison Avenue, between 85th & 86th Streets (1-212 734 7711/www.pinoluongo.com). Subway 4, 5, 6 to 86th Street. **Open** noon-3.30pm, 5.30-11pm Mon-Fri; 6-11pm Sat; noon-3.30pm, 6-10pm Sun. **$$$. Italian. Map** p137 D2 ⓬

'Up or down?' the host will probably ask when you arrive. Head upstairs, where potted sunflowers light up a room overlooking Madison Avenue. The service is delightful; waiters offer advice and don't hesitate to mention prices for specials. The menu includes a variety of inventive pastas as well as traditional dishes such as veal milanese.

Big Daddy's Diner p143

NEW YORK BY AREA

This is Jeffrey Chodorow's new-ish place (he was the evil partner in NBC's short-lived series *The Restaurant*). Framed with a wall of leather strings and 2,000 samurai swords positioned on the high ceiling, the dark bar area is perfect for the S&M fetishist. It's near impossible to leave without spending around $300 per couple.

Lollipop

27 E 61st Street, between Madison & Park Avenues (1-212 752 8900). Subway 4, 5, 6 to 59th Street. **Open** 5pm-3.30am Mon-Sat. **$$**. **Vietnamese**. Map p137 D5 ⑮

This underground lounge features sumptuous touches like a see-through bar and red velvet banquettes. Expense-account businessmen and high-heeled women sip herb-muddled cocktails, chow down on kobe beef and coconut-prawn skewers, and blather beneath low-volume house music.

Ginger

1400 Fifth Avenue, at 116th Street (1-212 423 1111). Subway 2, 3 to 116th Street-Lenox Avenue; 6 to 116th Street-Lexington Avenue. **Open** 5.30-10.30pm Mon-Thur; 5.30-11.30pm Fri; 11.30am-4.30pm, 5.30-11.30pm Sat; 5.30-10pm Sun. **$$**. **Chinese**. Map p139 D4 ⑬

What's novel about this recently opened organic Chinese restaurant is what executive chef James Marshall won't do to the food: there will be no deep-frying and no excessive use of oil or salt. Instead, fresh vegetables and lean meats are doused in citrusy sauces; the menu lists pineapple-and-mango-glazed pork chop as well as apricot-glazed chicken.

Kobe Club

68 W 58th Street between Fifth & Sixth Avenues (1-212 644 5623). Subway F to 57th Street; N, R, W to Fifth Avenue-59th Street. **Open** 5.30pm-midnight Mon-Wed; 5.30pm-2am Thur-Sat. **$$$$**. **Steakhouse**. Map p137 D5 ⑭

Payard Pâtisserie & Bistro

1032 Lexington Avenue, between 73rd & 74th Streets (1-212 717 5252). Subway 6 to 77th Street. **Open** noon-3pm, 5.45-10.30pm Mon-Thur; noon-3pm, 5.45-11pm Fri, Sat. Tea 3.30-5pm Mon-Sat. **$-$$$**. **French**. Map p137 D4 ⑯

Glance past the espresso machines at this Parisian-style bakery and restaurant, and you'll spy an elegant panelled dining room with glittering belle epoque mirrors. Contemporary dishes such as seared scallops in vanilla nage, and classics like rack of lamb and a steak in four-peppercorn sauce are winners.

Pudding Stones

1457 Third Avenue, between 82nd & 83rd Streets (1-212 717 5797). Subway 4, 5, 6 to 86th Street. **Open** 5pm-2am daily. **$$**. **Wine bar**. Map p137 E3 ⑰

Oenophiles know that pudding stones are found in rocky soils and help nurture grapes. Wine-lovers can discuss this while perusing more than 100 options available by the bottle, glass and flight. Bistro fare, artisanal cheeses and a downstairs tasting room are added incentives.

Ancient treasures

It's an exhibition so ambitious that it was years in the making. 'Beyond Babylon: Art, Trade, And Diplomacy in the Second Millennium BC' brings more than 400 objects from the world's earliest civilisations to the Met. Most of the treasures were excavated in Turkey, Syria, Lebanon, Iraq, Greece, Egypt and Cyprus, and many have never been seen outside these countries.

The show reveals the fascinating cultures and far-flung connections behind these cultures. 'Individual civilisations are viewed not in isolation, but in relation to one another,' explains curator Dr Joan Aruz. 'In the Bronze Age, there was intense interaction across the Mediterranean Sea, which brought the great royal houses from Babylonia to Egypt and the Aegean into contact, through the exchange of diplomatic gifts.'

Aruz says the logistics of mounting such an exhibition are very difficult, and jokes that 'some people think we just throw these things into a glass case.' In fact, the curatorial team had to request and photograph each of the hundreds of objects they wished to use. The most challenging aspect was convincing certain authorities to lend some of the most precious and important works in their collections.

Among the rarities is incredibly rich cargo from wreckage of the world's oldest seagoing ship, found off the southern coast of Turkey. The cargo included hippopotamus ivory canines and incisors, copper and glass ingots, and even a rare golden scarab of queen Nefertiti.

■ www.metmuseum.org, 18 November 2008-15 March 2009.

Subway Inn

143 E 60th Street, between Lexington & Third Avenues (1-212 223 8929). Subway N, R, W to Lexington Avenue-59th Street; 4, 5, 6 to 59th Street. **Open** 8am-4am daily. **Bar**. **Map** p137 D5 ⑱

The bar near the Lexington Avenue and 60th Street subway exit is a 73-year-old watering hole that really is a hole. And we like it that way. The clientele varies based on the time of day, but you're likely to see a mix of what appear to be Bowery-bum-like boozers, regular guys and confused tourists seated in decrepit booths or at the bar. Drinks are lost in a time warp – beer starts at $3.50.

Uva

1486 Second Avenue, at 77th Street (1-212 472 4552). Subway 6 to 77th Street. **Open** noon-1am Mon-Thur, Sun; noon-2am Fri, Sat. **Wine bar**. **Map** p137 E3 ⑲

A great wine bar requires more than a well-stocked cellar: the well selected, not-too-pricey wines (35 of them available by the glass) come in just the right package – a rustic brick-walled room dimly lit with chandeliers and flickering ruby-red tea lights. Along with the extensive leather-bound wine list comes a comprehensive dinner menu.

Shopping

Barneys New York

660 Madison Avenue, at 61st Street (1-212 826 8900/www.barneys.com). Subway N, R, W to Fifth Avenue-59th Street; 4, 5, 6 to 59th Street. **Open** 10am-8pm Mon-Fri; 10am-7pm Sat; 11am-6pm Sun. **Map** p137 D5 ⑳

All the top designers are represented at this bastion of New York style. At Christmas time, Barneys has the most provocative windows in town. Its Co-op boutique branches carry young designers as well as secondary lines from heavyweights like Marc Jacobs and Theory. Every February and August the Chelsea Co-op (236 West 18th Street, 1-212 593 7800) hosts the Barneys Warehouse Sale, when prices are reduced by up to 80%.

Charlotte Moss

NEW *20 E 63rd Street, between Madison & Fifth Avenues (1-212 308 3888/www.charlottemoss.com) Subway 4, 5, 6 at 59th Street.* **Open** 10am-6pm Mon-Sat. **Map** p137 D5 ㉑

If your idea of fun is snooping around a rich person's fancy townhouse – and you're not likely to get an invitation to Donald Trump's house soon – then have we got a store for you. The luxuriously appointed digs of this shop are set up like a real residence. Not only can you walk away with a prize purchase, you'll also learn a thing or two about how to put a room together just by walking through the place.

Conran Shop

407 E 59th Street, between First & York Avenues (1-212 755 9079/ www.conran.com). Subway N, R, W to Lexington Avenue-59th Street; 4, 5, 6 to 59th Street. **Open** 11am-8pm Mon-Fri; 10am-7pm Sat; noon-6pm Sun. **Map** p137 E5 ㉒

Nestled under the Queensboro Bridge, Terence Conran's shop stocks a vast selection of trendy products for every room of the house. The range includes cabinets, dishes, lighting, rugs, sofas, draperies, beds, linens, kitchen gadgets and much more.

Donna Karan New York

819 Madison Avenue, between 68th & 69th Streets (1-212 861 1001/www.donnakaran.com). Subway 6 to 68th Street-Hunter College. **Open** 10am-6pm Mon-Wed, Fri, Sat; 10am-7pm Thur; noon-6pm Sun. **Map** p137 D4 ㉓

Created around a central garden with a bamboo forest, Donna Karan's upscale flagship caters to men, women and the home. Check out the organic café at the nearby DKNY store, as well as Donna-approved reads, clothing, shoes and vintage furniture.

Edit

NEW *1368 Lexington Avenue, between 90th & 91st Streets (1-212 876 1368). Subway 4, 5, 6, to 86th Street.* **Open** 10.30am-6.30pm Mon-Sat. **Map** p137 D2 ㉔

Edit

This London-based naughty-nineties emporium Myla sells elegant lingerie and boudoir accessories, including tasteful (yet nipple-exposing) 'peep-hole' bras, silk wrist-ties and blindfolds, plus a handful of sculptural, Brancusi-esque vibrators.

Roger Vivier

750 Madison Avenue, at 65th Street (1-212 861 5371). Subway 6 to 68th Street. **Open** *10am-6pm Mon-Sat.* **Map** *p137 D5* ②⑦
Francophiles who celebrate shoes as petite works of art will feel right at home at the new-ish Roger Vivier store on a chic stretch of Madison Avenue, where the boutique's sleek, artful design rivals the footwear.

Upper West Side

This four-mile-long stretch west of Central Park is culturally rich and cosmopolitan in a moneyed sort of way. As on the Upper East Side, New Yorkers were drawn here in the late 19th century, after the completion of Central Park, the opening of local subway lines and Columbia University's relocation to Morningside Heights. The gateway to the Upper West Side is Columbus Circle, where Broadway meets 59th Street, Eighth Avenue, Central Park South and Central Park West – a rare roundabout in a city that is largely made up of right angles.

Scanning the racks at this handsome bi-level townhouse is akin to peeking into a socialite's closet. Luxe labels like Derek Lam and Michael Kors mix with less expensive ones such as J Brand and Nili Lotan. We wish we could move into its posh digs.

La Maison du Chocolat

1018 Madison Avenue, between 78th & 79th Streets (1-212 744 7117/www. lamaisonduchocolat.com). Subway 6 to 77th Street. **Open** *10am-7pm Mon-Sat; noon-6pm Sun.* **Map** *p137 D3* ②⑤
This suave cocoa-brown boutique, the creation of Robert Linxe, packages refined examples of edible Parisian perfection as if it were fine jewellery. A small café serves hot and cold chocolate drinks and a selection of sweets.

Myla

20 E 69th Street, between Fifth & Madison Avenues (1-212 570 1590). Subway 6 to 68th Street-Hunter College. **Open** *10am-6pm Mon-Sat.* **Map** *p137 D4* ②⑥

The Upper West Side's seat of highbrow culture is **Lincoln Center**, a complex of concert halls and auditoria built in the 1960s. It is home to the New York Philharmonic, the New York City Ballet and the Metropolitan Opera, along with a host of other arts organisations. The big circular fountain in the central plaza is a popular gathering spot, especially in summer, when amateur dancers converge on it to dance alfresco at Midsummer Night Swing.

Sights & museums

American Museum of Natural History/Rose Center for Earth & Space

Central Park West, at 79th Street (1-212 769 5100/www.amnh.org). Subway B, C to 81st Street-Museum of Natural History. **Open** 10am-5.45pm daily. **Admission** $13 suggested donation; free-$10 reductions. **Map** p136 C3 ㉓

The thrills begin when you cross the threshold of the Theodore Roosevelt Rotunda, where you're confronted with a towering Barosaurus rearing up to protect its young from an attacking Allosaurus. This impressive welcome to the world's largest museum of its kind acts as a reminder to visit the dinosaur halls on the fourth floor.

The rest of the museum is equally dramatic. The Hall of Biodiversity examines the world's ecosystems, and a life-size model of a blue whale hangs from the cavernous ceiling of the Hall of Ocean Life. The impressive Hall of Meteorites was brushed up and reorganised in 2003. From October to May, the museum installs a tropical butterfly conservatory in the Hall of Oceanic Birds, where visitors can mingle with 500 live specimens.

The spectacular $210 million Rose Center for Earth and Space – dazzling at night – is a giant silvery globe where you can discover the universe via 3-D shows in the Hayden Planetarium and light shows in the Big Bang Theater. An IMAX screens larger-than-life nature programmes, and you can always learn something new from the innovative temporary exhibitions, an easily accessible research library (with vast photo and print archives) and several cool gift shops.

Cathedral Church of St John the Divine

1047 Amsterdam Avenue, at 112th Street (1-212 316 7540/www.stjohn divine.org). Subway B, C, 1 to 110th Street-Cathedral Parkway. **Open** 8am-6pm daily. **Admission** $5; $4 reductions. **Map** p138 B4 ㉙

Construction on 'St John the Unfinished' began in 1892 in Romanesque style, was put on hold for a Gothic revival redesign in 1911, then ground to a halt in 1941, when the US entered World War II. It resumed in earnest in 1979, but a fire in 2001 destroyed the church's gift shop, further delaying completion. In addition to Sunday services, the cathedral hosts concerts and tours. It bills itself as a place for all people – and it means it: annual events include both winter and summer solstice celebrations; the Blessing of the Animals during the Feast of St Francis, which draws pets and their people from all over the city; and, would you believe it, the Blessing of the Bikes, which kicks off the bicycle season each spring.

General Grant National Memorial

Riverside Drive, at 122nd Street (1-212 666 1640). Subway 1 to 125th Street. **Open** 9am-5pm daily. **Admission** free. **Map** p138 A3 ㉚

Who's buried in Grant's Tomb? Technically, no one – the crypts of Civil War hero and 18th president Ulysses S Grant and his wife Julia are in full above-ground view. Note: the memorial is closed on Thanksgiving, Christmas and New Year's days.

Museum of Arts & Design

NEW *From autumn 2008: 2 Columbus Circle, at Broadway (1-212 956 3 535/www.madmuseum.org). Subway A, B, C, D, 1 to 59th Street-Columbus Circle.* **Open** 10am-6pm Mon, Tue, Wed, Fri-Sun; 10am-8pm Thur. **Map** p136 C5 ㉛

Formerly the American Crafts Museum, the Museum of Arts & Design is the country's leading museum of contemporary crafts in clay, cloth, glass, metal and wood. It changed its name to emphasize the harmonious relationships between art, design and craft. The museum plans to open in September 2008, where it will finally be able to display a sizable portion of its permanent collection of more than 2,000 objects. The ten-floor building (originally designed by modernist architect Edward Durell Stone to house the Gallery of Modern Art) will have a restaurant, glassed-walled artists' studios and the first contemporary jewellery gallery in the US.

New-York Historical Society

170 Central Park West, between 76th & 77th Streets (1-212 873 3400/www. nyhistory.org). Subway B, C to 81st Street-Museum of Natural History. **Open** 10am-6pm Tue-Sun. **Admission** $10; free-$5 reductions. No credit cards. **Map** p136 C3 ㉜

New York's oldest museum, founded in 1804, was one of America's first cultural and educational institutions. Highlights in the vast Henry Luce III Center for the Study of American Culture include George Washington's Valley Forge camp cot, a complete series of watercolours from Audubon's *The Birds of America* and the world's largest collection of Tiffany lamps.

Riverside Park

Map p136 A1-A4/p138 A1-A5 ㉝
A sinuous stretch of riverbank that starts at 72nd Street and ends at 158th Street, between Riverside Drive and the Hudson River. The stretch of park below 72nd Street, called Riverside Park South, has a pier and beautiful patches of grass with park benches. You'll see yachts, along with several houseboats, berthed at the 79th Street Boat Basin. In the summertime, there's an open-air café in the adjacent park where New Yorkers unwind with a beer and watch the sun set over the Hudson River.

Time Warner Center

10 Columbus Circle, at Broadway. Subway A, B, C, D, 1 to 59th Street-Columbus Circle. **Open** 8am-10pm daily. **Map** p136 C5 ㉞

The Shops at Columbus Circle takes up the first seven levels of this enormous glass complex and include dozens of retail outlets, including J Crew, Borders Books, Whole Foods and numerous bars and gourmet restaurants.

Eating & drinking

Alice's Teacup

102 W 73rd Street, between Columbus & Amsterdam Avenues (1-212 799 3006/www.alicesteacup.com). Subway B, C, 1, 2, 3 to 72nd Street. **Open** 8am-8pm Mon-Thur; 8am-10pm Fri; 10am-10pm Sat; 10am-8pm Sun. **$**. **Café**. **Map** p136 B4 ㉟

A quaint, homely space with mismatched furniture and scribbles from Lewis Carroll's classic book on the walls. Tea snobs will appreciate the impressive menu of 140 black, green and white blends from all over the globe, and cakes on proper stands.

Barcibo Enoteca

2020 Broadway, between 69th & 70th Streets (1-212 595 2805). Subway 1 to 66th Street. **Open** 5pm-midnight daily. **$$**. **Italian wine bar**. **Map** p136 B4 ㊱

The Upper West Side's latest wine bar offers more than just 100 vinos; the menu features rare spirits and some good small plates too.

Bar Boulud

NEW *1900 Broadway, between 63rd & 64th Streets (1-212 595 0303). Subway 1 to 66th Street-Lincoln Center.* **Open** noon-3.30pm, 5-11pm Mon-Thur; noon-3.30pm, 5pm-midnight Fri; 11am-3.30pm, 5pm-midnight Sat; 11am-3.30pm, 5-11pm Sun. **$$$**. **French**. **Map** p136 B5 ㊲

With Bar Boulud, the formidable Daniel Boulud has uncorked what must be America's first restaurant centered on terrines. There's more here than potted meats, of course: specifically, a heavy dose of bistro standards like coq au vin, escargots and blood sausage.Though the prices here are reasonable by Boulud standards, heavy wine sampling can add up.

Bouchon Bakery

3rd Floor, Time Warner Center, 10 Columbus Circle, at Broadway (1-212 823 9366). Subway A, C, B, D, 1 to 59th Street-Columbus Circle. **Open** 7am-7.30pm daily. **$**. **French**. **Map** p136 C5 ㊳

It has taken chef Thomas Keller, of Per Se (on the floor above), three years to open the New York outpost of his famous French bistro and boulangerie. The sleek 60-seat café also has a chic takeaway shop around the corner. The menu – served throughout the space whether you sit at the espresso/wine bar, the communal table or a marble four-top – includes savoury tartines, hearty soups, rustic pâtés, chocolate tarts and other affordable treats.

Community Food & Juice

NEW *2893 Broadway, between 112th & 113th Streets (1-212-665-2800). Subway 1 to 110th Street-Cathedral Parkway.* **Open** 8am-3.30pm, 6-11pm Mon-Thur; 8am-midnight Fri; 9am-midnight Sat; 9am-4pm Sun. **$$**. **American**. **Map** p138 B4 ❸❾

Clinton Street Baking Company's UWS sibling is quickly becoming a brunch destination. But there's more to eating here than eggs and pancakes: there's a formidable matzo-ball soup and a top-notch grass-fed burger that comes with caramelized onions and Vermont cheddar. Vegetarians will be pleased by the range of creative salads.

Dovetail

NEW *103 W 77th Street at Columbus Avenue (1-212 362 3800). Subway B, C to 81st Street-Museum of Natural History; 1 to 79th Street.* **Open** 5.30-11pm Mon-Sat; 5.30-10pm Sun. **$$**. **American**. **Map** p136 B3 ❹⓪

This upscale gem joins a small class of UWS restaurants that could justify a special trip uptown. Though the earth-toned look smacks of a hotel restaurant and service is dispassionate, the successful menu from chef John Fraser (Compass) has a rich, seasonal emphasis. Foie gras and butter infuse many dishes and meat, such as a charred sirloin accompanied by beef cheek lasagne layered with paper-thin slices of turnips, is equally hearty.

Good Enough to Eat

483 Amsterdam Avenue, between 83rd & 84th Streets (1-212 496-0163). Subway 1 to 86th Street. **Open** 8am-10.30pm Mon-Thur; 8am-11pm Fri; 9am-11pm Sat; 9am-10.30pm Sun. **$**. **American**. **Map** p136 B3 ❹❶

Brunchers crowd Good Enough to Eat's farmhouse-style space for the fluffy eggs, fruit-packed apple pancakes and plump buttermilk biscuits with strawberry butter. Everything – even the chopped salad tossed with bacon and a pinch of sugar – is aimed at hearty appetites and served in grizzly-bear portions. If home cooking were really this good, we'd still be living there.

Gray's Papaya

2090 Broadway, at 71st Street (1-212 799 0243). Subway 1, 2, 3 to 72nd Street. **Open** 24hrs. **$**. **American**. **Map** p136 B4 ❹❷

Many New Yorkers think that Gray's Papaya serves up the classic New York hot dog. The meat itself (all beef) boasts the ever-alluring combination of salty and sweet. Toppings are another matter – debates rage on about how you should garnish your wiener – but you'll find mustard, sauerkraut, sautéed onions and ketchup on the counter.

Kefi

222 W 79th Street, between Amsterdam Avenue & Broadway (1-212 873 0200). Subway 1 to 79th Street. **Open** 5-10pm Tue-Thur, Sun; 5-11pm Fri, Sat. **$$**. **Greek**. No credit cards. **Map** p136 B3 ❹❸

A casual eaterie serving rustic Hellenic cuisine. The equally artful yet laid-back food includes a variety of memorable meze, and flavorful spreads (tsatsiki, aubergine, fava and a top-notch taramasalata). Beverage director Kostas Damianos is vastly knowledgeable about the all-Greek wine list and makes excellent recommendations.

Mermaid Inn

NEW *568 Amsterdam Avenue at 88th Street (1-212 799 7400). Subway 1 to 86th Street.* **Open** 5.30-11pm Mon-Thur; 5-11.30pm Fri, Sat; 5-10pm Sun. **$$**. **Seafood**. **Map** p136 B2 ❹❹

With its nautical theme and fish-shack feel entirely intact, the new Inn offers aquatic fare. Skate wing is here sautéed

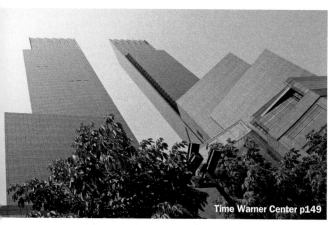

Time Warner Center p149

in fish broth and served with sweet figs. A mélange of beets, Brussels sprouts and hazelnuts alongside two tender monkfish filets suggests why reservations are difficult to score.

Porter House New York

4th Floor, Time Warner Center, 10 Columbus Circle, at 60th Street (1-212 823-9500/www.porterhousenewyork. com). Subway A, C, B, D, 1 to 59th Street-Columbus Circle. **Open** 5-10.30pm Mon-Thur; noon-4.30pm, 5-11pm Fri; 5-11pm Sat; 5-10pm Sun. **$$$. Steakhouse. Map** p136 C5
The latest restaurant from chef Michael Lomonaco has large portions and fair prices, all things considered. The steaks get a glorious char, though it can sometimes overpower the flavour of the meat. The wine list doesn't offer much at the lower end of the price spectrum, but there are plenty of half-bottles.

Telepan

72 W 69th Street, at Columbus Avenue (1-212 580 4300). Subway B, C to 72nd Street; 1 to 66th Street-Lincoln Center. **Open** 5-11pm Mon, Tue; 11.30am-2.30pm, 5-11pm Wed, Thur; 11.30am-2.30pm, 5pm-midnight Fri; 11am-2.30pm, 5pm-midnight Sat; 11am-2.30pm, 5-10.30pm Sun. **$$$. American. Map** p136 B4

The place isn't fancy, but it does get the basic things right. Diners can customise their $55 prix fixe dinners by selecting three dishes from any three columns on the menu; they can ask for assistance and get smart feedback; and they can count on fresh, Greenmarket-inspired fare featuring ingredients such as hen of the woods mushrooms, brook trout and organic lamb.

Toast

NEW *2737 Broadway at 105th Street (1-212 663 7010). Subway 1 to 103rd Street.* **Open** 5-11pm Mon-Wed; 5pm-midnight Thur, Fri; 11am-4pm, 5pm-midnight Sat; 11am-4pm, 5-11pm Sun. **$. American. Map** p138 B5
Raise a bruschetta to the wonder of Toast, where the pasta with chicken and pesto cream sauce is awesome. The mesquite-smoked barbecued-pork sandwich rules. The skirt-steak appetizer rocks. The raspberry swirl cheesecake kicks ass.

Shopping

H&H Bagels

2239 Broadway, at 80th Street (1-212 595 8003/www.hhbagels.com). Subway 1 to 79th Street. **Open** 24hrs daily. **Map** p136 B3

For a taste of the real, old-fashioned (boiled and baked) thing, head straight to H&H, which lays claim to being the city's largest bagel purveyor.

Zabar's

2245 Broadway, at 80th Street (1-212 787 2000/www.zabars.com). Subway 1 to 79th Street. **Open** 8am-7.30pm Mon-Fri; 8am-8pm Sat; 9am-6pm Sun. **Map** p136 B3 ➍➒

Zabar's is more than just a food store, it's a true New York landmark. You might leave the place feeling a little light in the wallet, but you can't beat the top-flight foods on offer. Besides the famous smoked fish and rafts of Jewish delicacies, Zabar's has fabulous selections of bread, cheese and coffee – and an entire floor of well-priced gadgets and housewares.

Nightlife

Dizzy's Club Coca-Cola: Jazz at Lincoln Center

Broadway, at 60th Street (1-212 258 9595/www.jazzatlincolncenter.org). Subway A, B, C, D, 1 to 59th Street-Columbus Circle. **Shows** at 7.30pm, 9.30pm. **Map** p136 C5 ➎➊

Seductively lit, decorated with elegant photography and blessed with clear sight lines and a gorgeous view of 59th Street and Central Park South, Dizzy's Club Coca-Cola might be a Hollywood cinematographer's ideal vision of what a Manhattan jazz club ought to be. The swanky, intimate club – a regular hangout for some of the most outstanding players in the business – is a class act in everything but its clunky, commercialised name.

Smoke

2751 Broadway, between 105th & 106th Streets (1-212 864 6662/www. smokejazz.com). Subway 1 to 103rd Street. **Shows** 9pm, 11pm, 12.30am Mon-Sat; 6pm Sun. **Map** p138 B5 ➎➊

Not unlike a swanky living room, Smoke is a classy little joint that acts as a haven for local jazz legends and any touring artists looking to play an intimate space. Early in the week,

evenings are themed: on Sunday, it's Latin jazz; Tuesday, organ jazz. On weekends, internationally renowned jazzers (Hilton Ruiz, Tom Harrell, Eddie Henderson) hit the stage, relishing the opportunity to play informal gigs uptown.

Arts & leisure

Lincoln Center

Columbus Avenue, at 65th Street (1-212 546 2656/www.lincolncenter.org). Subway 1 to 66th Street-Lincoln Center. **Map** p136 B5 ➎➋

The listing above is the main entry point for Lincoln Center, although the venues that follow are spread out across the square of blocks from 62nd to 66th Streets, between Amsterdam and Columbus Avenues.

Built in the 1960s, this massive complex is the nexus of Manhattan's performing arts scene. Lincoln Center hosts lectures and symposia in the Rose Building, in addition to events in the main halls: Alice Tully Hall, Avery Fisher Hall, Metropolitan Opera House, New York State Theater, the Vivian Beaumont and Mitzi E Newhouse Theaters and the Walter Reade Theater. **Alice Tully Hall** *1-212 875 5050.* Home to the Chamber Music Society of Lincoln Center (1-212 875 5788, www.chambermusicsociety.org), Alice Tully Hall somehow manages to make its 1,096 seats feel cosy. It has no centre aisle, and the seating offers decent legroom. The venue's 'Art of the Song' series ranks among Lincoln Center's most inviting offerings.

Avery Fisher Hall *1-212 875 5030.* This handsome, comfortable 2,700-seat hall is the headquarters of the New York Philharmonic (1-212 875 5656, www.nyphilharmonic.org), the country's oldest symphony orchestra (founded in 1842) and one of its finest. The acoustics, which range from good to atrocious depending on who you ask, stand to be improved. Look for the inexpensive, early evening 'rush hour' concerts and open rehearsals that are presented on a regular basis.

Metropolitan Opera House *1-212 362 6000/www.metopera.org.*

The Met is the grandest of the Lincoln Center buildings, so it's a spectacular place to see and hear opera. It hosts the Metropolitan Opera from September to May, and major visiting companies during the summer. Opera's biggest stars (think Domingo, Fleming and Voigt) appear here regularly, and artistic director James Levine has turned the orchestra into a true symphonic force. Audiences are knowledgeable and fiercely partisan, with subscriptions remaining in families for generations. Still, the Met has become more inclusive; digital English-language subtitles, which appear on screens affixed to railings in front of each seat, are convenient for the novice and unobtrusive to their more seasoned neighbour. Tickets are expensive, and unless you can afford good seats, the view won't be great; standing-room-only tickets start at $15, and you'll have to queue on Saturday morning to buy them. At least you'll be able to see the eye-popping, gasp-inducing sets that remain the gold standard.

New York State Theater *1-212 870 5570.*

NYST houses the New York City Ballet (www.nycballet.com) as well as the New York City Opera (www.nyc-opera.com). The opera company has tried to overcome its second-best reputation by being both ambitious and defiantly populist. Rising young American singers often take their first bows at City Opera (many of them eventually make the trek across the plaza to the Met), where casts and productions tend to be younger and sexier than those of its more patrician counterpart. Known for its fierce commitment to the unconventional – from modern American works and musical-theatre productions to intriguing Handel stagings and forgotten bel canto gems – City Opera is considerably cooler than its neighbour and, more importantly, about half the price. But truly splashy grand spectacle remains the province of the Met.

Walter Reade Theater *1-212 875 5600/www.filmlinc.com.* **No credit cards.**

The Walter Reade Theater's acoustics are less than fabulous; still, the Chamber Music Society uses the space regularly, and the 'Great Performers' series offers Sunday morning events fuelled by pastries and hot beverages sold in the lobby.

Merkin Concert Hall

Kaufman Center, 129 W 67th Street, between Broadway & Amsterdam Avenue (1-212 501 3330/www. kaufman-center.org). Subway 1 to 66th Street-Lincoln Center. **Map** p136 B4 ⑤⑨

Tucked away on a side street in the shadow of Lincoln Center, this unimposing gem of a concert hall offers a robust mix of early music and avant-garde programming, as well as an increasing amount of jazz, folk and some more eclectic fare. Here the New York Festival of Song has finally found a comfortable home, while regular performances sponsored by WNYC-FM afford opportunities for casual interaction with composers and performers.

Miller Theatre at Columbia University

Broadway, at 116th Street (1-212 854 7799/www.millertheatre.com). Subway 1 to 116th Street-Columbia University. **Map** p138 B4 ⑥④

Columbia's Miller Theatre has single-handedly made contemporary classical music sexy in New York. The credit belongs to executive director George Steel, who proved that presenting challenging fare by composers such as Babbitt, Ferneyhough and Scelsi in a casual, unaffected setting could attract a young audience – and hang on to it. Miller's early-music offerings, many conducted by Steel, are also exemplary.

Symphony Space

2537 Broadway, at 95th Street (1-212 864 5400/www.symphonyspace.org). Subway 1, 2, 3 to 96th Street. **Map** p136 B1 ⑥⑤

Despite its name, Symphony Space provides concerts that are anything but symphony-centric: recent seasons have featured saxophone quartets, Indian classical music and politically astute performances of Purcell's *Dido and Aeneas*. The annual 'Wall to Wall' marathons serve up a full day of free music focusing on a particular composer, from Bach to Sondheim.

Harlem & beyond

Harlem is not just a destination on Manhattan island – it's the cultural capital of black America. West Harlem, between Fifth and St Nicholas Avenues, is the Harlem of popular imagination, and 125th Street is its lifeline. Harlem's historic districts continue to gentrify. The Mount Morris Historic District (from 119th to 124th Streets, between Malcolm X Boulevard (Lenox Avenue) & Mount Morris Park West) contains charming brownstones and a collection of religious buildings in a variety of architectural styles.

These days, new boutiques, restaurants and pavement cafés dot the walk down the double-wide **Malcolm X Boulevard** (Lenox Avenue). Another area with a historic past is **Strivers' Row**, also known as the St Nicholas Historic District. Running from 138th to 139th Streets, between Adam Clayton Powell Jr Boulevard (Seventh Avenue) and Frederick Douglass Boulevard (Eighth Avenue), these blocks of majestic houses were developed in 1891. East of Fifth Avenue is East Harlem, sometimes called Spanish Harlem but better known to its primarily Puerto Rican residents as El Barrio.

At the northern tip of Manhattan in pretty Fort Tryon Park, you'll find the **Cloisters**, a museum built in 1938 incorporating segments of medieval cloisters shipped from Europe by the Rockefeller clan. It currently houses the Metropolitan

Museum of Art's permanent medieval art collection, including the exquisite *Unicorn Tapestries*, woven around 1500.

Sights & museums

Abyssinian Baptist Church

132 W 138th Street, between Malcolm X Boulevard (Lenox Avenue) & Adam Clayton Powell Jr Boulevard (Seventh Avenue) (1-212 862 7474/www. abyssinian.org). Subway 2, 3 to 135th Street. **Open** 9am-5pm Mon-Fri. **Admission** free. **Map** p138 C1 ⑤
The place where Harlem's controversial 1960s congressman Adam Clayton Powell Jr once preached is celebrated for its history, political activism and rousing gospel service. A small museum is dedicated to Powell, the first black member of New York's City Council.

Cloisters

Fort Tryon Park, Fort Washington Avenue, at Margaret Corbin Plaza (1-212 923 3700/www.metmuseum.org). Subway A to 190th Street, then M4 bus. **Open** *Mar-Oct* 9.30am-5.15pm Tue-Sun. *Nov-Feb* 9.30am-4.45pm Tue-Sun. **Admission** $15 suggested donation (includes admission to the Metropolitan Museum of Art on the same day); free-$10 reductions.
Set in a lovely park overlooking the Hudson River, the Cloisters houses the Met's medieval art and architecture collections. A path winds through the peaceful grounds to a castle that seems to have survived from the Middle Ages. (It was built a mere 70 years ago, using pieces from five medieval French cloisters.) Be sure to see the famous *Unicorn Tapestries* and Robert Campin's *Annunciation Triptych*.

Hispanic Society of America

Audubon Terrace, Broadway, between 155th & 156th Streets (1-212 926 2234/www.hispanicsociety.org). Subway 1 to 157th Street. **Open** 10am-4.30pm Tue-Sat; 1-4pm Sun. **Admission** free.
The Hispanic Society has the largest assemblage of Spanish manuscripts

and art and outside Spain. Look for two portraits by Goya and the lobby's bas-relief of Don Quixote. The collection is dominated by religious artefacts, but there are also decorative art objects and thousands of photographs documenting Spanish and Latin-American life from the 19th century to the present.

Morris-Jumel Mansion

65 Jumel Terrace, between 160th & 162nd Streets (1-212 923 8008/www. morrisjumel.org). Subway C to 163rd Street-Amsterdam Avenue. **Open** 10am-4pm Wed-Sun. **Admission** $4; free-$3 reductions. No credit cards.
Built in 1765, Manhattan's only surviving pre-Revolutionary manse was originally the heart of a 130-acre estate that stretched from river to river (on the grounds, a stone marker points south with the legend 'new york, 11 miles'). George Washington planned the Battle of Harlem Heights here in 1776, after the British colonel Roger Morris moved out. The handsome 18th-century Palladian-style villa offers fantastic views.

Studio Museum in Harlem

144 W 125th Street, between Malcolm X Boulevard (Lenox Avenue) & Adam Clayton Powell Jr Boulevard (Seventh Avenue) (1-212 864 4500/www.studio museum.org). Subway 2, 3 to 125th Street. **Open** noon-6pm Wed-Fri, Sun; 10am-6pm Sat. Guided tours by appointment. **Admission** suggested donation $7; free-$3 reductions. No credit cards. **Map** p138 C3 ⑤⑦
When the Studio Museum opened in 1968, it was the first black fine arts museum in the country, and it remains the place to go for historical insight into African-American art and that of the African diaspora. It's also the city's most exciting showcase for contemporary African-American artists.

Eating & drinking

Coogan's

4015 Broadway, at 169th Street (1-212 928 1234). Subway A, C, 1 to 168th Street-Washington Heights. **Open** 11am-4am daily. **Bar**.

Clap your hands!

'From the drumbeats of Mother Africa to the work songs and spirituals created in a new land, a path is traced to the blues, gospel, jazz, rhythm and blues, soul, and hip-hop expressions of African Americans that are celebrated throughout the world.' So goes the press release for 'Honor! A Celebration of the African American Cultural Legacy', a music festival that kicks off in early March 2009. New York is America's first city when it comes to music, and African American musicians, singers and songwriters, in particular, have shone brightly on city stages, in music halls, in churches and on street corners for decades. It's only fitting that such a celebration of African American popular music takes place here. The event is curated by Jesse Norman, the four-time Grammy award winner, and Ms Norman invites participants to concerts, recitals, lectures, discussions and exhibitions hosted by the Apollo Theater (p157) and other sites around the city. Jesse Norman will pay homage to Duke Ellington in a concert that will also feature a jazz ensemble, string quartet, gospel choir and a dancer. She adds: 'The vast cultural fabric of the African American experience consists not only of the music, but also the words, the images, and the dances of a people, all providing rich fulfillment of the Langston Hughes credo: "Hold fast to dreams".'
■ www.carnegiehall.org

Harlem p154

families and Columbia brainiacs. Fried chicken soaked in buttermilk and honey is plump and moist. Each main dish scores two sides, such as wilted greens and four-cheese macaroni.

New Leaf Café

Fort Tryon Park, 1 Margaret Corbin Drive (1-212 568 5323). Subway A to 190th Street; take elevator to Fort Washington Avenue, then walk into Fort Tryon Park. **Open** 6-10pm Tue; noon-3pm, 6-10pm Wed-Sat; 11am-4pm, 5.30-9.30pm Sun. **$$. American.** Whether you enjoy smoked trout and pear salad on the garden patio, or a Bloody Mary with brunch in the dining room of the 1930s stone building, you'll be surrounded by the park's natural beauty, and you'll be helping to conserve it. The views are more dazzling than the mildly adventurous food, but this is one case where everybody wins.

Soundz Lounge

3155 Broadway, between Tiemann Place & La Salle Street (1-212 537 7660). Subway 1 to 125th Street. **Open** 4pm-4am daily. **Bar. Map** p138 B3 ⑤⑨ During happy hour, this comfortable, cavelike hangout serves fresh watermelon martinis, sugary 'shotz' like the Bomb Diggity Bomb (blue curaçao, Myers's rum and pineapple juice) and 24 varieties of $3 pints. And, when it comes to those 'soundz', you'll hear 1980s, retro, neo-soul or reggae.

All types pop up at this uptown Irish bar. Tuesdays and Saturdays are dedicated to belting out bilingual karaoke (in Spanish and English).

809 Sangria Bar & Grill

112 Dyckman Street, between Nagle & Post Avenues (1-212 304 3800). Subway 1 to Dyckman Street. **Open** 11.45am-11pm Mon-Wed; 11.45am-midnight Thur, Fri; 11.45am-1am Sat; 5-11pm Sun. **$$. Latin.** An upscale Latin restaurant near the top of Manhattan. Patrons feast on modern updates of classic dishes and take in original oil paintings by Dominican artists. This is sangria heaven, with half a dozen varieties on the menu.

Kitchenette Uptown

1272 Amsterdam Avenue, between 122nd & 123rd Streets (1-212 531 7600). Subway 1 to 125th Street. **Open** 8am-11pm Mon-Fri; 9am-11pm Sat, Sun. **$. American. Map** p138 B3 ⑤⑧ Uptown emphasises the rich side of country fare, which is fine with local

Shopping

Everything Must Go

2281 First Avenue, between 117th & 118th Streets (1-212 722 8203). Subway 6 to 116th Street. **Open** noon-7pm Tue-Sun. **Map** p139 E4 ⑥⓪ A skateboarder's haven, Everything Must Go is a welcome addition to the neighbourhood. This cool shop also carries Vigilantee and Billionaire Boys Club T-shirts and charm necklaces.

Harlemade

174 Malcolm X Boulevard (Lenox Avenue), between 118th & 119th Streets (1-212 987 2500/www.

*harlemade.com). Subway 2, 3 to 116th
Street.* **Open** 11.30am-7.30pm Tue-Sat;
noon-5pm Sun. **Map** p138 C4 ⑥①
Sells T-shirts with Afro- and Harlem-
centric messages and images, along
with postcards, books and other neighbourhood memorabilia.

Hue-Man
Bookstore & Café

*2319 Frederick Douglass Boulevard
(Eighth Avenue), between 124th &
125th Streets (1-212 665 7400/
www.huemanbookstore.com). Subway
A, B, C, D to 125th Street.* **Open**
10am-8pm Mon-Sat; 11am-7pm Sun.
Map p138 C3 ⑥②
The emphasis is on African-American
work at this spacious Harlem bookstore and café, which features frequent
readings as well as in-store appearances by authors and other events.

N

*114 W 116th Street, between Malcolm
X Boulevard (Lenox Avenue) & Adam
Clayton Powell Jr Boulevard (Seventh
Avenue) (1-212 961 1036/www.
nharlemnewyork.com). Subway 2, 3
to 116th Street; A, C, E to 116th
Street.* **Open** 11.30am-8pm Tue-Thur;
11.30am-9pm Fri, Sat; noon-5pm Sun.
Map p138 C4 ⑥③
N aspires to pioneer upscale retail in
Harlem just as the downtown fashion
megastore did in the Meatpacking
District. Owners Larry Ortiz, Nikoa
Evans and Lenn Shebar provide locals
with 4,000sq ft of elegant urban garb.

Nightlife

Apollo Theater

*253 W 125th Street, between Adam
Clayton Powell Jr Boulevard (Seventh
Avenue) & Frederick Douglass
Boulevard (Eighth Avenue) (1-212
531 5305/www.apollotheater.com).
Subway A, B, C, D, 1 to 125th
Street.* **Map** p138 C3 ⑥④
The city's home of R&B and soul
music is much cosier than it looks on
TV's *Showtime at the Apollo*. Known
for launching the careers of Ella
Fitzgerald, Michael Jackson and
D'Angelo, to name just a few, the

Apollo continues to bring in veteran
talent while offering wannabe stars a
legendary stage on which to perform.

Lenox Lounge

*288 Malcolm X Boulevard (Lenox
Avenue), between 124th & 125th
Streets (1-212 427 0253/www.
lenoxlounge.com). Subway 2, 3 to
125th Street.* **Open** noon-4am daily.
Map p138 C3 ⑥⑤
This classy art deco lounge in Harlem
once hosted Billie Holiday and has
been drawing stars since the late 1930s.
Saxist Patience Higgins's Sugar Hill
Jazz Quartet jams on Monday nights.

Uptown Jazz Lounge at
Minton's Playhouse

*20 W 118th Street, between St Nicholas
Avenue & Adam Clayton Powell Jr.
Boulevard (1-212 864 8346/www.
uptownatmintons.com) Subway B, C to
116th Street.* **Open** 2pm-4am daily.
Map p138 C4 ⑥⑥
One of the true jewels in Harlem's
crown, Minton's Playhouse reopened
recently after being boarded up for
more than 30 years. Few clubs in the
city can boast as rich a history as
Minton's, which Miles Davis once
dubbed 'the black jazz capital of the
world.' During the 1940s, when
Thelonious Monk was the resident
pianist, late-night jams brought such
luminaries as Dizzy Gillespie and
Charlie Parker to the club, giving birth
to bebop. Minton's presents five house
bands from Sunday through
Thursday, with guest acts like Joe
Chambers at weekends.

Arts & leisure

Schomburg Center for
Research in Black Culture

*515 Malcolm X Boulevard (Lenox
Avenue), at 135th Street (1-212 491
2200). Subway 2, 3 to 135th Street.*
Open noon-8pm Tue, Wed; noon-6pm
Thur, Fri; 10am-6pm Sat. **Admission**
free. **Map** p138 C2 ⑥⑦
A trove of vintage literature and historical memorabilia relating to black
culture and the African diaspora.

Brooklyn Bridge

The Outer Boroughs

Bronx

Bronx Zoo/Wildlife Conservation Society

Bronx River Parkway, at Fordham Road (1-718 367 1010/www.bronxzoo.org). Subway 2, 5 to West Farms Square-East Tremont Avenue. **Open** *Apr-Oct* 10am-5pm Mon-Fri; 10am-5.30pm Sat, Sun, holidays. *Nov-Mar* 10am-4.30pm daily. **Admission** $14; $12 reductions. Voluntary donation Wed. (Some rides and exhibitions are extra.)

The elusive snow leopard wanders across the peaks of the Himalayan Highlands, and more than 30 species of Rodentia co-exist in the Mouse House. Birds, giraffes, lions and reptiles abound in a zoo that is home to more than 4,500 creatures. For visitors who want a bird's-eye view, the 'Skyfari', an aerial tram ride over the zoo, is won-derful. Groundcrawlers can jump on the Zoo Shuttle, which provides rides (for a few dollars) through the zoo. Tiger Mountain is a three-acre perma-nent display devoted to Siberian tigers, the largest of the big cats. Highlights include an underwater viewing area, kiosks to educate visitors about tigers and conservation, as well as talks and demonstrations. The Butterfly Garden is a big hit with children, featuring more than 1,000 colourful butterflies fluttering about in an enclosed habitat.

New York Botanical Garden

Bronx River Parkway, at Fordham Road (1-718 817 8700/www.nybg.org). Travel: B, D to Bedford Park Boulevard, then take the Bx26 bus to Garden gate; or Metro-North (Harlem Line local) from Grand Central Terminal to Botanical Garden.

Warm Up at P.S.1 Contemporary Art Center p164

Open *Mar-Oct* 10am-6pm Tue-Sun, Mon federal holidays. *Jan, Feb* 10am-5pm Tue-Sun. **Admission** $20; $18 seniors, students; $7 2-12s; free under-2s. Grounds only $6; free 10am-5pm Wed; 10am-noon Sat.

As well as access to 250 acres of flora, the $20 you pay for your ticket buys entry to all the current exhibitions, the Adventure Garden, the Haupt Conservatory and tram tours. If you're coming from Manhattan, look into specials from Metro-North's Harlem line train from Grand Central Terminal, which may include a round-trip ticket with admission.

New York Yankees

Yankee Stadium, River Avenue, at 161st Street, Bronx (1-718 293 6000/ www.yankees.com). Subway B, D, 4 to 161st Street-Yankee Stadium. **Open** Box office 9am-5pm Mon-Sat; 10am-4pm Sun; and during games.
Tickets $8-$95.

Yankee fans bid farewell to the iconic 84-year old stadium in 2008. The new stadium, right next door, 'will present new comforts, new features and be state-of-the-art in every way,' Yankees president Randy Levine said. 'It will be the most spectacular fan-friendly stadium ever built.'

Brooklyn

Brooklyn Botanic Garden

900 Washington Avenue, at Eastern Parkway, Prospect Heights (1-718 623 7200/www.bbg.org). Subway B, Q, Franklin Avenue S to Prospect Park; 2, 3 to Eastern Parkway-Brooklyn Museum. **Open** *Apr-Sept* 8am-6pm Tue-Fri; 10am-6pm Sat, Sun. *Oct-Mar* 8am-4.30pm Tue-Fri; 10am-4.30pm Sat, Sun. **Admission** $8; $4 reductions; free Tue; free late Nov-Feb Tue-Fri.

Fifty-two acres of greenery await you at Brooklyn Botanic Garden. During spring hightail it out here for the blooming of more than 220 cherry blossoms. The newly renovated Eastern Parkway entrance and the Osborne Garden – a three-acre Italian-style formal garden – are also worth a peek.

New York Botanical Garden p158

Brooklyn Museum

200 Eastern Parkway, at Washington Avenue, Prospect Heights, Brooklyn (1-718 638 5000/www.brooklynmuseum. org). Subway 2, 3 to Eastern Parkway-Brooklyn Museum. **Open** *10am-5pm Wed-Fri; 11am-6pm Sat, Sun. 1st Sat of mth (except Sept) 11am-11pm.* **Admission** *$8; free-$4 reductions; free 5-11pm 1st Sat of mth.*

Brooklyn's premier institution is a tranquil alternative to Manhattan's big-name exhibition spaces and it's rarely crowded. Among the museum's many assets is a rich, 4,000-piece Egyptian collection, which includes a gilded ebony statue of Amenhotep III and, on a ceiling, a large-scale rendering of an ancient map of the cosmos. You can even view a mummy preserved in its original coffin.

Masterworks by Cézanne, Monet and Degas, part of an impressive European painting and sculpture collection, are displayed in the museum's skylighted Beaux Arts Court. On the fifth floor, American paintings and sculptures include native son Thomas Cole's *The Pic-Nic* and Louis Rémy Mignot's *Niagara*, a stunning vista of the falls. Don't miss the renowned Pacific Island and African galleries (this was the first American museum to display African objects as art). A new centre devoted to feminist art opened in 2007.

Brooklyn Tourism & Visitor Center

Brooklyn Borough Hall, 209 Joralemon Street, between Court & Adams Streets (1-718 802 3846/www.visitbrooklyn. org). Subway 2, 3, 4, 5 to Borough Hall; M, R to Court Street; A, C, F to Jay Street (Borough Hall is 3 blocks west). **Open** *10am-6pm Mon-Fri.*

Studio B

259 Banker Street, between Meserole & Calyer Streets, Greenpoint, Brooklyn (1-718 389 1880). Subway L to Bedford Avenue. **Open** *10pm-4am Fri, Sat.*

It's way off the normal beaten track – in the deep, dark outskirts of Brooklyn's Greenpoint neighbourhood,

Bronx Zoo p158

to be precise – but since opening at the end of 2006, the one-time Polish disco Studio B has been regularly packing hundreds of cool kids on to its ample dance floor. The secret to Studio B's success is simple: zero attitude, an ace sound system and a forward-thinking booking policy. The list of DJs and bands who have played at Studio B is a sterling one, with techno deity Carl Craig, electro-house duo Booka Shade, neo-disco band Escort and the nu-ravey Klaxons just a small sampling of those who have braved the G train to rock the house.

Queens

Aqueduct Racetrack
110-00 Rockaway Boulevard, at 110th Street, Jamaica, Queens (1-718 641 4700/www.nyra.com). Subway A to Aqueduct Racetrack. **Races** Thoroughbred Oct-May Wed-Sun. **Admission** *Clubhouse* $2. *Grandstand* $1. Free early Jan-early Mar. No credit cards.

The Wood Memorial – a test run for promising three-year-old horses – is held here each spring. Betting is, of course, legal at all New York tracks.

New York Mets
Shea Stadium, 123-01 Roosevelt Avenue, at 126th Street, Flushing, Queens (1-718 507 8499/www.mets.com). Subway 7 to Willets Point-Shea Stadium. **Open** Box office 9am-5.30pm Mon-Fri; 9am-2pm Sat, Sun. **Tickets** $5-$53.

The Mets are New York's 'other' baseball team. Not to be outdone by the Yankees, the team is also opening a new stadium in 2009: Citi Field will open next to Shea Stadium.

Noguchi Museum
9-01 33rd Road, between Vernon Boulevard & 10th Street, Long Island City, Queens (1-718 204 7088/www.noguchi.org). Subway N, W to Broadway, then take Q104 bus to 11th Street; or 7 to Vernon Boulevard-Jackson Avenue, then take Q103 bus to 10th Street.

Williamsburg beer crawl

Gutter

'He couldn't understand why we don't serve Budweiser.' We smiled at the bartender's remark, ordered an Allagash White, and knew that the **Gutter** (200 North 14th Street, between Berry Street & Wythe Avenue, 1-718 387 3585) is the right bar to begin our Williamsburg beer crawl. This eight-lane bowling alley that looks straight out of early-1980s Milwaukee not only offers up a chance to make an ass of yourself as you attempt to make balls meet pins but they have a dozen killer microbrews to numb your low-score shame. Excellent choices are Maine's Allagash White or anything from the nearby Brooklyn Brewery.

South 11 blocks is **Radegast Hall & Biergarten** (113 N 3rd Street, at Berry Street, 1-718 963 3973). This new-to-the-'hood beer garden pours a primarily German and Czech selection of suds – 13 on tap and 41 by the bottle. Down a refreshing Gaffel Kölsh under the retractable roof or take a seat at one of the 16-foot-long communal tables made from salvaged fir. Snacks, like weisswurst, a veal and pork sausage, are sourced from local butchers. A mug of BrauCzech from a durndel-clad waitress makes the perfect pairing to the bratwurst and sauerkraut.

In contrast to the buzzing Radegast, the unmarked **Spuyten Duyvil** (359 Metropolitan Avenue, at Havemayer Street, 1-718 963 4140) provides a secluded setting in which to enjoy its selection of brews. Admire the precise pour of a Trappistes Rochefort 10, and toast your pals out back on the deck. Follow that Rochefort with Coniston Bluebird Bitter and get ready for game time.

Barcade (388 Union Avenue, between Ainslie & Powers Streets, 1-718 302 6464) is a made-in-heaven match of microbrews and classic arcade games. A 25-strong beer menu is a brilliant match-up to the 27 cult games here, which include violence-free Q*Bert and '80s racing fave Out Run. With any luck, after several beers Super Mario lovers will remember where the hidden stars are.
■ www.Beerlord.com.

Open 10am-5pm Wed-Fri; 11am-6pm Sat, Sun. **Admission** $10; $5 reductions. No credit cards.
In addition to his famous lamps, artist Isamu Noguchi (1904-88) designed stage sets for Martha Graham and George Balanchine, as well as large-scale sculptures. The museum is located in a 1920s-era factory in Queens; galleries surround a serene sculpture garden that was designed by Noguchi himself. The building, which was recently renovated to the tune of $13.5 million, now stays open year-round. Look for the second-floor galleries devoted to Noguchi's interior design, a new café and a shop. A shuttle service

from Manhattan is available at weekends (call the museum or visit the website for further information on this).

US Open

USTA National Tennis Center, Flushing Meadows-Corona Park, Queens (1-866 673 6849/www.usopen. org). Subway 7 to Willets Point-Shea Stadium. **Tickets** $22-$120. Late Aug.
Tickets go on sale late in the spring for this Grand Slam, hard court thriller, which the United States Tennis Association (USTA) claims to be the highest-attended annual sporting event in the world. Check the website for match schedules and prices.

NEW YORK BY AREA

Brooklyn Museum p160

P.S.1 Contemporary Art Center

22-25 Jackson Avenue, at 46th Avenue, Long Island City, Queens (1-718 784 2084/www.ps1.org). Subway E, V to 23rd Street-Ely Avenue; G to 21st Street-Jackson Avenue; 7 to 45th Road-Court House Square. **Open** *noon-6pm Mon, Thur-Sun.* **Admission** *suggested donation $5; $2 reductions.*

Cutting-edge shows and an international studio programme make each visit to this freewheeling art space an experience. In a Romanesque revival building that still bears some resemblance to the public school it once was, P.S.1 mounts shows that appeal to adults and children. P.S.1 became an affiliate of the Museum of Modern Art in 1999, but it has a wholly independent schedule of temporary exhibitions, along with a decidedly global outlook. Be sure to check out the summer Warm Up dance party series.

Queens Museum of Art

New York City Building, park entrance on 49th Avenue, at 111th Street, Flushing Meadows-Corona Park (1-718 592 9700/www.queensmuseum.org). Subway 7 to 111th Street. Walk south on 111th Street, then turn left on to 49th Avenue. Continue into the park and over Grand Central Parkway Bridge. **Open** *26 June-5 Sept 1-8pm Wed-Sun. 6 Sept-25 June 10am-5pm Wed-Fri; noon-5pm Sat, Sun.* **Admission** *$5; $2.50 seniors, students; free under-5s. No credit cards.*

Studio B p160

Located in the grounds of the 1939 and 1964 World's Fairs, the QMA holds one of the area's most amazing sights: a 9,335sq ft scale model of New York City, accurate down to the square inch – at least up to 1994, the date of its last major renovation. In early 2007, the Panorama unveiled a long-overdue upgrade: an updated lighting system now mimics the arc of the sun as it passes over NYC, while a new 13-minute multimedia presentation explores the Panorama's construction and spotlights various NYC attractions, including Shea Stadium, Times Square and the Triborough Bridge.

Essentials

6 Columbus p181

Hotels

Undersupplied – that's the word the experts reach for when trying to explain why hotel rates continue to break records in leaps and bounds. It seems there are many more people wanting to sleep in Manhattan than there are beds. Occupancy rates here continue to hover around 85 per cent, compared to 65 per cent in the rest of the US. By and large, a place to rest your head, or at least store your luggage while you're out on the town, will cost you, on average, somewhere in the region of $325. Still, there is hope that rates will eventually level off, as 13,000 new (or renovated) hotel rooms are expected to be available by 2010; though your guess is as good as ours when it comes to predicting how things will play out in the long run. In the meantime, the mini hotel-boom in Brooklyn should soften the blow of rising rates in Manhattan (see box p178).

Stylish and pricey hotels are opening all the time in New York. Recent openings include Robert De Niro's long awaited **Greenwich Hotel** (p172) — though don't expect to be tucked in by the former *Goodfellas* star, or even to see him walking the halls; he's a silent partner. The folks behind the glamorous **60 Thompson** (p173) have launched not one but four new hotels in less than two years, including **6 Columbus** (p181). If you're after something a little more off the radar, but no less stylish, than check out Tribeca's **Duane Street Hotel** (p172).

Happily, there is one bright spot for budget-minded travellers: the colourful **Pod Hotel** (p180), which opened not long ago in the old Pickwick Arms Hotel on Midtown's east side. At press time, rooms could be had here for as little as $140 a night – plus you're within walking distance of the Museum of Modern Art and the Rockefeller Center.

Whatever your hotel needs we've included a hotel to fit the bill. Price categories are as follows: Deluxe $300+ **$$$$**; Expensive $200-$300 **$$$**; Moderate $100-$200 **$$**; Budget $100 and under **$**.

The hunt

Your chances of finding a room will be boosted if you start looking a few months before you intend to travel. Decide on your price range and choose a neighbourhood that interests you. Be sure to include New York's 13.625 per cent room tax and a $2 to $6 per-night occupancy tax when planning your budget. And be warned: many smaller hotels in the city adhere to a strict three-night minimum booking policy.

Pre-booking blocks of rooms allows reservation companies to offer reduced rates. The following agencies don't charge for their services: **Hotel Reservations Network** (1-214 369 1264, 1-800 246 8357, www.hotels.com); **Quikbook**, 3rd Floor, 381 Park Avenue South, New York, NY 10016 (1-212 779 7666, 1-800 789 9887, www.quikbook.com).

Downtown

Abingdon Guest House

13 Eighth Avenue, between Jane & W 12th Streets (1-212 243 5384/www. abingdonguesthouse.com). Subway A, C, E to 14th Street; L to Eighth Avenue. $$.
This charming guesthouse is a good option if you want to be near the Meatpacking District but can't afford

---

S H O R T L I S T

Best new
- Greenwich Hotel (p172)
- Gild Hall (p172)

Best for hipsters
- Chelsea Hotel (p169)
- Hotel 17 (p172)
- Hotel on Rivington (p172)

Fashion shoot favourites
- Bowery Hotel (p169)
- Hotel Gansevoort (p172)
- 60 Thompson (p173)

Most stellar restaurants
- Mercer (p173)
- Four Seasons Hotel (p176)

Best hotel bars
- Dream Hotel (p176)
- Maritime Hotel (p173)
- W New York-Times Square (p180)

Best super-cheap
- Jazz on the Park Hostel (p181)
- Central Park Hostel (p181)
- East Village Bed & Coffee (p172)
- Chelsea Star Hotel (p171)

Cheap for the location
- Pod Hotel (p180)
- Hotel Beacon (p181)
- Hotel Pennsylvania (p177)
- Hudson (p178)

Best old New York
- The Waldorf-Astoria (p180)
- The Pierre (p181)
- The Algonquin (p175)

Cosy comfort
- Inn on 23rd Street (p172)
- Abingdon Guest House (p167)

Best for theatre buffs
- 414 Hotel (p176)
- Big Apple Hostel (p175)
- Hotel Edison (p176)

the Gansevoort. The nine-room town-house offers European ambience at reasonable prices. The Brewbar Coffee doubles as a check-in desk and café.

Bowery Hotel

335 Bowery at E 3rd Street (1-212 505 9100/www.boweryhotel.com). Subway B, D, F, V to Broadway-Lafayette Street; 6 to Bleecker Street. **$$$**.

The renaissance of the Bowery continues with the opening of this boutique hotel, which garnered a glowing profile in *Vanity Fair* magazine. Rooms are plush and the views of the neighbourhood are stunning. The buzz has kept scene-seekers lining up to eat, drink and sleep here. If you're lucky enough to pop in during a lull, cosy up by the fire in the wood-panelled lobby.

Bowery's Whitehouse Hotel of New York

340 Bowery, between 2nd & 3rd Streets (1-212 477 5623/www. whitehousehotelofny.com). Subway B, D, F, V to Broadway-Lafayette Street; 6 to Bleecker Streets. **$**.

Although the Bowery these days is more sleek than seedy, the Whitehouse Hotel remains unapologetically basic. This no-frills hostel offers semi-private cubicles (ceilings are an open lattice-work, so be warned that snorers or sleep-talkers may interrupt your slumber) at unbelievably low rates. Towels and linens are provided.

Chelsea Hotel

222 W 23rd Street, between Seventh & Eighth Avenues (1-212 243 3700/ www.hotelchelsea.com). Subway C, E, 1 to 23rd Street. **$$**.

Built in 1884, the Chelsea has a long (and infamous) past: Nancy Spungen was murdered in Room 100 by her boyfriend, Sex Pistol Sid Vicious. In 1912, Titanic survivors stayed here, and former residents include Mark Twain, Thomas Wolfe and Madonna. Rooms are generally well-worn with high ceilings, but some of the amenities – such as flatscreen TVs, washer-dryers and marble fireplaces – vary. The lobby doubles as an art gallery.

Duane Street Hotel p171

ESSENTIALS

Chelsea Lodge

318 W 20th Street, between Eighth & Ninth Avenues (1-212 243 4499/www. chelsealodge.com). Subway C, E to 23rd Street. **$$.**

If Martha Stewart decorated a log cabin, it would look not unlike this 22-room inn, housed in a landmark brownstone. All rooms have new beds, televisions, showers and air-conditioners. Although most are fairly small, the rooms are so seductively charming that reservations fill up quickly.

Chelsea Star Hotel

300 W 30th Street, at Eighth Avenue (1-212 244 7827/1-877 827 6969/ www.starhotelny.com). Subway A, C, E to 34th Street-Penn Station. **$.**

To keep costs down, opt for one of the 16 themed rooms – but be warned, they're on the small side and lavatories are shared. Ultra-cheap, shared hostel-style dorm rooms are also available. A recent renovation more than doubled the hotel's size – there are now 18 superior rooms and deluxe suites with custom mahogany furnishings, flatscreen TVs and private baths.

Cosmopolitan

95 West Broadway, at Chambers Street (1-212 566 1900/1-888 895 9400/ www.cosmohotel.com). Subway A, C, 1, 2, 3 to Chambers Street. **$$.**

Despite the name, you won't find any pink cocktails at this well-maintained hotel (or indeed even a bar to drink them in). That's because the Cosmopolitan is geared towards budget travellers who don't expect luxury. Open continuously since the 1850s, it remains a tourist favourite because of its Tribeca address and affordable rates. Mini-lofts – multi-level rooms with sleeping lofts – start at $119.

Duane Street Hotel

NEW *130 Duane Street, at Church Street (1-212 964 4600/www. duanestreethotel.com). Subway A, C, 1, 2, 3 to Chambers Street.* **$$$.**

Set on a quiet corner in Tribeca this newcomer to the neighbourhood has a lofty, airy vibe. Minimalist artist Donald

Green room

It took a while, but the eco-revolution has finally got a hold of New York's hotel business. In spring 2009, **Greenhouse 26**, the city's first green boutique hotel, will open on 26th Street – fittingly, in Chelsea's former flower district. The developers are aiming to cram every nook and cranny with enviro-friendly design elements.

'First of all, our concept is to use the least toxic building materials and reduce waste when ever possible,' says Steven Ancona, president of Flatiron Real Estate Advisors, the project's principal developer. Not only will the hotel use eco-friendly materials, it will also boast a geothermal heating and cooling system. Greenhouse 26 will also feature energy-conserving thermal breaks on room terraces, thereby preventing the transfer of outdoor heat or cold inside. Ancona says that they will apply for Leadership in Energy and Environmental Design (LEED) Gold status – the industry's green seal of approval.

Rooms at the hotel will average about 325 square feet, larger than usual in New York. And they'll be stocked with certified organic products, from the toiletries right down to the mattress and linens. According to Ancona the hotel will also have an outdoor garden and veggie restaurant serving organic fare. 'I live here too,' says Ancona, 'and the greener the city is, the better off we'll all be.' Amen to that.

■ www.greenhouse26.com

Judd would feel right at home in the 45-room boutique hotel, designed by Gene Kaufman. Just off the lobby is 'beca, a sleek 40-seat restaurant and bar.

East Village Bed & Coffee

110 Avenue C, between 7th & 8th Streets (1-212 533 4175/www. bedandcoffee.com). Subway F, V to Lower East Side-Second Avenue; L to First Avenue. **$**.
Popular with European travellers, this unassuming East Village B&B (minus the full breakfast as the name makes clear) is a great place in which to immerse yourself in downtown culture without dropping too much cash. The nine guest rooms come with eclectic furnishings and quirky themes. Shared areas include three separate loft-like living rooms, bathrooms and fully equipped kitchens.

Gild Hall

NEW *15 Gold Street, at Platt Street (1-212 232 7700/www.thompsonhotels. com). Subway A, C to Broadway-Nassau Street; J, M, Z, 2, 3, 4, 5 to Fulton Street.* **$$$**.
This 18-storey hotel adds a European sheen to lower Manhattan's Gold Street. A split-level wood-panelled library offers a welcome retreat from the harried New Yorkers pounding the sidewalks outside. Raise a pint at the in-house English tavern before heading off to bed in rooms that are stylish and cosmopolitan.

Greenwich Hotel

NEW *377 Greenwich Street at N. Moore Street (1-212 941 8900/ www.greenwichhotel.com). Subway 1 to Franklin Street.* **$$$**.
Co-developed by Robert De Niro, this hotel offers 88 individually designed rooms featuring such distinctive touches as oak floors, hand-loomed Tibetan silk rugs and Swedish Dux beds, plus an upscale Tuscan restaurant.

Hotel Gansevoort

18 Ninth Avenue, at 13th Street (1-212 206 6700/1-877 726 7386/www. hotelgansevoort.com). Subway A, C, E to 14th Street; L to Eighth Avenue. **$$$$**.

It's hard to miss this soaring, 14-floor structure set against the cobblestone streets and warehouse storefronts of the Meatpacking District. Opened in early 2004, this full-service luxury hotel gets strong marks for style. The private roof garden features a glassed-in heated pool complete with underwater music and 360-degree views of the city. The latest addition to the hotel is the subterranean G Spa & Lounge.

Hotel on Rivington

W107 Rivington Street, between Essex & Ludlow Streets (1-212 475 2600/ www.hotelonrivington.com). Subway F to Delancey Street; J, M, Z to Delancey-Essex Streets. **$$$**.
Hotel on Rivington has a high cool factor: floor-to-ceiling windows are a theme throughout, the second-floor lobby overlooks Rivington Street, and every room has an unobstructed city view.

Hotel 17

225 E 17th Street, between Second & Third Avenues (1-212 475 2845/ www.hotel17ny.com). Subway L to Third Avenue; N, Q, R, W, 4, 5, 6 to 14th Street-Union Square. **$-$$**.
Equivalent to a good dive bar, Hotel 17 has a grungy cachet that draws you in. Except for a recent sprucing-up of the lobby, the place remains a little rough around the edges, although with a funky vibe. Labyrinthine corridors lead to tiny high-ceilinged rooms filled with discarded dressers and mismatched 1950s wallpaper. Expect to have to share the hallway bathroom with other guests.

Inn on 23rd Street

131 W 23rd Street, between Sixth & Seventh Avenues (1-212 463 0330/ www.innon23rd.com). Subway A, C, E to 14th Street; L to Eighth Avenue. **$$$**.
This B&B in the heart of Chelsea gives you a warm feeling from the moment you enter. Owners and innkeepers Annette and Barry Fisherman renovated a 19th century townhouse into this homey hostelry with 14 themed rooms (all accessible by elevator and each with its own private bathroom).

Maritime Hotel

363 W 16th Street, between Eighth & Ninth Avenues (1-212 242 4300/ www.themaritimehotel.com). Subway A, C, E to 14th Street; L to Eighth Avenue. **$$$**.

In 2002 this nautical-themed building was spun into the high-gloss Maritime Hotel; the decor blends the look of a luxury yacht with a chic 1960s airport lounge. Modelled after ship cabins, each room features one large porthole window and lots of glossy teak panelling. The hotel offers four food and drink spaces: Matsuri, a gorgeous Japanese restaurant; La Bottega, an Italian trattoria with a lantern-festooned patio; Cabana, an airy rooftop bar; and Hiro, a basement lounge that draws a buzzing crowd.

Mercer

147 Mercer Street, at Prince Street (1-212 966 6060/1-888 918 6060/www. mercerhotel.com). Subway N, R, W to Prince Street. **$$$$**.

Almost a decade on, Soho's first luxury boutique hotel is still a notch above nearby competitors. Rooms are large by New York standards and feature furniture by Christian Liagre, spacious washrooms with tubs for two and Face Stockholm products. The lobby, with oversized white sofas and book-lined shelves, acts as a bar, library and lounge – open exclusively to guests. The restaurant, Mercer Kitchen, serves Jean-Georges Vongerichten's stylish version of casual American cuisine.

St Mark's Hotel

2 St Mark's Place, at Third Avenue (1-212 674 0100/www.stmarkshotel.qpg. com). Subway 6 to Astor Place. **$$**.

Positioned among the tattoo parlours and piercing shops of St Mark's Place, this small hotel is unexpectedly bright, clean and understated. The basic rooms have double beds with their own private baths. St Mark's biggest asset, however, is its location – it's perfectly situated for immersing yourself in the East Village's historic punk-rock culture and burgeoning restaurant scene.

Mercer

Note that the hotel is in a pre-war walk-up building, which means there are no elevators.

60 Thompson

60 Thompson Street, between Broome & Spring Streets (1-212 431 0400/1-877 431 0400/www.60thompson.com). Subway C, E to Spring Street. **$$$$**.

Don't be surprised if you have to walk through a fashion shoot when you enter this hotel – it's a favourite fashionista haunt. A60, the exclusive guests-only rooftop bar, offers commanding city views. The modern rooms are dotted with pampering details like pure down duvets and pillows, and a 'shag bag' filled with fun items to get you in the mood. The highly acclaimed restaurant Kittichai serves creative Thai cuisine beside a pool filled with floating orchids.

Wall Street Inn

9 South William Street, at Broad Street (1-212 747 1500/www.thewallstreetinn. com). Subway 2, 3 to Wall Street; 4, 5 to Bowling Green. **$$**.

The area surrounding this boutique hotel in the Financial District has seen a reincarnation in recent years, sprouting new pâtisseries, bars and restaurants along its cobblestone streets. To lure travellers beyond financiers, the hotel offers hefty discounts at weekends. There's no restaurant or room service, but breakfast is included.

Washington Square Hotel

103 Waverly Place, between MacDougal Street & Sixth Avenue (1-212 777 9515/1-800 222 0418/www. washingtonsquarehotel.com). Subway A, B, C, D, E, F, V to W 4th Street. **$$**.
Bob Dylan and Joan Baez both lived here back when they sang for change in nearby Washington Square Park. Today the century-old hotel remains popular with travellers aiming to soak up Village life. Recently, the deluxe rooms were expanded into larger chambers decked out with art deco furnishings and leather headboards. Rates include a complimentary continental breakfast – or you can splurge on the Sunday jazz brunch at North Square (1-212 254 1200), the hotel's restaurant.

Midtown

The Algonquin

59 W 44th Street, between Fifth & Sixth Avenues (1-212 840 6800/1-800 555 8000/www.thealgonquin.net). Subway B, D, F, V to 42nd Street-Bryant Park; 7 to Fifth Avenue. **$$$**.
This landmark hotel with a strong literary past (greats like Alexander Woollcott and Dorothy Parker gathered in the infamous Round Table Room to gossip) is beautifully appointed with upholstered chairs, old lamps and large paintings of important figures of the Jazz Age. In 2004 the entire hotel underwent renovations but it retains its character; hallways are covered with New Yorker-cartoon wallpaper to commemorate Harold Ross, who secured funding for the magazine over long meetings at the Round Table. Quarters are on the small side and the decor is a bit dated, but the feel is still

classic New York. Catch readings by local authors on some Mondays; cabaret performers take over in the Oak Room from Tuesday to Saturday.

Americana Inn

69 W 38th Street, at Sixth Avenue (1-212 840 6700/www.newyorkhotel.com). Subway B, D, F, N, Q, R, V, W to 34th Street-Herald Square; B, D, F, V to 42nd Street. **$$**.
This budget hotel, situated close to Times Square, has a speakeasy feel: the signage is very discreet, and you'll have to ring the doorbell to enter through the second-floor lobby. What the Americana might lack in ambience (with its linoleum floors and fluorescent lighting), it makes up for in location (a rhinestone's throw from the major Broadway shows) and reasonable prices (rooms start at just under $100). Although all bathrooms are shared, rooms come with a mini-sink and large walk-in closets.

Big Apple Hostel

119 W 45th Street, between Sixth & Seventh Avenues (1-212 302 2603/www.bigapplehostel.com). Subway B, D, F, V to 42nd Street; N, Q, R, S, W, 1, 2, 3, 7 to Times Square-42nd Street. **$**.
This basic hostel may be lacking in frills, but the rooms are spotless and as cheap as they come – especially given the location. The Big Apple puts you just a few steps from the Theater District and the bright lights of Times Square. Beware if you're travelling in high summer: dorm rooms have no air-conditioning.

Carlton Arms Hotel

160 E 25th Street, at Third Avenue (1-212 679 0680/www.carltonarms.com). Subway 6 to 23rd Street. **$**.
A bohemian hotel boasting themed spaces (check out the 'English cottage' room). Discounts are offered for students, overseas guests and patrons on weekly stays. Most guests share baths; tack on an extra $15 for a private lavatory. Rooms are usually booked early, so reserve in advance.

Casablanca Hotel

147 W 43rd Street, between Sixth Avenue & Broadway (1-212 869 1212/1-800 922 7225/www. casablancahotel.com). Subway B, D, F, V to 42nd Street-Bryant Park; N, Q, R, W, 42nd Street S, 1, 2, 3, 7 to 42nd Street-Times Square. **$$**.

This 48-room boutique hotel has a cheerful Moroccan theme. The lobby is an oasis in the middle of Times Square: walls are adorned with blue and gold Mediterranean tiles, and giant bamboo shoots stand in tall vases. The theme is diluted in the basic rooms, but wicker furniture, wooden shutters and new carpets and sofas warm up the space.

Dream Hotel

210 W 55th Street, between Broadway & Seventh Avenue (1-212 247 2000/ 1-866 437 3266/www.dreamny.com). Subway N, Q, R, W to 57th Street. **$$$**.

In 2004, hotelier Vikram Chatwal enlisted boldfaced names to turn the old Majestic Hotel into a luxury lodge with a trippy slumberland theme. David Rockwell dressed up the restaurant, an outpost of Serafina; Deepak Chopra conceived the Ayurvedic spa. The lobby sums up the resulting aesthetic – walls are cloaked in Paul Smith-style stripes and a crystal boat dangles from the ceiling. Rooms are more streamlined, with white walls, satin headboards and an ethereal blue backlight that glows under the bed. Rooftop bar Ava has panoramic views.

414 Hotel

414 W 46th Street, between Ninth & Tenth Avenues (1-212 399 0006/ www.414hotel.com). Subway A, C, E to 42nd Street-Port Authority. **$$**.

This small hotel's affordable rates and reclusive location (tucked away on the Theater District's Restaurant Row) make it feel like a well-kept secret. Immaculate rooms are tastefully appointed with suede headboards, vases full of colourful roses and framed black-and-white photos of the city. There's a glowing fireplace, and a computer available to guests in the lobby, plus a leafy outdoor courtyard.

Four Seasons Hotel

57 E 57th Street, between Madison & Park Avenues (1-212 758 5700/1-800 332 3442/www.fourseasons. com). Subway N, R, W to Lexington Avenue-59th Street; 4, 5, 6 to 59th Street. **$$$$**.

New York's quintessential hotel hasn't slipped a notch from its heyday. Everybody who's anybody – from music-industry executives to international political figures – continues to drop in for a dose of New York luxury. Renowned architect IM Pei's sharp geometric design (in neutral cream and honey tones) is sleek and modern, and rooms are among the largest in the city. The hotel is renowned for catering to guests' every need: your 4am hot fudge sundae is only a phone call away.

Gershwin Hotel

7 E 27th Street, between Fifth & Madison Avenues (1-212 545 8000/ www.gershwinhotel.com). Subway N, R, W, 6 to 28th Street. **$**.

Rates are extremely reasonable for a location just off Fifth Avenue. All rooms received a facelift in 2005. If you can afford a suite, book the Lindfors, which has screen-printed walls and a sitting room. Just off the lobby, but unaffiliated, is Gallery at the Gershwin, a bar and lounge with glowing countertops and mod Lucite orbs.

Hotel Chandler

12 E 31st Street, between Fifth & Madison Avenues (1-212 889 6363/ www.hotelchandler.com). Subway 6 to 33rd Street. **$$$**.

Rooms at this delightful hotel are style-conscious, with checked carpeting, black-and-white photographs of New York streetscapes on the walls, and Frette robes and Aveda products in the bathroom. The in-house 12:31 bar offers cocktails and light nibbles.

Hotel Edison

228 W 47th Street, at Broadway (1-212 840 5000/1-800 637 7070/ www.edisonhotelnyc.com). Subway N, R, W to 49th Street; 1 to 50th Street. **$$**.

Theatre-lovers flock to this newly renovated art deco hotel for its affordable rates and convenient location. Rooms are standard sized, but decidedly spruced-up. Café Edison, a classic diner just off the lobby known as the 'Polish Tea Room', is a long-time favourite of Broadway actors and their fans – Neil Simon was so smitten that he set his play '45 Second From Broadway' there.

Hotel 41

206 W 41st Street, between Seventh & Eighth Avenues (1-212 703 8600/ www.hotel41.com). Subway N, Q, R, W, 42nd Street S, 1, 2, 3, 7 to 42nd Street-Times Square. **$$**.

Although its looks are decidedly cool, this tiny boutique hotel feels comfy, warm and welcoming: reading lamps extend from the dark-wood headboards, and triple-paned windows effectively filter out the cacophony from the streets below. The penthouse suite has a large private terrace with potted trees and views of Times Square. Bar 41 serves meals all day.

Hotel Metro

45 W 35th Street, between Fifth & Sixth Avenues (1-212 947 2500/1-800 356 3870/www.hotelmetronyc.com). Subway B, D, F, N, Q, R, V, W to 34th Street-Herald Square. **$$**.

It may not be posh, but the Metro offers its guests good service and a retro vibe. Black-and-white portraits of Hollywood legends adorn the lobby, and the tiny rooms are clean. You can take in views of the Empire State Building from the rooftop bar of the Metro Grill.

Hotel Pennsylvania

401 Seventh Avenue, between 32nd & 33rd Streets (1-212 736 5000/1-800 223 8585/www.hotelpenn.com). Subway A, C, E, 1, 2, 3 to 34th Street-Penn Station. **$$**.

The Pennsylvania is one of the city's largest hotels. Its reasonable rates and convenient location (it stands directly opposite Madison Square Garden and Penn Station) make it a highly popular choice with tourists. Rooms are fairly basic but pleasant. Jazz fans, take note: the hotel's Café Rouge

Pod Hotel p180

Brooklyn calling

Hotel Le Bleu

TIme was when tourists in Brooklyn were people needing better directions. Local resident Tom Botti, who runs bus tours into the borough, recalls: 'Usually it was someone who got confused on the subway and wanted help getting back to Manhattan.' Now visitors are coming to Brooklyn on purpose. That burgeoning interest has led to a spike in hotel construction. When the **New York Marriott Brooklyn** (333 Adams Street, 1-718 246 7000, www.marriott.com) opened in 1998, it was the borough's first new hotel in 68 years. Since then, Brooklyn has gained another 600 or so hotel rooms, and 2,000 more are said to be on the way.

Once flats in Williamsburg or DUMBO started fetching million dollar price tags, it was inevitable that luxury boutique hotels would follow. The first opened in late 2007: **Hotel Le Bleu** (370 4th Avenue, 1-718 625 1500,

www.hotelbleu.com), located in Park Slope, offers 48 rooms, many with breathtaking views of the Manhattan skyline.

Summer 2008 saw the opening of the **Smith Hotel** (75 Smith Street, 1-718 338 2500, www. 75smith.com) on the edge of Brooklyn Heights. Towards the end of 2008, look for a 300-room Sheraton Hotel (www.sheraton. com) and a 200-room Aloft Hotel – a spinoff of the W Hotel chain (www.alofthotels.com).

'Brooklyn is a more real and culturally interesting part of the city,' says Miguel Garcia, who was visiting the area from Madrid. 'About once a week someone on one of the tours will say they plan to check out of their hotel in Manhattan and stay in Brooklyn instead,' Botti adds. 'They're absolutely charmed by the place, and they figure they can save a few bucks to boot.'

Ballroom once hosted such luminaries of swing such as Duke Ellington and the Glenn Miller Orchestra.

Hotel QT

125 W 45th Street, between Sixth & Seventh Avenues (1-212 354 2323/ www.hotelqt.com). Subway N, Q, R, W, 42nd Street S, 1, 2, 3, 7 to 42nd Street-Times Square. **$$**.

Celebrity hotelier André Balazs has taken a stab at a youth hostel, albeit one kitted out with flatscreen TVs and a lobby pool with underwater music. This ultra-hip hotel is the last thing you'd expect to find in the middle of Times Square.

Hotel Thirty Thirty

30 E 30th Street, between Madison Avenue & Park Avenue South (1-212 689 1900/1-800 497 6028/ www.thirtythirty-nyc.com). Subway 6 to 28th Street. **$$**.

Ambient music sets the tone in the spare, fashionable, block-long lobby. Rooms are small but sleek and complemented by clean lines and textured fabrics. Executive-floor rooms are slightly larger, with nifty workspaces and slate bathrooms. The hotel's restaurant, Zanna, serves Mediterranean fare.

Hudson

356 W 58th Street, between Eighth & Ninth Avenues (1-212 554 6000/ www.hudsonhotel.com). Subway A, B, C, D, 1 to 59th Street-Columbus Circle. **$$**.

Outside of its teeny bedrooms the Hudson has lots to offer. A lush courtyard is shaded with enormous potted trees, a rooftop terrace overlooks the Hudson River, and a glass-ceilinged lobby with imported English ivy is crawling with beautiful people.

London NYC

151 W 54th Street, between Sixth & Seventh Avenues (1-866 690 2029/ www.thelondonhotel.com). Subway B, D, E to Seventh Avenue. **$$$$**.

Formerly the Rihga Royal Hotel, this 54-storey high rise was completely done over and reopened as the London NYC in early 2007. The onsite concierge service promises to provide guests with any indulgence great or small. If you can't afford the sky-high rates, you can always pop in for a look-see: the inviting lobby is done up as a grand London residence. The spot also boasts the London Bar and Gordon Ramsay at the London – the first US eaterie for the UK's foul-mouthed chef.

Murray Hill Inn

143 E 30th Street, between Lexington & Third Avenues (1-212 683 6900/ 1-888 996 6376/www.nyinns.com). Subway 6 to 28th Street. **$**.

A recent renovation added hardwood floors and new bathrooms – most of which are private – to this affordable inn. Discounted weekly and monthly rates are available. It's advisable to book well in advance.

Night Hotel

132 W 45th Street, between Sixth & Seventh Avenues (1-212 835 9600). Subway N, Q, R, W, 42nd Street S, 1, 2, 3, 7 to 42nd Street-Times Square. **$$$**.

At Midtown's Night Hotel, the recently opened 72-room boutique property from Vikram Chatwal (of Dream and Time fame), out-of-town guests will see the city through the romantic lens of 21st-century 'gothic Gotham'. The hotel's stylish black-and-white motif extends beyond the loungey lobby to the handsome rooms.

Park South Hotel

122 E 28th Street, between Park Avenue South & Lexington Avenue (1-212 448 0888/1-800 315 4642/www.parksouthhotel.com). Subway 6 to 28th Street. **$$$**.

Everything about this quaint boutique hotel says 'I love New York'. The mezzanine library is crammed with books on historic Gotham, and the walls are covered with images from the New York Historical Society. Rooms are appointed in warm amber and brown tones, and some have dazzling views of the Chrysler Building. The hotel's bar-restaurant, Black Duck (1-212 204 5240), serves live jazz with brunch.

Pod Hotel

230 E 51st Street, at Third Avenue (1-212 355 0300/www.thepodhotel.com). Subway E to Lexington Avenue-53rd Street; 6 to 51st Street. **$**.

This hotel opened in early 2007 and offers cheap and cheerful rooms perfect for people who are looking for a little style without having to part with a sizeable chunk of their life savings. The rooftop café is great for an afternoon snack. A short walk away you'll find the Museum of Modern Art, Rockefeller Center and plenty of shopping on Fifth Avenue.

Roosevelt Hotel

45 E 45th Street, at Madison Avenue (1-212 661 9600/1-888 833 3969/ www.theroosevelthotel.com). Subway 42nd Street S, 4, 5, 6, 7 to 42nd Street-Grand Central. **$$**.

Several films have been shot here, including *Wall Street*, *The French Connection* and *Maid in Manhattan*. Built in 1924, the enormous hotel was once a haven for celebs and socialites, and a certain nostalgic grandeur lives on in the lobby.

Waldorf-Astoria

301 Park Avenue, at 50th Street (1-212 355 3000/1-800 924 3673/ www.waldorf.com). Subway E, V to Lexington Avenue-53rd Street; 6 to 51st Street. **$$$**.

First built in 1893, the Waldorf-Astoria was the city's largest hotel, but it was demolished to make way for the Empire State Building. The current art deco Waldorf opened in 1931 and has protected status as a historic hotel. It still caters to the high and mighty (guests have included Princess Grace, Sophia Loren and many US presidents). Check your attire before entering – you won't be allowed in if you're wearing a baseball cap, T-shirt or ripped jeans.

W New York-Times Square

1567 Broadway, at 47th Street (1-212 930 7400/1-877 976 8357/www. whotels.com). Subway N, R, W to 49th Street; 1 to 50th Street. **$$$**.

NYC's fifth and flashiest W has a street-level vestibule with a waterfall (reception is on the seventh floor). To your right, the Living Room is a

Marrakech

massive sprawl of white leather seating. Every private room features a floating-glass desk and an ultra-sleek bathroom stocked with Bliss spa products. However it's the bed-to-ceiling headboard mirrors and sexy room service menu that really get the pulse racing. Steve Hanson's Blue Fin (p117) serves stellar sushi and cocktails. The second hotel bar, Living Room Bar, is on the seventh floor.

Uptown

Central Park Hostel

19 W 103rd Street, at Central Park West (1-212 678 0491/www.central parkhostel.com). Subway B, C to 103rd Street. **$**.

Housed in an attractively renovated brownstone, this tidy little hostel offers dorm-style rooms that sleep four, six or eight people; private chambers with two beds are also available. All baths are shared.

Hostelling International New York

891 Amsterdam Avenue, at 103rd Street (1-212 932 2300/www.hinew york.org). Subway 1 to 103rd Street. **$**.

This budget lodging is New York's only genuine hostel – that's to say it offers non-profit accommodation belonging to the International Youth Hostel Federation. It's also one of the most architecturally stunning – the Gothic-inspired building spans an entire city block. The immaculate rooms are spare but air-conditioned, and there is a shared kitchen and a large backyard.

Hotel Beacon

2130 Broadway, between 74th & 75th Streets (1-212 787 1100/1-800 572 4969/www.beaconhotel.com). Subway 1, 2, 3 to 72nd Street. **$$**.

The Hotel Beacon offers good value in a desirable residential uptown neighbourhood just a short walk from both Central and Riverside Parks. Rooms are clean and spacious and include marble baths.

Jazz on the Park Hostel

36 W 106th Street, between Central Park West & Manhattan Avenue (1-212 932 1600/www.jazzhostels.com). Subway B, C to 103rd Street. **$**.

Jazz on the Park might be the trendiest hostel in the city – the lounge is outfitted like a space-age techno club and sports a piano and pool table. Make sure to double-check your room type and check-in date before you arrive.

Marrakech

2688 Broadway, at 103rd Street (1-212 222 2954). Subway 1 to 103rd Street. **$$**.

Nightclub and restaurant designer Lionel Ohayon was enlisted to take over this newly renovated Upper West Side hotel. Rooms are warm-toned with simple Moroccan embellishments. The clean no-frills hotel is likely to appeal to twentysomethings who are not that interested in amenities, or bothered by the fact that there is no elevator.

Pierre

2 E 61st Street, at Fifth Avenue (1-212 838 8000/1-800 743 7734/www. fourseasons.com/pierre). Subway N, R, W to Fifth Avenue-59th Street. **$$$$**.

A landmark of New York glamour, the Pierre marked its 75th birthday in 2005. A black-and-white checked pavement leads up to the gleaming gold lobby. Front rooms overlook Central Park, and wares from fancy neighbouring stores are on display in the lobby. There are three restaurants, including the opulent Café Pierre.

6 Columbus

NEW *6 Columbus Circle (1-212 204 3000/www.sixcolumbus.com). Subway 1, A, C, 59th Street-Columbus Circle.* **$$$$**.

It's a mod, mod, mod world indeed at 6 Columbus: teak, chrome, pony skins, the works. But despite all the cool, the hotel doesn't skimp on comfort with 400 thread count linens and super plush terry-cloth robes. Local color consists of goodies and snacks from hometown gourmet markets Dean & Deluca and Zabar's.

Getting Around

Arriving & leaving

By air

For a list of transport services between New York City and its major airports, call 1-800 247 7433. Public transport is the cheapest method, but it can be both frustrating and time-consuming. None of the airports is particularly close or convenient. Private bus or van services (a selection is listed below) are usually the best bargains. Medallion (city-licensed) yellow cabs, which can be flagged on the street or picked up at designated locations at airports, are more expensive but take you all the way to your destination for a fixed, zoned price, with any tolls on top. (Not so in reverse.)

New York Airport Service
1-212 875 8200/
www.nyairportservice.com
CoachUSA 1-877 894 9155/
www.coachusa.com
SuperShuttle 1-212 209 7000/
www.supershuttle.com

Airports

Three major airports service the New York City area, plus the smaller MacArthur airport on Long Island, served by domestic flights only.

John F Kennedy International Airport

1-718 244 4444/www.panynj.gov
At $2, the bus and subway link from JFK is dirt cheap but it can take up to two hours to get to Manhattan. At the airport, look for the yellow shuttle bus to the Howard Beach station (free), then take the A train to Manhattan. Thankfully, JFK's AirTrain now offers a faster service between all eight airport terminals and the A, E, J and Z subway lines, as well as the Long Island Rail Road, for $5. Visit www.airtrainjfk.com for more information. Private bus and van services are a good compromise between value and convenience (see above). A medallion yellow cab from JFK to Manhattan will charge a flat $45 fare, plus toll (varies by route, but usually $4) and tip (if service is fine, give at least $5). Although metered (not a flat fee), the fare to JFK from Manhattan will be about the same. Check out www.nyc.gov/taxi for cab rates.

La Guardia Airport

1-718 533 3400/www.panynj.gov
Seasoned New Yorkers take the M60 bus ($2), which runs between the airport and 106th Street at Broadway. The ride takes 40 minutes to an hour (depending on traffic) and runs from 4.30am to 1.30am daily. The route crosses Manhattan at 125th Street in Harlem. Get off at Lexington Avenue for the 4, 5 and 6 trains; at Malcolm X Boulevard (Lenox Avenue) for the 2 and 3; or at St Nicholas Avenue for the A, B, C and D trains. You can also disembark on Broadway at 116th or 110th Street for the 1 train. Less time-consuming options: private bus services cost around $14; taxis and car services charge about $30, plus toll and tip.

Newark Liberty International Airport

*1-973 961 6000/
www.newarkairport.com*
Although it's in next-door New Jersey, Newark has good public transport links to NYC. The best bet is a 40-minute, $11.55 trip by the New Jersey Transit to or from Penn Station. The airport's monorail, AirTrain Newark (www.airtrain newark.com), is now linked to the NJ Transit and Amtrak train systems. For inexpensive buses, see the bus services below. A car service or a taxi will set you back about $45, plus toll and tip.

By bus

Buses are an inexpensive means of getting to and from New York City, though the ride takes longer and is sometimes uncomfortable. Buses are particularly useful if you want to leave in a hurry; many don't require reservations. Most out-of-town buses come and go from the Port Authority Bus Terminal.

Port Authority Bus Terminal

625 Eighth Avenue, between 40th & 42nd Streets (1-212 564 8484/www. panynj.gov). Subway A, C, E to 42nd Street-Port Authority.

This somewhat unlovely terminus is the hub for many transportation companies offering commuter and long-distance bus services to and from New York City. If you have an early departure, bring your own breakfast, as the concessions don't open until around 7am. As with transport terminals anywhere in the world, watch out for petty criminals, especially late at night.

Long-distance bus lines

Greyhound Trailways

1-800 229 9424/www.greyhound.com
Greyhound offers long-distance bus travel across North America.

New Jersey Transit

1-973 762 5100/1-800 772 2222/ www.njtransit.com
NJT provides bus services to nearly everywhere in New Jersey and some destinations in New York State; most buses run around the clock.

Peter Pan

1-800 343 9999/www.peterpanbus.com
Peter Pan runs extensive services to cities across the North-east; its tickets are also valid on Greyhound.

By car

If you drive to the city, you may encounter delays at bridge and tunnel crossings (it's a good idea to check out websites www.nyc.gov and www.panynj.gov before driving in). Tune your car radio to WINS (1010 on the AM dial) for up-to-the-minute traffic reports. Delays can last anywhere from 15 minutes to two hours – plenty of time to get your money out for the toll ($4 is average). It makes sense, of course, to time your arrival and departure against the commuter flow. For parking garages, see p185.

By train

America's national rail service is run by Amtrak. Nationwide routes can be slow-moving and infrequent, but there are some good fast services linking the eastern seaboard cities. For information about commuter rail services serving New York and New Jersey, see p184.

Grand Central Terminal

From 42nd to 44th Streets, between Vanderbilt & Lexington Avenues. Subway 42nd Street S, 4, 5, 6, 7 to 42nd Street-Grand Central.
Grand Central is home to Metro North, which runs trains to more than 100 stations throughout New York State and Connecticut. Schedules are available at the terminal. As well as one of New York's loveliest buildings, it's a big retail centre with some excellent eating and drinking venues, including the famous Oyster Bar.

Penn Station

31st to 33rd Streets, between Seventh & Eighth Avenues. Subway A, C, E, 1, 2, 3 to 34th Street-Penn Station.
Amtrak, Long Island Rail Road and New Jersey Transit trains depart from this terminal, which has printed schedules available.

In the city

Manhattan is divided into three major sections: Downtown, which includes all neighbourhoods south

ESSENTIALS

of 14th Street; Midtown, roughly the area between 14th and 59th Streets; and Uptown, north of 59th Street. Generally, avenues run north-south along the length of Manhattan. They are parallel to one another and are logically numbered, with a few exceptions, such as Broadway, Columbus and Lexington Avenues. Manhattan's centre is Fifth Avenue, so all buildings located east of it will have 'East' addresses, with numbers getting higher towards the East River, and those west of it will have 'West' numbers that get higher towards the Hudson River. Streets are also parallel to one another, but they run east to west, or crosstown, and are numbered, from 1st Street up to 220th Street.

The neighbourhoods of lower Manhattan – including the Financial District, Tribeca, Chinatown and Greenwich Village – were settled prior to urban planning and can be confusing to walk through. Their charming lack of logic makes frequent reference to a map essential.

Public transport

Metropolitan Transportation Authority (MTA)

Travel info 1-718 330 1234/updates 1-718 243 7777/www.mta.info
The MTA runs the subway and bus lines, as well as a number of alternative commuter services to points outside Manhattan. You can get news of service interruptions and download current MTA maps from the website. Schedule changes can occur at the last minute, so look out for posters in stations announcing time alterations.

City buses

These are white and blue and display a digital destination sign on the front, along with a route number preceded by a letter (M for Manhattan). The $2 fare is payable with a MetroCard (see below) or with exact change (coins only; no pennies).

Subway

The fare is $2 per ride. Trains run around the clock, but with sparse service and fewer passengers around at night, it's advisable (and usually quicker) to take a cab after 10pm.

To enter the subway system, you need a **MetroCard** (it also works on buses), which you can buy from a booth inside the station entrance or from one of the brightly coloured MetroCard vending machines, which accept cash, debit and credit cards and can usually give change when available. Free transfers between buses and subways are available only with a MetroCard.

Trains are identified by letters or numbers and are colour-coded according to the line on which they run. Stations are most often named after the street on which they're located. Entrances are marked with a green globe (24 hours) or a red globe (limited hours). Many stations have separate entrances for the Uptown and Downtown platforms – look before you pay. Local trains stop at every station; express trains make major-station stops only.

Train services

The following commuter services ply NY's hinterland.

Long Island Rail Road (LIRR)

1-718 217 5477/www.lirr.org.
LIRR provides rail services from Penn Station, Brooklyn and Queens.

Metro-North

1-800 638 7646/www.mnr.org.

Commuter trains service towns north of Manhattan and leave from Grand Central Terminal.

New Jersey Transit
1-800 772 2222/www.njtransit.com.
Service from Penn Station reaches most of New Jersey, some points in New York State and Philadelphia.

PATH Trains
1-800 234 7284/www.pathrail.com.
PATH (Port Authority Trans-Hudson) trains run from six stations in Manhattan to various places across the Hudson River in New Jersey, including Hoboken, Jersey City and Newark. The system is automated, and entry costs $1.50; you need change or crisp bills for the ticket machines. Trains run 24 hours a day. Manhattan PATH stations are marked on the subway map (see back flap).

Taxis & car services

Taxis carry up to four people for the same price: $2.50 plus 40¢ per fifth of a mile, with an extra 50¢ charge from 8pm to 6am and a $1 surcharge during rush hour (weekdays from 4 to 8pm). The average fare for a three-mile ride is $9-$11, depending on the time of day and on traffic (the meter adds another 20¢ per minute while the car is idling). Below is a selection of call-out car services.

Carmel *1-212 666 6666*
Dial 7 *1-212 777 7777*
Limores *1-212 777 7171/
1-212 410 7600*

Car rental

Avis *US 1-800 230 4898/
www.avis.com; UK 0870 606
0100/www.avis.co.uk*

Budget *US 1-800 527 0700/
www.budget.com; UK 0870 153
170/www.budget.co.uk*

Enterprise *US 1-800 261 7331/
www.enterprise.com; UK 0870 350
3000/www.enterprise.com/uk*

Hertz *US 1-800 654 3131/
www.hertz.com; UK 0870 844
8844/www.hertz.co.uk*

National *US 1-800 227 7368;
UK 0116 217 3884. Both:
www.nationalcar.com*

Thrifty *US 1-800 847 4389/
www.thrifty.com; UK 01494
51600/www.thrifty.co.uk*

Parking

Parking on the street is generally problematic and car theft not unheard of. Garages are plentiful but expensive. If you want to park for less than $15 a day, try a garage outside Manhattan and take public transport into the city. Listed below are Manhattan's better deals. For other options, see the *Yellow Pages*.

Central Kinney System
www.centralparking.com. **Open** 24hrs daily, most locations.
This is one of the city's largest parking companies. Kinney is both accessible and very reliable, though it is not the cheapest option available in town. Rates do vary, so it's best to call ahead for relevant prices.

GMC Park Plaza
1-212 888 7400. **Open** 24hrs daily, most locations.
GMC has more than 70 locations in the city. At $23 overnight, including tax, the one at 407 E 61st Street, between First and York Avenues (1-212 838 4158), is the cheapest.

Icon Parking
1-877 727 5464/www.iconparking.com.
Open 24hrs daily, most locations.
Choose from more than 160 locations via the website to guarantee a spot and price ahead of time.

Standard Parking
Pier 40, West Street, at W Houston Street (1-212 989 9536). **Open** 24hrs daily.
Mayor Parking, another large chain, offers indoor and outdoor parking. Call for details of other locations.

ESSENTIALS

Resources A-Z

Accident & emergency

For ambulance, fire brigade or police in the event of a serious emergency, dial 911. The hospitals listed below have 24-hour Accident & Emergency departments.

Cabrini Medical Center
227 E 19th Street, between Second & Third Avenues (1-212 995 6000). Subway L to Third Avenue; N, Q, R, W, 4, 5, 6 to 14th Street-Union Square.

Mount Sinai Hospital
Madison Avenue, at 100th Street (1-212 241 7171). Subway 6 to 103rd Street.

New York – Presbyterian Hospital/Weill Cornell Medical Center
525 E 68th Street, at York Avenue (1-212 746 5454). Subway 6 to 68th Street.

St Luke's – Roosevelt Hospital
1000 Tenth Avenue, at 59th Street (1-212 523 6800). Subway A, B, C, D, 1 to 59th Street-Columbus Circle.

St Vincent's Hospital
153 W 11th Street, at Seventh Avenue (1-212 604 7998). Subway F, V, 1, 2, 3 to 14th Street; L to Sixth Avenue.

Age restrictions

In NYC, you must be 18 to buy tobacco products and 21 to buy or to be served alcohol. Some bars and clubs admit patrons between 18 and 21, but you will be ejected if you're caught drinking alcohol in the venue. Always carry photo ID as even those who are well over 21 can be asked to show proof of age and identity.

Credit card loss

American Express
1-800 528 2122

Diners Club
1-800 234 6377

Discover
1-800 347 2683

MasterCard/Maestro
1-800 826 2181

Visa/Cirrus
1-800 336 8472

Customs

For allowances, see US Customs (www.customs.gov).

Disabled travellers

New York can be challenging for a disabled visitor. *Access for All* is a useful guide to the city's cultural institutions, which is published by Hospital Audiences Inc (www.hospaud.org). The database is also on its website.

All Broadway theatres are equipped with devices for the hearing-impaired; call **Sound Associates** (1-212 582 7678, 1-888 772 7686) for more info. There are a number of other stage-related resources for the disabled. **Telecharge** (1-212 239 6200) reserves tickets for wheelchair seating in Broadway and Off Broadway venues, while Theatre Development Fund's **Theatre Access Project** (1-212 221 1103, www.tdf.org) arranges sign-language interpretation and captioning in American Sign Language for Broadway and Off Broadway shows.

Electricity

The US uses 110-120V, 60-cycle alternating current rather than the 220-240V, 50-cycle AC used in Europe and elsewhere. The transformers that power or recharge many newer electronic devices such as laptop computers are designed to handle either current and may need nothing more than an adaptor for the wall outlet.

Embassies & consulates

Check the phone book for a full list.

Australia
1-212 351 6500

Canada
1-212 596 1628

Great Britain
1-212 745 0200

Ireland
1-212 319 2555

New Zealand
1-212 832 4038

Insurance

If you're not an American citizen, it is advisable to buy comprehensive insurance before you travel, as insurance for foreigners is almost impossible to arrange once you are in the US. Make sure your insurance includes adequate health coverage as medical costs are high.

Internet

Cyber Café
250 W 49th Street, between Broadway & Eighth Avenue (1-212 333 4109). Subway C, E, 1 to 50th Street; N, R, W to 49th Street. **Open** 8am-11pm Mon-Fri; 11am-11pm Sat, Sun. **Cost** $6.40/30mins; 50¢/printed page.

This is a standard internet-access café that also happens to serve great coffee and snacks.

FedEx Kinko's
1-800 463 3339/www.fedex.com
Outposts of this ubiquitous and very efficient computer and copy centre can be found throughout the city.

NYCWireless
www.nycwireless.net
This group has established 113 nodes in the city for free wireless access. (For example, most parks below 59th Street are now covered.) Visit the website for more information.

Starbucks
www.starbucks.com
Many branches of Starbucks offer pay-as-you-go wireless internet access. Check online for enabled stores.

Money

All denominations except for the $1 bill have recently been updated by the US Treasury. One dollar ($) equals 100 cents (¢). Coins include copper pennies (1¢) and silver-coloured nickels (5¢), dimes (10¢) and quarters (25¢). Half-dollar coins (50¢) and the gold-coloured dollar coins are less commonly seen, except as change from vending machines. All paper money is the same size. It comes in denominations of $1, $2, $5, $10, $20, $50 and $100.

ATMs

Automated teller machines (ATMs) are located throughout the city in bank branches, delis and many small shops. Most of them accept American Express, MasterCard and Visa as well as the major bank cards, if they have been registered with a personal identification number (PIN). Commonly, there is a usage fee of between $1.50 and $3 to withdraw money.

Banks & currency exchange

Banks are generally open from 9am to 3pm Monday to Friday; some stay open later and on Saturdays. Many banks will not exchange foreign currency, and the bureaux de change, limited to tourist-trap areas, close between 6pm and 7pm.

People's Foreign Exchange

3rd Floor, 575 Fifth Avenue, at 47th Street (1-212 883 0550). Subway E, V to Fifth Avenue-53rd Street; 7 to Fifth Avenue. **Open** *9am-6pm Mon-Fri; 10am-3pm Sat, Sun.*

Travelex

29 Broadway, at Morris Street (1-212 363 6206/www.travelex.com). Subway 4, 5 to Bowling Green. **Open** *9am-5pm Mon-Fri.*

Travellers' cheques

Travellers' cheques are routinely accepted at stores and restaurants. You will usually need to show a photo ID such as your driver's licence or passport. If cheques are lost or stolen, contact:

American Express

1-800 221 7282

Thomas Cook

1-800 223 7373

Visa

1-800 336 8472

Pharmacies

Be aware that pharmacies will not repeat foreign prescriptions.

Duane Reade

224 W 57th Street, at Broadway (1-212 541 9708/www.duanereade.com). Subway N, Q, R, W to 57th Street. **Open** *24hrs daily.*
This chain operates all over the city, and some stores are open 24 hours. Check website for additional branches.

Post

For a complete list of NYC post offices visit www.usps.com.

General Post Office

421 Eighth Avenue, between 31st & 33rd Streets (24hr information 1-800 275 8777/www.usps.com). Subway A, C, E to 34th Street-Penn Station. **Open** *24hrs daily.*

Smoking

New Yorkers live under some of the strictest anti-smoking laws on the planet. The 1995 NYC Smoke-Free Air Act makes it illegal to smoke in virtually all indoor public places, including the subway and cinemas. Recent legislation went even further, banning smoking in nearly all restaurants and bars.

Tax & tipping

In restaurants, it is customary to tip at least 15 per cent, and since NYC tax is 8.625 per cent, a quick method for calculating the tip is to double the tax. In many restaurants, when you are with a group of six or more, the tip will be included in the bill. In taxis, tipping ten per cent is typical.

Telephones

Dialling & codes

As a rule, you must dial 1 + the area code before a number, even if the place you are calling is in the same area code. The area codes for Manhattan are 212 and 646; Brooklyn, Queens, Staten Island and the Bronx are 718 and 347; 917 is reserved mostly for mobile phones and pagers.

Numbers preceded by 800, 877 and 888 are free of charge when dialled from anywhere in the US.

For international calls, dial 011 + country code (Australia 61; New Zealand 64; UK 44) and the number.

Directory assistance

Dial 411 or 1 + area code + 555 1212. For a directory of toll-free numbers, dial 1-800 555 1212.

Operator services

To reverse the charges (make a collect call) or pay by credit card, dial 0 followed by the number, or dial AT&T's 1-800 225 5288, MCI's 1-800 265 5328 or Sprint's 1-800 663 3463.

Public phones

Payphones take any combination of silver coins: local calls usually cost 25¢ for three minutes; a few require 50¢ but allow unlimited time on the call. The best way to make long-distance calls is with a phonecard, available from post offices, delis and newspaper kiosks.

Tickets

With the exception of the major cultural institutions, which have in-house box offices, most venues subcontract their ticket sales out to agencies. To find out which one, see the venue's website. Between them, Ticketmaster (1-212 307 4100, www.ticketmaster.com) and Ticket Central (1-212 279 4200, www.ticketcentral.org) represent most venues, for a fee (to you).

Time

New York is on Eastern Standard Time, which extends from the Atlantic coast to the eastern shore of Lake Michigan and south to the Gulf of Mexico. This is five hours behind Greenwich Mean Time. In 2007, clocks are set forward one hour on 11 March for Daylight Saving Time and back one hour on 4 November. Going from east to west, Eastern Time is one hour ahead of Central Time, two hours ahead of Mountain Time and three hours ahead of Pacific Time.

Tourist information

NYC & Company

810 Seventh Avenue, between 52nd & 53rd Streets (1-800 NYC VISIT/ www.nycvisit.com). Subway B, D, E to Seventh Avenue. **Open** 8.30am-6pm Mon-Fri; 9am-5pm Sat, Sun.
This is the city's official visitors' and information centre.

Visas

Some 27 countries participate in the Visa Waiver Program (VWP). Citizens of Andorra, Australia, Austria, Belgium, Brunei, Denmark, Finland, France, Germany, Iceland, Ireland, Italy, Japan, Liechtenstein, Luxembourg, Monaco, the Netherlands, New Zealand, Norway, Portugal, San Marino, Singapore, Slovenia, Spain, Sweden, Switzerland and the UK do not need a visa for stays in the US shorter than 90 days as long as they have a machine-readable passport valid for the full 90-day period and a return ticket. If you do not qualify for entry under the VWP, you will need a visa; check before travelling.

What's on

Several free listings magazines are distributed around town, but the weekly *Time Out New York* ($3.99), which hits newsstands on Wednesdays and contains listings for Thursday to Wednesday, is the essential arts and entertainment guide. For gay listings, look out for *HX* magazine in venues.

ESSENTIALS

Index

Sights & Areas

a
ABC Television
Studios p116
Abyssinian Baptist
Church p154
African Burial Ground
p55
AIA Center for
Architecture p91
American Folk Art
Museum p121
American Museum of
Natural History/Rose
Center for Earth
& Space p148
Aqueduct Racetrack
p161

b
Bloomingdales p132
Broadway p116
Bronx p158
Bronx Zoo/Wildlife
Conservation Society
p158
Brooklyn p159
Brooklyn Botanic
Garden p159
Brooklyn Bridge p55
Brooklyn Museum p160
Brooklyn Tourism &
Visitor Center p160

c
Cathedral Church of St
John the Divine p148
Central Park p135
Chelsea p101
Chinatown p72
Circle Line Cruises p127
City Hall p55
Cloisters p154
Cooper-Hewitt, National
Design Museum p140

d
Downtown p54

e
Eastern States Buddhist
Temple of America
p72
East Village p85
Empire State Building
p122

f
Federal Reserve Bank
p60
Fifth Avenue p121
Financial District p54
Flatiron Building p111
Flatiron District p111
Fraunces Tavern
Museum p60
Frick Collection p141

g
Garment District p114
General Grant National
Memorial p148
Gracie Mansion
Conservancy p141
Grand Central Terminal
p131
Greenwich Village p91
Ground Zero p60

h
Harlem p154
Herald Square p114
Hispanic Society of
America p154

i
Intrepid Sea-Air-Space
Museum p128

j
Jewish Museum p141

l
Little Italy p72
Lower East Side p76
Lower East Side
Tenement Museum p76

m
Macy's p114
Madame Tussaud's New
York p116
Meatpacking District
p95
Metropolitan Museum
of Art p141
Midtown p101
Midtown East p130
Midtown West p127
Morgan Library p111
Morris-Jumel Mansion
p155
Museo del Barrio, El p142

Museum of American
Finance p60
Museum of Arts
& Design p148
Museum of Chinese
in the Americas p73
Museum of the City of
New York p142
Museum of Modern Art
(MoMA) p122
Museum of Sex p101
Museum of Television
& Radio p123

n
National Museum of
the American Indian
p61
NBC p123
Neue Galerie p142
New Museum
of Contemporary
Art p76
New York Botanical
Garden p158
New York City Fire
Museum p66
New-York Historical
Society p149
New York Mets p161
New York Public
Library p123
New York Stock
Exchange p61
New York Yankees
p159
Noguchi Museum p161
Nolita p72

o
Outer Boroughs, The
p158

p
P.S.1 Contemporary
Art Center p164

q
Queens p161
Queens Museum
of Art p164

r
Radio City Music Hall
p123
Riverside Park p149
Rockefeller Center p124

ESSENTIALS

Arts & Leisure

ESSENTIALS

WWW.VISITBROOKLYN.ORG   718.802.3846

THE BROOKLYN TOURISM & VISITORS CENTER
HISTORIC BROOKLYN BOROUGH HALL, GROUND FLOOR
209 JORALEMON ST. (BTW COURT/ADAMS), BROOKLYN, NY 11201
SUBWAY - BOROUGH HALL STOP: M R 2 3 4 5 A C F
OPEN MONDAY-FRIDAY 10AM-6PM (SATURDAY SEASONAL)

BROOKLYN TOURISM IS AN INITIATIVE OF BOROUGH PRESIDENT MARTY MARKOWITZ & BEST OF BROOKLYN, INC.